Timothy C. Daughtry, Ph.D.
Gary R. Casselman, Ph.D.

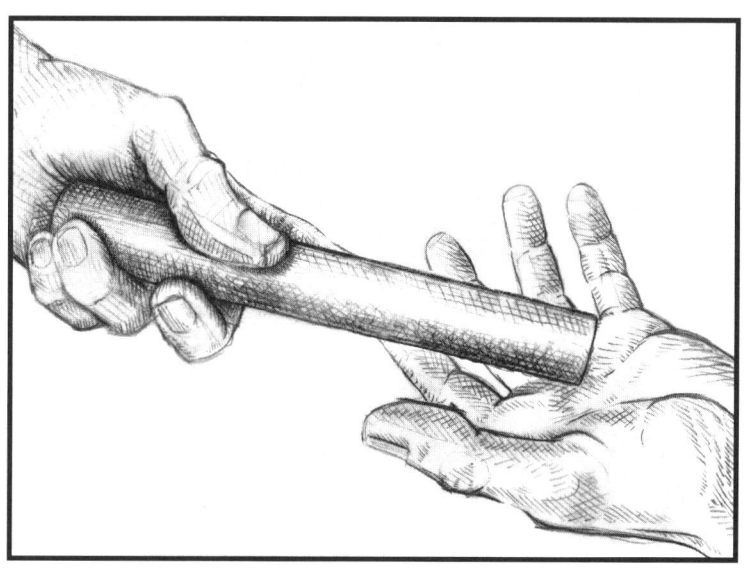

Passing the Baton:
Winning the Race for
Strategic Execution

Copyright © 2008 by Timothy C. Daughtry, Ph.D.,
and Gary R. Casselman, Ph.D.

All rights reserved. No part of this book may be reproduced or utilized in any form or by any means, electronic or mechanical, including photocopying, recording, or by any information storage or retrieval system, without permission in writing from the publisher.

Authors:
Timothy C. Daughtry, Ph.D.
Gary R. Casselman, Ph.D.

Edited by:
Corrie Lisk-Hurst

Cover design, page layout, and illustrations by:
East 14th Creative, Inc.

Printed by:
Cushing-Malloy, Inc., Ann Arbor, MI

Library of Congress Control Number 2008923495

ISBN 978-0-9815996-0-1

Printed and bound in the United States of America.

Table of Contents

Table of Contents i

Acknowledgements ix

Introduction 1
Outline of the Book 2

Chapter 1
The Baton and Three Handoff Zones 5

Strategic Execution and the Handoff Zone 5

Common Problems in Executing Strategy 7
    Lack of Strategic Focus (Trying to Be Everything) 7
    Failure to Prioritize (Trying to Do Everything) 8
    Failure to Develop Managers. 9
    Dumping and Micromanaging 9
    Avoiding Accountability 10

The Strategic Baton 11
    The Environmental and Organizational
    Context That Shaped the Strategy. 11
    The Organizational Vision 11
    The Strategy Itself (the Value Proposition,
    Major Trade-offs, and Strategic Paths). 12
    The Barriers to Execution and
    Plans to Address Those Barriers 13
    The Personal Implications of the Strategy,
    Performance Expectations, and Accountabilities 14

i

The Organizational Values and Team Agreements That
Will Form the Behavioral Boundaries for Execution 14

Overview of the Handoff Process 15
    Preparing for the Pass 15
        The First Challenge 15
        The Second Challenge 16
        The Third Challenge 16
    Making the Handoff 16
        The Fourth Challenge 16
        The Fifth Challenge 17
    Following through after the Handoff 17
        The Sixth Challenge 18
        The Seventh Challenge 18

Chapter 2

The First Challenge: Sizing Up the Field 19

Biggs & Bucks Financial Services 19

Systems and Stages: The Context for the Race 22
    Understanding Systems 22
    Systems View of Biggs & Bucks 26
    Stages of Organizational Development 28

From Personality to P&L: Three S-Curves 31
    The Organizational S-Curve 31
    The Leadership S-Curve 32
    The Personal S-Curve 32

How the Personal Ends up in the P&L 33

Three S-Curves at Biggs & Bucks:
How Personality Ends up in the P&L 37

Chapter 3

The Second Challenge: Sizing up the Team 43

Right Runners, Right Roles.......................... 43

Three Management Levels and Three Handoff Zones....... 44
    Senior or Systems Level........................... 44
    Middle or Organizational Level:
    The First Translators of Strategy.................... 47
    Line or Operational Level......................... 52

Guaranteeing a Fumble: Failing to Develop
Managers for Their Roles............................ 53
    Where Senior Managers Drop the Baton 54
    Where Middle Managers Drop the Baton............. 55
    Where Line Managers Drop the Baton............... 56
    The Invisible Levels: Three Handoff Zones 57

The Talent Base at Biggs & Bucks Financial Services........ 61

Chapter 4

The Third Challenge:
Anticipating Problems in the Handoff Zone 65

Understanding the Handoff Process 65

Ideal Alignment and Ideal Handoffs 67
    The Environmental and Business
    Context of the Strategy 69
    The Company's Vision 70
    The Strategy 70
    Barriers to Execution and Solution Paths 70
    Personal Implications, Performance Expectations,
    and Accountabilities 71

The Organizational Values as They
Apply at Each Level 72

Common Problems with the Handoff................... 73
Scenario 1: All Levels Working Beneath
Ideal Role (or Are They?) 73
Scenario 2: Strong Line, but Senior and
Middle Management Underperforming 75
Scenario 3: Fumbling in the Middle Ranks 78

Defining the Handoff Zone at Biggs & Bucks............. 81

Your Execution is Only as Good as Your Weakest Links 85

A Brief Preview of the Players 87

Chapter 5
The Fourth Challenge: The Strategic Baton 89

Seven Elements of Strategy 89
The Business Context: What are We Facing? 90
Environmental Scanning at Biggs & Bucks............ 91
Defining the Business Case at Biggs & Bucks.......... 95
Stages of Growth and Organizational History
at Biggs & Bucks 98
Organizational Vision: Where Are We Going? 103
The Relevance of Vision at Biggs & Bucks 106
Strategy: What is Our Path? 108
A Strategy Map for Biggs & Bucks 110
Organizational Value Proposition and Major
Trade-offs: How Will We Differentiate Ourselves? 114
The Barriers to Execution and Solution Paths:
What Could Stop Us?............................ 118
An Assessment of Barriers to Execution
at Biggs & Bucks 120

Personal Implications and Performance Expectations:
What Does This Mean For Me? 121

Organizational Values and Team Agreements:
How Will We Get There? 123

Chapter 6

The Fifth Challenge: Translating Strategy into Expectations 127

Translation of Strategy: Senior Management
to the Organization 127

Translation of Strategy: Senior Management
to Middle Management 130

A General Process for Managing the Handoff 133

    Here's How We Do It 133

    The First Handoff Zone at Biggs
    & Bucks: Senior to Middle Strategy and Themes 136

    Look at Your Team, but Remember
    Not All Runners Are Equal 139

    Drill Down to the Individual 140

Translation of Strategy: Middle Management
to Line Management 144

    Meet Myra Bennis, Supervisor of Training
    and Development 144

Translation of Strategy: Line Management
to Organization 147

    Meet Tracey Collins, Anchor Runner 147

Chapter 7

The Sixth Challenge: Coaching for Performance 153

Factors to Consider Before You Start Coaching........... 153
    Two Kinds of Performance 153
    People and Systems............................ 156

A Guide to Performance Development 158
    Performance Hurdle #1: Expectations 158
    Four Dimensional Leadership© 161
    Performance Hurdle #2: Commitment 172
    Performance Hurdle #3: Skill..................... 178
    Performance Hurdle #4: Confidence............... 184
    Performance Hurdle #5: Personality and Motivation.... 189
    Performance Hurdle #6: The Organizational
    Support Systems 198

Chapter 8

The Seventh Challenge: Guiding Execution without Micromanaging...................... 205

What's the Difference?.............................. 205
    Guiding Execution at the Senior Management Level ... 207
    Guiding Execution at the Middle Management Level... 210
    Guiding Execution at the Line Management Level..... 214

Chapter 9

Creating Your Handoff Plan 219

The First Challenge: Sizing up the Field 219
    Environmental Scan 220
    Organizational Scan 221

The Second Challenge: Sizing up the Team 222

The Third Challenge: Anticipating Problems
in the Handoff Zones 226

The Fourth Challenge: Defining the Strategic Baton 229
    The Business Context 230
    Organizational Vision 230
    The Strategy 231
    Value Proposition and Major Trade-offs 232
    Barriers to Execution and Solution Paths 233
    Personal Implications and
    Performance Expectations 234
    Organizational Values and Team Agreements 234

The Fifth Challenge: Translating Strategy
into Expectations 235

The Sixth Challenge: Coaching for Performance 237

The Seventh Challenge: Guiding Execution
without Micromanaging 248

Some Final Thoughts 250

Passing the Baton: Winning the Race for Strategic Execution

Acknowledgements

If ever there were an example of a book that was years in the making, this would be it. This book represents the culmination of our experiences and learnings that we have derived from working with corporate clients over the past twelve years, particularly with the delivery of our *Passing the Baton*: **Winning the Race for Strategic Execution**© workshop.

This workshop started out a number of years ago as a straightforward leadership development program for mid-managers and front-line supervisors. We want to thank Mr. Wayne L'Heureux, who was the vice president of human resources at Volvo Cars of North America at the time we began this journey. Wayne saw the value of what we were endeavoring to do and of providing this kind of development to the managers of his organization. Now the senior executive vice president of human resources at ULTA Salon, Cosmetics & Fragrance, Inc., Wayne continues to work with us.

Along the same lines, we wish to thank Mr. John Hipp, who has been the CEO of several banks over the course of his remarkably effective banking career. John also saw the value of supporting mid- to front-line management in developing their leadership acumen.

What both of these gentlemen did was to provide us with venues in which to test out our ideas, and thereby give us the initial opportunity to learn, and to develop and hone our message, as well as our process. Without those venues, we would not be where we are today.

The next step in the evolution of the concepts behind this book was catalyzed by the work of Dr. Robert Kaplan and Dr. David Norton in their seminal work on the balanced scorecard and strategy mapping, and by Dr. Peter Senge's work on systems theory. Their highly creative and influential work complements and augments our organizational development paradigm, serving as a springboard for taking our model to a qualitatively new level, as reflected in this book. We wish to thank these authors for providing that springboard.

With the integration of the strategy mapping process into our work, we needed other venues in which to field test and refine the paradigm. For that, we wish to thank two more executives: Mr. Bob Bruggeworth, CEO of RFMD, Inc., and Mr. Frank Sherron, who was at that time the president and chief operating officer of LSB Bancshares, Inc. Both worked intensively with us to develop the principles put forth in this book, in ways that were apropos to their respective organizations at the time. They both took significant time out of their packed schedules to co-facilitate our workshops in their companies. Without their support and involvement, we don't know that this book would have been possible.

And where would we be without our editor, Ms. Corrie Lisk-Hurst, who worked with us from the very first draft? When we got tangled up in the initial effort to get all of those ideas into a manuscript, she would come in with a fresh set of eyes and a clear set of insights that helped us find our way out of the confusion we had created for ourselves with the initial drafts. If it weren't for Corrie, we would probably still be wandering around in the wilderness of those initial drafts. We have developed a deep professional respect for what she has brought to our table.

After two years and nine drafts of this book, we felt we finally had it ready to distribute to a select few of our closest clients and colleagues as a pre-publication review draft. We were humbled and honored that they took to the task of reviewing this work with great commitment, dedication, and interest. The feedback that they provided us was incredibly valuable. Specifically, we wish to thank for their preview work: Mr. John Hipp, group president, Ameris Bank; Mr. Dave Dyer, chief operating officer, Concept Packaging Group; Mr. Jeff Frye, vice president and general manager, Gap, Inc.; Dr. Ralph Knupp, vice president, RFMD, Inc.; Mr. Wayne L'Heureux, senior executive vice president, ULTA Salon, Cosmetics & Fragrance, Inc.; Mr. John Schlich, senior vice president, National Envelope Company; Mr. Frank Sherron, president, LSB Banc-shares, Inc.; Mr. Jim Ethier, chairman and CEO, Bush Brothers & Company, Inc.; and Mr. Keith Sirois, formerly the CEO of Checkers Corporation. We wish to extend a deep and sincere "thank you" to all of you for your support in this process.

To our graphic designers, Ms. Denise Kanir and Ms. Betsy Crawford of East 14th Creative, we are appreciative of their very professional guidance in getting this book into final form, ready to hit the press.

And, in saving the best for last (but first in our hearts), we wish to thank from the bottom of our hearts our wonderful, patient, tolerant, and most capable office manager, Ms. Joanne (Jo) Bostick. She does it all — staying focused and centered the entire time. Jo is never reluctant to step up and challenge us when we are about to derail ourselves, is always there when we need her, and provides unending support to both of us. She is an invaluable and immeasurable asset to our practice in general, and to this publication specifically. Jo, know that you are immensely important to us, and we value all that you bring to the table.

Introduction

At the sound of the starter's gun, runners spring from the starting blocks in a classic relay race. Conventional wisdom teaches that the team with the fastest runners on the field will win the day, but that is not always the case in a relay race. In addition to speed, which is of course important, a team of four in a relay race has to execute three passes of the baton. The first runner passes to the second, the second to the third, and the third to the fourth (or "anchor") runner.

For each pass, the approaching runner and the outgoing runner have to match speeds and coordinate their movements in the handoff zone. Fumbles or improper handoffs can cost precious time and even penalties, more than making up for the advantages of pure speed alone. So important is skill in the handoff zone that a team's skill in passing the baton can actually offset another team's speed advantage. In fact, the baton's travel time around the track can actually be slightly less than the combined lap times for each of the four runners on the team (the baton "gains" a step in a well-executed pass). Successful coaches know that fast runners are important, but having the best talent is only the first step. The talent has to work well in the handoff zone to reap the full benefits of their speed. Successful relay coaches make sure they have the right runners in the right legs of the race, but then they drill their teams to succeed in the handoff zone.

This book offers an introduction to one of the most critical aspects of the leadership role: guiding the translation and execution of strategy from the senior ranks of the organization down to the level of individual employees. As is the case with a relay race, successful execution of strategy requires successful passing of information and priorities through each level of the organization. Vision and strategy, critical though they are, are virtually useless without consistent execution right down to the front lines. In developing this image of strategic execution as a relay race, throughout this book we put special emphasis on the handoff zone — the space in which the baton is passed from one runner to the next (or from one management level to the next).

For the purposes of this book, we have identified three primary management levels — senior, middle, and line — as well as a level beneath line management consisting of all other non-managerial employees of an organization. We describe the typical promotion path, along with the shifts in role and skills that define each step. We also offer simple steps that managers at each level can take in order to successfully receive, translate, and pass the strategic baton.

In addition, we present a simple process that will help you analyze a receiver's ability to take the handoff and then fit your coaching approach to his or her needs. Often, simply having a structured process such as the one we present can remind a busy manager to be sure that the receiver understands what is expected and has the resources to carry it out.

Many of the tools in this book ultimately help in managing accountability. If the strategic focus is clear, priorities are reasonably established, and managers are developed, it can be easier to recognize and define accountability issues.

Outline of the Book

Chapter One provides an overview of what information is in the strategic baton that must be passed from top to bottom of an organization, and gives an introduction to each of the three handoff zones: senior to middle, middle to line, and line to the non-managerial organization. We describe common problems we've seen clients face in executing strategy and begin to analyze the causes of these challenges.

Chapter Two covers the first challenge of strategic execution: sizing up the field. We introduce a hypothetical company, Biggs & Bucks, which we use as an illustration throughout the book. In particular, we use Biggs & Bucks to describe stages of organizational growth and introduce a simple systems perspective to better understand those stages. In order to continue growing, Biggs & Bucks has to integrate three growth perspectives: the organizational, the leadership, and the personal. No organization can outgrow its leadership; leaders must grow personally in order for the organization to continue to grow.

Chapter Three describes the second challenge, which involves sizing up your team and having the right runners in the right roles. We define the roles of senior, middle, and line managers as they are commonly described in various sources, and delve into more detail about each of the three handoff zones, describing the promotion path and common challenges that result in dropped strategic batons at each handoff.

Chapter Four describes the third challenge: anticipating problems in the handoff zones as they apply to your organization. We provide the Role Alignment and Handoff Model©, which illustrates both ideal role alignment across the three levels and common patterns of misalignment. In addition, we look at common ways that misalignment develops, each of which raises the likelihood of fumbles in the handoff of strategy through these three levels.

Chapter Five outlines the fourth challenge: translating the strategic baton. We provide a detailed analysis of what the content of the strategic baton should be — those things that each person in the organization needs to understand. And we return to the Biggs & Bucks case study, creating a strategy map to illustrate the importance of creating line-of-sight relationships among the major elements of strategy.

Chapter Six covers the fifth challenge: translating the strategy into expectations to avoid fumbles at each level. This is perhaps the most critical handoff challenge. In this chapter, we offer you a practical process for passing the strategic baton, looking at the translation of each of the elements of the baton into the language and goals of the respective levels. We present simple methods to aid in engaging people at each level to increase their commitment and to better translate the strategy into practical plans.

Chapter Seven gets down to the nitty-gritty of coaching and developing others to carry out their roles in strategic execution — the sixth challenge. We offer a primer on coaching and performance management, as these are central to smooth execution of strategy, and we introduce you to the six performance hurdles that must be cleared by each manager in your organization. We refer in this chapter to our Four Dimensional Leadership© model, which should help you understand the general role expectations that face each individual you are tasked with coaching. Finally, we provide a simple decision-tree process to help you identify and manage potential barriers to role performance.

Chapter Eight highlights the seventh challenge and one of the more difficult aspects of the management role: guiding execution without micromanaging. Finding the right balance between dumping and micromanaging is a core skill for working in the handoff zone. Many books and training programs have focused on the pitfalls of micromanagement; fewer have discussed the drawbacks to the other extreme management behavior of dumping. We believe this is one of the only resources that provides specific tools to help managers operate effectively somewhere between the two.

Chapter Nine will help to guide your thinking about the strategic hand-off. We have pulled all of the guidelines and tools discussed in this book together in summary form to make it easier for you to address each of the challenges facing you and your organization.

This book has been long in the making, and it has benefited from the input and support of many clients, friends, and colleagues. We hope that you find it as thought-provoking to read as we did to write.

Chapter 1

The Baton and Three Handoff Zones

Strategic Execution and the Handoff Zone

Like successful coaches in sports, successful CEOs understand that they must have the right talent in the right places in order to execute strategy, and they know that talent is only the beginning. Just as there are four legs in a relay race, there are four distinctive levels in most organizations: the senior management, middle management, line management, and non-management. And just as a relay team has to make three successful passes of the baton, strategy has to be passed like a baton from the senior ranks down to the front lines.

But there is a critical difference between the baton in a relay race and the baton of strategy. With each pass of the strategic baton, strategy has to be *translated* into the language and actions appropriate to each level in the organization. Senior management may make a strategic decision that "providing the lowest prices in our market" is the organization's best hope of success. This decision — to compete primarily on price — has to be translated into functional plans and priorities at the middle management level.

This will be the first pass of the strategic baton. Operational planning must translate "lowest price in our market" to "more time and effort on driving out cost from key processes and less on innovation and customer service." The sales area will translate the strategy into "targeting customers who are more price-sensitive and offering incentives for buying in volume and from standard stock." In human resources language, "lowest price in our market" translates into "using limited training resources to teach methods for driving out waste and inefficiencies."

As these and other functional groups translate the strategy into the language and priorities of their specialties, the second pass is made to line managers, who once again translate the functional language into work plans. The final pass of the strategic baton puts the strategy in the hands of the employees who will carry out the bulk of the work.

Remember, as is the case with a relay race, a fumble in any one of the handoff zones can cost the race. Failure at any organizational level to translate your organization's strategy into appropriate language and priorities means wasted time, effort, and resources, or misalignment between functional efforts. These fumbles can and do happen, even with talented people in each of the roles.

In making the handoff, there is a crucial moment in which both hands are on the baton; it belongs not solely to the runner making the pass nor to the runner taking the pass. If the runner making the pass lets go of the baton before the receiver is ready or fails to release the baton when the receiver has a firm grasp, the result is a fumbled baton. A fumbled or clumsy handoff, even between runners who are skilled as individuals, can cost the race. It is unlikely that one heroic runner can make up the lost time and penalties resulting from a dropped baton. Once again, having fast runners is necessary, but it is not sufficient for victory.

In an organization, the handoff zone is the white space between any two levels on the organization chart, in the space that does not clearly belong to either level. Too much involvement of the upper level is lamented as micromanagement, but too little involvement from above elicits cries of dumping. It is in this white space — this strategic handoff zone — that two management levels have to be clear about the implications of the strategy and the plans for implementation if the baton is to be passed without a fumble. In this handoff zone, there will be times when both hands will be on the strategic baton and it will not be clear which level has responsibility. A premature pass (dumping) or holding on too long (micromanaging) can cause a fumble, and a fumble can cost the race.

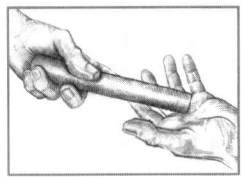

A premature pass (dumping) or holding on too long (micromanaging) can cause a fumble, and a fumble can cost the race.

Common Problems in Executing Strategy

In our work with executive teams, we have encountered several common problems with execution. Though they don't apply in every situation, we find them often enough to warrant a quick discussion.

Lack of Strategic Focus (Trying to Be Everything)

One of the biggest challenges facing executive teams is lack of strategic focus. As organizations grow, they bring with them the customers, products and services, and practices that got them to where they are. With growth in size and scope, however, things often change. For example, a high-maintenance customer may be profitable to an entrepreneur who has low overhead and is hungry for customers. That same customer may become more costly and distracting, however, as the entrepreneur's business grows. The same level of service now may have administrative support costs that were not there early on, and now there may be an opportunity cost because more profitable customers have to wait. We are not quick to suggest that "firing the customer" is the thing to do in such cases, but we do believe that growing organizations must be relentless in challenging the validity of the very practices that brought them growth.

We often challenge our clients to clarify their value propositions as one way of focusing attention on things that are strategically critical. We also encourage them to take a close look at the current growth stages of their companies in order to reveal what practices have reached the point of diminishing returns as the organization has matured.

Failure to Prioritize (Trying to Do Everything)

Because of the sheer number of demands from customers and stockholders, and because there is a difficult balance between short-term and long-term goals, it is tempting to executives to say "yes" to far too many initiatives and projects. We rarely have seen initiatives or projects that were clearly useless; somebody can usually make a good argument for every item on the corporate to-do list. But, usually, the "nice-to-have" list is longer than the "need-to-have" list.

These to-do lists are especially likely to pile up in the support areas such as Information Technology (IT). Of course we want faster computers and newer software. Who doesn't? Sales wants customized forms to speed up the sales process, and Manufacturing wants all kinds of information about process flows. Finance wants to keep IT costs down. And everyone can list numerous benefits to be reaped if they get what they request. Of course, IT (or any of the others) can do only so much, so the question is not, "Who is right?" but, "Whose perfectly sensible request is most critical from a strategic perspective?"

Failure to Develop Managers

The typical promotion path begins with demonstrated skill in some technical area. We then see the *promotion paradox* come into play as talented technicians move up into management roles that depend less and less on their technical skills and more and more on their management and leadership skills. Failure to prepare and develop managers as their roles shift can be a major cause of fumbles as the strategic baton is passed. As problems mount, unprepared managers often are pulled down into the familiar and comfortable technical areas that got them promoted and don't (or can't) step up to the less-familiar roles of managing and leading. The neglected parts of the role are usually those most critical to success in passing the strategic baton: translating strategy into relevant actions and priorities and managing the performance of their employees.

Dumping and Micromanaging

A logical result of lacking strategic focus, trying to do everything, and failing to develop managers is *inconsistency* as managers pass the baton to others down the line. Some managers approach delegation as a kind of default, believing their role to be primarily an assigner of tasks, but not recognizing they also must be developers of people. It is as if they toss the baton to the receiver and hope for a good catch. These are the managers described by their teams as dumping rather than delegating. Their teams typically flounder, trying to understand priorities or to figure out which solutions to problems are acceptable.

If things get difficult enough, however, the hands-off manager may morph into a hands-on manager who seizes control of the problem rather than use the occasion to develop others. Other managers seem to have trouble letting go of the strategic baton from the start. It is as if they follow the receiver out of the handoff zone and down the track, holding on for dear life to prevent a fumble. The irony, of course, is that such micromanaging almost guarantees a fumble because the manager gets so bogged down in details that he fails to step up to the critical roles of translating strategy and developing others.

Avoiding Accountability

Once the baton in a relay race is passed, it is up to the receiving runner to do his or her part. With the strategic baton, however, there is an added step for the manager: following up to see that the pass has in fact been successful. But following up — holding others accountable — is more of a problem for managers than it first appears. For a variety of reasons, many managers talk a better game than they play when it comes to accountability.

Sometimes this avoidance derives from a personality that is engaging and warm in dealing with others. On the upside, such managers are often seen as approachable and supportive. The downside, however, is that they may avoid the unpleasantness of confronting performance problems.

Others get caught in the hero trap. They are so busy stepping in to put out fires that they have little time to deal with the performance issues that cause the fires. Others work in a culture that sends subtle messages that it is better to work around a performance issue rather than to rock the boat. Unpleasant though it may be for many managers, fair and skillful management of accountability is critical to successful execution of strategy.

In later chapters we will go into detail about the contents of the strategic baton and the process for making the handoff. For now, a brief overview of each will be enough to get us started.

The Strategic Baton

The baton as we define it comprises all of those things that people throughout your organization need to know about strategy — what the strategy is and how they should behave in executing it — including:

The Environmental and Organizational Context That Shaped the Strategy

It is important for each individual to know where the organization is headed and what role he or she needs to play in that journey. Too often people do not understand why the organization is going where it is going. This misunderstanding is particularly common when that direction is different from the path that has led to success in the past. Without an understanding of the market and organizational drivers of the strategy, the changes required of each individual can appear, at best, arbitrary and, at worst, just downright wrong.

The Organizational Vision

The strategic baton certainly includes the vision, or the compelling description of the future, that the organization strives to create. It is virtually impossible to write anything new about vision or the need for visionaries if an organization is to thrive, so we have concentrated on the role of vision in the strategic handoff. After all, visioning is a mental process, but communication and translation of that vision happens in the handoff zone. Though common wisdom associates "visionary" with the senior executive level (and typically the founder, CEO, or president of a company), we emphasize the need for visionaries throughout the management ranks of the organization. Certainly the vision is different at different levels, but visionary thinking in some form is needed right down to the line management level.

The Strategy Itself — Value Proposition, Major Trade-offs, and Strategic Paths

We have worked with organizations ranging from those that have engaged in sophisticated strategic planning processes to those in which strategic planning is essentially annual goal setting, and even those who have no strategic plan at all! Few leadership topics raise as many passions as that of developing strategy — there are myriad perspectives within and outside of our clients' organizations about what it is and how to do it. In conducting interviews as part of the strategic planning process for clients, we hear these differing perspectives as a potential source of lively and productive debate that will provide great benefit to the organization, but we also hear lurking in the background the potential for a dropped strategic baton if differing opinions fail to create a coherent approach.

In years of introducing people in management positions to the demands of strategic leadership, the works we recommend most often are those by Michael Porter and by Robert Kaplan and David Norton.[1,2] In particular, because we have found leadership development to be most successful if there is a clear strategic context, we have adapted the strategy mapping process of Kaplan and Norton for use with our clients.

It's worth noting that the strategy map we use as an example here drills down to a more tactical level than those of Kaplan and Norton. Our goal is to introduce *strategic leadership*, so we want to stay as close as possible to the concept of translating strategy into individual work plans. Also, in our work with clients, we have found this more concrete approach to the strategy mapping process helpful in that the map may be used as a teaching tool in the organization.

---

1 Porter, M. (November-December, 1996). "What is Strategy?" *Harvard Business Review*, 61-64.

2 Kaplan, R. S. & Norton, D. P. (2004). *Strategy Maps: Converting Intangible Assets into Tangible Outcomes*. Boston, MA. Harvard Business School Publishing Corp.

Our focus on the tactical comes with a trade-off, because the map has to be revised more frequently to reflect tactical changes. Either way, an essential element of the strategic baton is the actual strategy and its implications for each person in the organization.

The Barriers to Execution and Plans to Address Those Barriers

When Robert Burns penned his famous line about the best laid plans of mice and men often going astray, he could well have been talking about strategic plans. Every strategy, no matter how well conceived and mapped out, will encounter barriers to execution. Those barriers may take the form of legacy processes and systems that have reached the point of diminishing returns, a talent base that does not fit well with new organizational requirements, or any number of other practical problems encountered in carrying out a plan.

A major element of the strategic baton is anticipating those barriers and developing plans to address them at each level in the organization. In fact, identifying barriers and developing solutions to address them is a major activity in the handoff zone — the area between management levels where it is not clear who owns the problem. We will cover a simple method for characterizing such barriers in systems terms and engaging the talents and skills of the people who have to confront those barriers.

Many of the potential barriers to execution lie in the horizontal relationships among functions. In fact, the handoff zones between functions are often more challenging than those between vertical levels. These functions are usually headed by middle managers, who feel the greatest pinch between the strategic perspective above them and the operational fire-fighting that occurs right under them. Especially in the middle ranks, managers may have to coordinate their work with peers whose goals appear to conflict with their own. We will offer a practical tool for clarifying the social and political network in which functional goals have to be coordinated and executed. Though this tool can be useful for managers at any level, we have found it especially suited to the peer relationship challenges faced by those working in the middle ranks.

The Personal Implications of the Strategy, Performance Expectations, and Accountabilities

Ultimately, strategic execution is the aggregated actions of multiple individuals. The strategy map allows line-of-sight among major strategic goals, and an effective handoff process should allow line-of-sight from each individual's priorities to those on the strategy map. A simple performance plan will provide such a connection from each individual at each level in the organization up to the major goals of the strategy. It is also important to clarify the accountabilities of *both* levels: what is expected of the higher level in terms of monitoring, support, and guidance, and what the deliverables are for the receiving level.

The Organizational Values and Team Agreements That Will Form the Behavioral Boundaries for Execution

The strategic baton comprises *what* will be accomplished, *why* it must be accomplished, and *by whom* it will be accomplished. But there is another critical element of the strategic baton—*how* the goals will be accomplished. Translating organizational values into language and examples that are relevant to each level ensures that those values are internalized and lived, not just recited.

Overview of the Handoff Process

Let's break the baton pass in a relay race into three distinct phases. Think of the process as involving an *approach* to the handoff zone, then the actual *passing of the baton* within the handoff zone, and finally *following through* to make sure that the pass was successful.

We can adapt these phases to the leadership process of handing off the responsibility for translating strategy into goals and actions appropriate to each level of the organization. Each phase carries with it particular challenges, and we have organized the rest of this book to describe the seven challenges we have observed and give you a series of practical tools for surmounting these challenges. Though we would not advocate a rigid, bureaucratic process for managing strategic execution, we do believe that thinking in terms of handing off a strategic baton can guide your thinking and help you spot potential problems.

Let's look at the three phases of the handoff and the leadership challenges in each.

Preparing for the Pass

Think of the first phase of the strategic handoff as similar to the approach in a relay race: One runner has the baton and has to make the pass to the next runner successfully. In the case of strategic execution, there are three challenges that must be met during the approach to the handoff zone:

- **The first challenge is to size up the field,** or the organizational context in which the strategic race will be run. Strategy is developed in anticipation of future trends, but it has to begin with where the organization is now. The process of sizing up the field requires taking a focused look at the forces that shaped the history of the organization and those that will act on it in the future. Especially in organizations that are facing significant change, this broad perspective can help make sense of the change for people who have become accustomed to the earlier ways of doing things.

- **The second challenge is to size up the team,** making sure you have the right players in the right roles. We can think of no better context for assessing your talent bench than the ability of that bench to execute your strategy.

- **The third challenge is to anticipate problems in the handoff zones.** Taking the time to walk the strategy mentally through the organization's structure often makes it possible to identify the areas where a fumble is likely. For example, if your organization's strategy calls for a different recruiting focus, but your Human Resources Department does not have particularly strong leadership, we can anticipate problems with the handoff in that part of the strategy. With some preparation and support, those fumbles can then be avoided.

Making the Handoff

In a relay race, the real challenges begin in the handoff zone. Having a good grasp of the baton and making a strong pass are essential. In strategic execution, the fourth and fifth challenges that occur in the handoff zone between any two management levels are as follows:

- **The fourth challenge is to translate the baton from the language and priorities of the level making the pass to that of the level receiving the pass.** This is the point when the hands of both the passer and the receiver are on the baton. Strategy has to be translated into functional plans before it can be translated into specific task assignments. At each pass or translation, the manager making the pass has to make sure that the receiver has a firm grasp on the baton before letting go. In business terms, that means ensuring that the receiving level understands the strategy and has adapted the plans and priorities of his or her area to align with the strategy.

- **The fifth challenge is to translate the strategy and plans into personal expectations so that the level making the handoff and the one receiving it understand the contribution each is to make.** That translation includes far more than goals and objectives. It is important that managers at each level in the organization educate their teams about the business context in which the strategy was developed. The more the strategy involves changing from comfortable habits that worked in the past, the more critical it is for managers at each level to understand their role as advocates for that change.

Following through after the Handoff

With the handoff of the strategic baton, the manager's job is not done. There is an ongoing obligation to follow through! Following the analogy of the relay race: after the handoff, the manager merely changes his or her role to fit the situation. The manager making the handoff has to develop the team and guide execution without micromanaging.

Unfortunately, the manager who has made the handoff often behaves as if his or her job has been finished! There is little or no follow-through. Or we see the opposite scenario, in which the manager who has supposedly made the handoff never lets go of the baton. With these managers, there is not enough delegation.

Either way, there are two additional challenges for the manager that a runner in a relay race does not face.

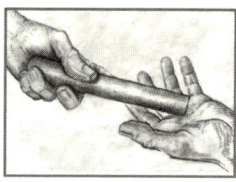

Unfortunately, the manager who has made the handoff often behaves as if his or her job has been finished. There is not enough follow-through. Or we see the opposite scenario, in which the manager who has supposedly made the handoff never lets go of the baton. With these managers, there is not enough delegation.

- **The sixth challenge is coaching for performance.** Typically, the managers who take the strategic handoff at the next level down have different skill and experience levels, so a "one size fits all" approach to delegation does not serve all equally well.

- **The seventh challenge is guiding execution without micromanaging.** In our experience, this is one of the toughest challenges that managers face in passing the baton to others. They still are responsible for ensuring that the receiving manager has a workable plan and executes that plan. If they fail to exercise enough oversight, there are likely to be fumbles at the receiving level. If they fail to delegate enough, the receiving level is hampered in their own development.

In order to execute strategy successfully and be positioned for continued success, your organization's managers have to meet each of these challenges. In the remaining chapters of this book, we hope to give you — and them — the tools needed to clear each hurdle.

Chapter 2

The First Challenge: Sizing Up the Field

Biggs & Bucks Financial Services

Welcome to Biggs & Bucks Financial Services, a fictional company we created to demonstrate the concepts and tools described in this book. We have pulled together in its story many of the challenges that we see most often in our work with real companies in a range of industries. Though Biggs & Bucks is fictional, we have incorporated in its story a variety of real challenges faced by our clients over the years. If you are willing to look beneath the surface, you will probably recognize your own organization's challenges in our description of Biggs & Bucks.

> *Biggs & Bucks Financial Services has grown from a small insurance agency in the 1960s to a provider of a wide array of financial consulting services, including insurance, financial planning, tax consulting and preparation, estate planning, and securities. Biggs & Bucks began as a partnership and grew as financial consultants worked their way up to equity partnership and also, more recently, by acquisition of smaller boutique financial planning and insurance firms.*

With 30 offices in eight states, each offering a mix of services based on the unique history of the office and expertise of the consultants, Biggs & Bucks has a strong reputation in each of its local markets. Local offices have adapted well to their own mix of available talent, local competition, and customer base. Some offices offer higher end estate planning and tax consulting to a mature, wealthy clientele. These offices tend to sell a wide range of securities and offer a high level of personalized service. Other offices have developed a larger base of younger professional clients just beginning to plan and invest seriously. Though they do not advertise as such, the consultants in those offices refer to the base package of mutual funds, life and disability insurance, and wills that they can sell in fairly large volume.

Even with these differences in approach, Biggs & Bucks has grown in overall footprint and profitability. The last two acquisitions, however, have gone much less smoothly than earlier ones. Margins are smaller than had been projected. Some board members have pushed for continuing growth, arguing that the time is right to expand the array of products and services into the real estate arena. However, CEO John Jefferson has fought strenuously against further expansion of any kind at this point, and he argues that the priority should be clarifying the company's direction and business model and taking time to digest its recent acquisitions.

In particular, the CEO and others believe that Biggs & Bucks needs greater standardization, as it has become painfully clear that the market identity of Biggs & Bucks depends heavily on the local offices' offerings. Jefferson and his supporters want more of a "one company" approach, as marketing data indicate that the local market identities are tapping fairly limited customer segments. Others, especially those who have come up through the local ranks from within the company, are arguing that the need for standardization in administrative systems is long overdue, as each office has its own IT systems, forms, processes, reporting formats, and HR procedures. These different local methods have simply been carried over from acquired offices. These same partners caution, however, against pushing standardization too much on the offering side, as Biggs & Bucks has been built on local response to local markets. They argue, so far convincingly, that flexibility, speed, and personal service are primary advantages against larger firms.

A concern that everyone shares is that they seem to have hit the wall in having successful financial consultants step into the roles of leading teams and running local markets. Some offices are thriving, but a growing number seem to be floundering from lack of local leadership.

Over a recent series of planning sessions, the board and senior management have agreed on a strategy. Under Jefferson's leadership, they wrestled with the questions of what sets Biggs & Bucks apart from other financial consulting firms in the minds of customers, and they faced the standardization versus local autonomy question head-on.

Systems and Stages: The Context for the Race

Understanding Systems

An organization is a complex system, and executing strategy requires the ability to understand which forces in that system will support execution and which ones will hamper it. In fact, the ability to think in systems terms — to understand how all the pieces of a complex system work together — is often cited as a critical leadership skill.[3] Some entire theories of executive leadership have as a core element the ability to form and work with complex causal maps of how various pieces work together in the business environment and the organization.[4] These causal maps — or more simply, having a mental picture of what drives what in a business or industry — are essential to the development and execution of strategy.

There are numerous patterns or systems that are so common that the influential business theorist Peter Senge calls them *systems archetypes*, and all of them are relevant in some way to strategic execution. But we are interested here in one particular type of system that produces a growth pattern called an S-curve.[5] An example of an S-curve is shown in Figure 2.1.

The S-curve depicts a system that grows up to a point and then encounters barriers to further growth. That is, the activities that produce an initial growth period reach a point of diminishing returns. Understanding S-curves, and the underlying system that produces them, is essential to strategic execution. Let's look at the case of Biggs & Bucks to illustrate:

---

3 Walton, M. (1986). *The Deming Management Method.* New York, NY. Perigee Books.

4 Zaccaro, S. J. (2001). *The Nature of Executive Leadership: A Conceptual and Empirical Analysis of Success.* Washington, DC. American Psychological Association.

5 Senge, P. M. (1990). *The Fifth Discipline.* New York, NY. Currency-Doubleday.

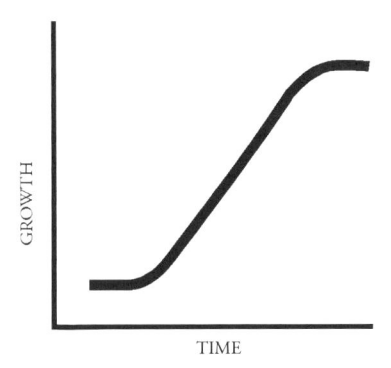

Figure 2.1 - Example of an S-Curve

- You need to understand where your organization is in its growth curve in order to develop and execute your strategy. Actions that work well at one stage of growth will actually begin to limit growth at a later point.

   Biggs & Bucks has grown in part because of the ability of local offices to adapt to local markets. The company has reached a size, however, at which the local flexibility is causing inefficiency and duplication, which in turn are limiting margins.

- To effect a smooth pass of the strategic baton from level to level, you need to be sure you know which forces in the organization will support that pass and which may cause a fumble.

   Though the need for standardization in administrative processes and, to a lesser extent, product and service offerings is recognized, efforts to standardize will encounter numerous internal barriers. Some of these will be technical (e.g., converting to a uniform IT system) and some will be human (e.g., preference for the old system). Failure to understand and address the barriers will limit the execution of the newer strategy.

- As you get close to the top of the growth curve, you need to focus more on removing the restraining forces. The human tendency is to work harder at doing what has always been done, because its always worked before. But this can be fatal. Continuing to push at that point will only increase the push back from the system.

If Biggs & Bucks were to continue doing what has worked in the past (acquiring new offices to expand footprint and product offerings) they would add to the local inconsistencies and inefficiencies that are squeezing margins. The acquisitions would not pay off as well as in the past, when a small but growing Biggs & Bucks could tolerate more local autonomy because the influences and inconsistencies had limited ramifications in the smaller organization.

The S-curve is produced by a system Senge called a Limits to Growth Archetype, which consists of a growing cycle that is eventually slowed by a second set of forces called a limiting cycle. The growing cycle works essentially like compounding interest in a savings account — growth creates more growth at an increasing rate. A limiting cycle, on the other hand, works to maintain itself within certain boundaries. In that sense, it works like a heating and cool-

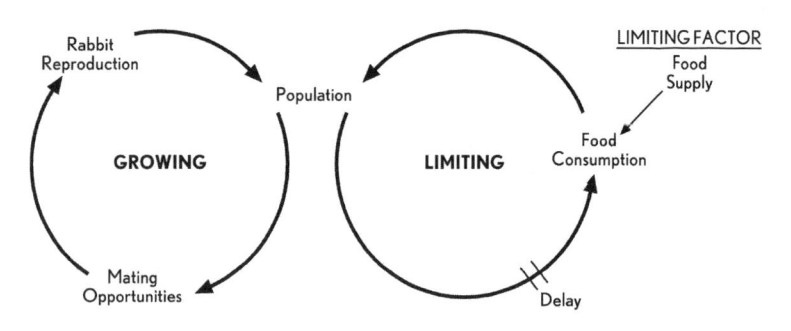

Figure 2.2 - Limits to Growth Applied to Rabbit Population on an Island

ing system controlled by a thermostat. The combined action of the two cycles produces initially slow growth, followed by an increasing rate of growth, followed by slowing and leveling off as seen earlier in the S-curve in Figure 2.1.

This pattern occurs frequently in nature, particularly as populations grow. An easy example of a natural system that produces an S-curve might be the growth of a rabbit population on an isolated island, as shown in Figure 2.2.

In this case, the rabbit population is the growing loop in that reproduction adds to the population, which in turn creates more opportunities for mating. In our population example, however, the growth will not continue without limits. Eventually, we see the effects of the second aspect of this basic system, the limiting cycle. As the rabbit population grows, so does the food consumption. Early on, when the population is easily supported by the available food, the limiting cycle has little or no effect. The rabbit population on the island enters the fast-growth part of the S-curve. But eventually, with some delay, the food consumption reaches the critical threshold of the food supply, and the limiting loop begins to show its effects. With less food there is less mating, so the rabbit population slows and then levels off, creating the flattened portion of the S-curve.

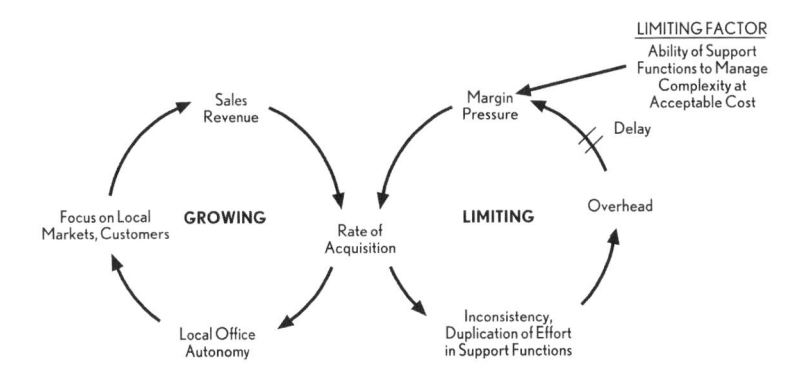

Figure 2.3 - Limits to Growth Applied to Biggs & Bucks Financial Services

Few things could be more relevant to strategic execution than understanding the growing and the limiting loops in your organization. Having a feel for where you are on the relevant S-curves is critical if you are to put your efforts in the right places.

Systems View of Biggs & Bucks

If all this sounds too theoretical, let's look for a moment at the practical implications for Biggs & Bucks. The diagram in Figure 2.3 tells the story of the early growth and current challenges of Biggs & Bucks, as we've described them so far.

This example illustrates the Biggs & Bucks business model of local autonomy, which allows close focus on local markets and adaptation to customer needs. The greater the focus on local customer needs, the greater the revenue, which then allows Biggs & Bucks to open or acquire more offices. These new offices, in turn, focus on their local markets. As such, we see in this simple diagram the growing cycle that drove the early success and growth of Biggs & Bucks.

With each additional office, however, the local autonomy that fuels growth is also fueling duplication, inconsistencies, and inefficiencies. You can easily visualize the pressures on the back room described so simply in the right-hand loop. Local offices use different reporting formats, which work for them but make it harder to track what is going on in the business. Local offices have different forms, different coding systems for customer accounts, different office hours, product offerings, and so on. Early on, even though these inefficiencies are there, they are more of a minor nuisance than a problem for the business. Because the benefits of local autonomy still outweigh the disadvantages, people simply work around the problems and keep the focus on growing the customer base. Some poor soul at corporate figures out a way to understand and use the patchwork of reports and the business keeps rolling.

Over time, however, with more offices, the patchwork of reports gets more tangled. Maybe additional staff are finally added to manage the patchwork of reports. Maybe errors in mailings to customers begin to pile up because of the different forms and coding systems in use. Slowly, the disadvantages of local autonomy make themselves felt in creeping overhead and squeezed margins. The growth curve of Biggs & Bucks begins to flatten out, and we have the familiar S-curve.

Few things could be more relevant to strategic execution than understanding the growing and the limiting loops in your organization. Having a feel for where you are on the relevant S-curves is critical if you are to put your efforts in the right places. If you are on the steep part of the S-curve, you can continue to do more of what you have done in the past, or you can do it better, and you will get more good results.

Early on, the success of Biggs & Bucks fueled revenue, which brought more offices, which brought more revenue, and so on. But you have to recognize the signs that the system is straining and that the curve is flattening out. If you are near the top of the S-curve — the point where the growing and limiting forces have built up past a critical threshold — doing more of what you've always done will make things worse, not better. If Biggs & Bucks were to make another acquisition at this point, or move into a new area such as real estate, the back room functions would stagger under the weight and eventually hurt customer experience. At this stage in your organization's growth you have to do something differently. In order to set the stage for strategic execution, your leaders must understand these growing and limiting forces.

Stages of Organizational Development

In sizing up the field, not only do you need to understand your organization from a systems perspective, but you must also know what stage of development your organization is in, as this will guide the development of your strategy. For the purpose of this book, we have adapted the language of Larry Greiner's important article on stages of organizational development, which shows that many companies go through periods of steady (or evolutionary) growth and periods of unstable (or revolutionary) growth.[6]

In the **Entrepreneurial Stage**, the entrepreneurs or founders are involved in the day-to-day activities of the organization. There is a clear focus on the customer and the product, and an air of informality usually is evident. Standardization of roles and procedures is minimal. People do what needs to be done to keep the organization running. Our description of the early days of Biggs & Bucks certainly fits here. Local autonomy allowed quick adaptation to local markets and focus on the needs of customers.

As is the case with Biggs & Bucks, however, the creativity and flexibility that drove success in the early stage has begun to accrue inconsistencies that eventually limit the continued growth.

To accommodate for this, the organization reaches a state of readiness to move to the next stage, the **Systems Stage**, which is characterized by increased standardization and clarification of roles, with senior management providing direction. Biggs & Bucks is clearly struggling with the challenges of the Systems Stage.

Standardization and clear direction from above bring order to the growing complexity and allow growth to continue. It becomes harder, however, for senior managers to exercise good control over the growing enterprise, especially as new product or service lines are added. Managers lower in the organization begin to feel constrained in their ability to manage their area. Following the systems perspec-

---

[6] Greiner, L. E. (May-June, 1998). "Evolution and Revolution as Organizations Grow." *Harvard Business Review*. From Reprint 98308.

tive above, the clear direction that has driven growth now begins to constrain growth. The S-curve begins to level off, signaling the organization's need to move into the next stage.

The **Delegation Stage** is characterized by the need for senior managers to rise to the challenge and to delegate more responsibility to lower levels so that the organization can respond more quickly to local demands. Senior managers then focus more on finding opportunities to expand the business, while lower managers handle the details. Growth is again driven by delegation and local flexibility until, as you might expect by now, the benefits begin to be outweighed by the resulting problems. In this case, local actions can become less coordinated and more siloed. If senior managers hold on to the baton, the growth of the organization is limited to the size that can be managed at the top. Though Biggs & Bucks has not yet focused on building its management bench, the tightest pinch they feel currently is from the lack of consistent systems. Once those issues are addressed and the company starts to grow again, they will soon feel the pinch from their limited management ranks.

Since it is beyond our purpose here to cover Greiner's model in full, suffice it to say that there are two further stages as organizations develop, each presenting its organizational and leadership challenges as leaders grapple with growing size and specialization. The point here, simply, is that there is a constant challenge to find the right balance between the benefits of local autonomy and delegation on the one hand, and standardization and centralized direction on the other. This balance takes different forms for organizations at different sizes and stages of growth, but the implications of these growth stages are profound. At some point in an organization's life, the challenge is to get better at whatever is working now (e.g., entrepreneurial spirit, standardization, delegation, and so on). Eventually, however, the success created by those evolutionary improvements reaches a point of diminishing returns, and it is time for revolutionary change. Your job is to be aware of that shift and act upon it to continue the growth curve.

Successful execution of strategy must take into account the systems dynamics and stages of development of the organization. We have used this information to make several important points in working with our clients:

- **If you understand stages of growth, you will better appreciate the factors that contributed to your organization's growth thus far and, at the same time, make the case for needed change.** Framing discussions around stages of growth can ease some of the ego involvement of key players who helped to create the past successes. Just as there is nothing intrinsically better about third gear than second gear, there is nothing intrinsically better about more local flexibility or more standardization. With organizations as with cars, the question is simply which gear or which approach fits the needs of the current situation.

- **Knowing where you are in these stages can help guide the development of strategy because you'll have an understanding of when and how your organization needs to change.** At Biggs & Bucks, for example, the CEO and the board of directors recognize that they are reaching the point of diminishing returns on local autonomy. A major challenge in their strategic planning is to provide enough consistency and standardization to manage growing complexity without stifling the ability of local offices to adapt to their local conditions. If they overshoot on the control side, they run the risk of hobbling local offices. If they undershoot, their margins will continue to be squeezed by excessive costs.

- **Using these stages and the systems perspective can also help in explaining the need for change and the meaning of change to others.** Human nature being what it is, the local office managers at Biggs & Bucks are likely to hear "we need to standardize some of our administrative processes" as "Corporate is coming with the leg irons." If they view the strategic changes as a serious threat to their freedom of action, they are likely to resist in a number of overt and covert ways.

From Personality to P & L: Three S-Curves

Against this backdrop we now can look at how strategic execution depends on alignment of three S-Curves.

The Organizational S-Curve

Organizations go through fairly predictable phases of growth. An entrepreneurial organization will grow because a specific set of actions and habits work well in that stage. Doing the same things better and more efficiently further fuels the growth. But those actions and habits will eventually work so well that they reach a point of diminishing returns — when continuing on the same path no longer will continue to drive the growth of the organization. The stage is set for a new phase, which will continue until *it* reaches a point of diminishing returns. Senior management's failure to recognize the point of diminishing returns for any set of organizational actions almost guarantees a fumbled handoff.

Unless the organization's leadership understands stages of growth, they won't know when to do the same thing better and when it is time to do something differently.

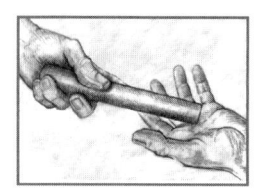

> Unless the organization's leadership understands stages of growth, they won't know when to do the same thing better and when it is time to do something differently.

The Leadership S-Curve

What it takes for successful leadership is different at different stages of an organization's growth. A manager whose skills work well at one stage of growth may flounder as the organization moves into the next stage, and floundering managers are more likely to drop the strategic baton.

Just as an organization's leadership needs to change with growth, a manager moving up within the organization goes through predictable career stages, and at each stage, the demands for success change. As you'll see, the organization cannot outgrow its leadership . . . at least for long.

The Personal S-Curve

Sometimes the barriers to a smooth handoff lie in the organization — in systems and processes that don't deliver results like they used to. Sometimes the barriers to a smooth handoff lie in the skill sets of leadership, i.e., their ability to provide the kind of leadership that the organization needs at the time. But often, the barriers to a smooth handoff lie inside us as individuals — in habits and beliefs that get in the way of changing what we need to change.

There's an old Indian proverb that says, "What you're filled with spills when you're bumped." Few situations will show what you're filled with quite as much as trying to lead other people in a complicated and difficult undertaking. If you're filled with anger, your anger will show in times of stress. If you are filled with doubt, your doubt will surface when you're faced with tough decisions. If you are filled with ego, your ego will flare and get in the way when you're working in a team.

When individuals fail to understand and manage themselves (i.e., their own personalities and egos), attention is shifted away from smoothly passing the baton and onto personal issues. Sometimes the handoff is fumbled because someone won't let go of it, or because someone won't take the handoff. Sometimes it's fumbled because two people can't seem to connect in the handoff zone.

In our experience, someone who fails to grow and adapt personally is as likely to have problems in their role or in the handoff zone as someone who lacks the skill set. We have often seen the careers of bright executives limited because of their failure to manage and adapt their personalities to the changing demands of their roles.

How the Personal Ends up in the P & L

Let's look for a minute at a local office director at Biggs & Bucks. In its early history, Biggs & Bucks grew because local office directors were star performers with customers. They reached their current role because of their demonstrated ability to serve customers and deliver the highest level of billable hours. Under the emerging strategy, local office directors will be encouraged to delegate more account management and billable work to consultants working in their offices. In turn, the local office director's role will shift to developing business and feeding more of the billable work to consultants.

It is likely that the local office directors are smart enough to understand the logic of the desired change . . . and smart enough to give multiple good reasons why they cannot make the change. Pressing problems and inadequate resources would be common reasons:

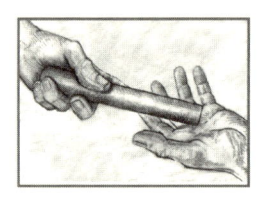

There is no delegation, because no one is prepared to address the problems and the manager is too tied up addressing problems to prepare anyone to take the delegation. As you move down the hierarchy, the specifics might change but the pattern would be the same: managers who are too busy doing what got them promoted to do what they were promoted to do.

"We've had some major problems with some big accounts and I've been tied up in firefighting mode." Another is talent: "You can't imagine how much I wish I could delegate the account management and get out to develop the business. I just don't have anybody right now who I can comfortably turn loose to handle clients of this size. They're just too inexperienced." If you were to recommend developing that next level down, the likely response would be in keeping with those above: "I don't have time for coaching because I'm too busy taking care of clients."

Note the potential for a limiting loop there. There is no delegation, because no one is prepared to address the problems and the manager is too tied up addressing problems to prepare anyone to take the delegation. As you move down the hierarchy, the specifics might change but the pattern would be the same: managers who are too busy doing what got them promoted to do what they were promoted to do.

At one level, each individual would be right. They cannot step up in their own role without having solid performers in the role beneath them. But that is a common problem faced by all managers. There is a solution to that problem. Why not develop the people at the level below so that they can take on more? And if they cannot be developed, then why not take appropriate action to get the right people in the right roles? Put another way, why do some managers face the challenge and develop their direct reports while others continue to get pulled down into doing work that should be done by their direct reports?

There are a limited number of reasons why any individual is not performing at a desired level. In a later chapter we will go into more detail about the process for finding the reasons, so a brief walk-through here will suffice:

1) The first and simplest reason is awareness. The manager does not yet fully understand the demands and expectations of the current role. That one is easy enough to solve if someone takes the time to teach the manager.

2) The second reason is that the manager doesn't believe that the desired behaviors will actually work better than the current behaviors. Lack of commitment to the new behavior just requires someone to make a convincing case. Again, this is not that hard. The case here is usually in the numbers. We once saw the case made for a role shift with two questions before a group of new partners in a large consulting firm: "How many hours can you individually bill per month? And then, how many hours can your team bill per month if you're developing both the business and the team, and the team is actually doing the work?"

3) The third reason is that the person lacks the skill to fulfill the role even if they understand it and believe it is important. Either the person can learn the skills or they can't. And everyone can find out which it is, provided someone has taken the time to teach.

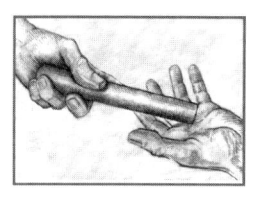

...the personal comfort zone ends up in the P&L. Growing an organization usually means that managers have to move up in their own personal growth curve.

4) Maybe the person has the skill to step into the new role but is uncertain and lacking confidence. Building confidence, again, is not impossibly difficult, if someone has recognized the need and taken reasonable steps to develop the confidence.

5) If all of the above have been addressed, but the person still is not performing as desired, we are now into more difficult territory. The next possible reason is that the demands of the role just don't fit well with the personality and motivation of the individual. If that is the case, the options will be limited.

6) Finally, if you have ruled out all of the reasons discussed above, then the barrier is in the system. There are conflicting priorities or real resource problems that cannot be addressed by the individual alone.

Whatever the personal barrier to desired performance is, overcoming it will depend on the willingness to do something that is personally uncomfortable. That is, growing into a new role usually requires getting out of the personal comfort zone, to face and manage the emotional discomfort of changing your behavior to fit the demands of the new role instead of relying on behaviors that worked well in a previous role. Failure to do so keeps leadership performing below what is needed by the organization. Put another way, the personal comfort zone ends up in the P&L. Growing an organization usually means that managers have to move up in their own personal growth curve.

Three S-Curves at Biggs & Bucks: How Personality Ends Up in the P&L

Let's look briefly at a systems view of the challenges at Biggs & Bucks, especially the connections among the three S-curves. First, let's look again at our simplified diagram showing the forces that drive growth at Biggs & Bucks and the forces restraining or slowing growth (Figure 2.4).

Note that the local office autonomy drives client focus which, in turn, drives sales revenue. The revenue drives further acquisitions

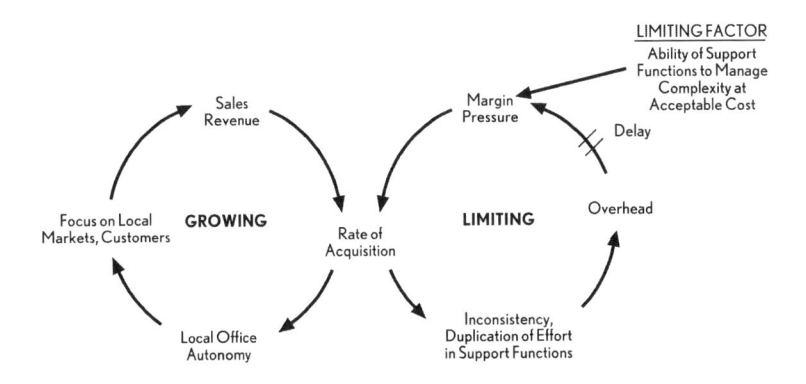

Figure 2.4 - Systems Model of the Organizational Challenges at Biggs & Bucks

which, in turn, allows for the local autonomy that, in turn, allows for the satisfaction of clients, and so on. As these forces work over time to drive the growth of the firm, the same local autonomy that drives growth also increases the amount of duplication of effort and other inefficiencies, which drive up overhead.

At first, the growth outweighs the costs of the duplication in support functions, and growth continues. Eventually, however, the benefits of local autonomy reach the point of diminishing returns as duplication and inefficiency in support functions start to squeeze margins. Tighter margins would then slow the rate of acquisitions. Just as food supply would limit the rate of growth of a rabbit population on an island, the capacity of the support functions would begin to limit the growth of Biggs & Bucks.

Now let's turn to the implications for local office directors. Continued growth will require the local office directors to increase the productivity of their offices by using standardized processes and developing the pool of experienced consultants. But, as Figure 2.5 shows, these local office directors have been promoted into management roles because of their success in producing revenue from sales and service to clients.

The more time these managers spend in the familiar territory of direct billable work, the greater the short-term benefit in terms of

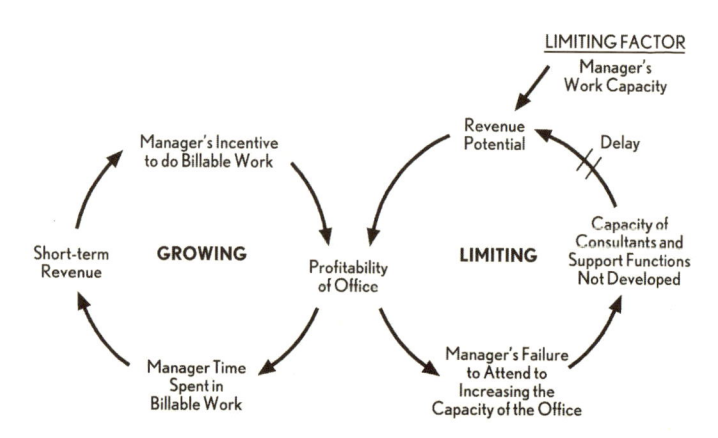

Figure 2.5 - Systems Model of the Local Leadership Challenges at Biggs & Bucks

revenue. The manager then feels greater incentive to stay close to the billable work and sales activity, and thus helps drive the profitability of the office. This pattern continues to feed on itself, all the while drawing the manager's time away from work on growing the capacity of the office, activities such as improving the standardization, coaching those in consulting roles to grow their client lists, and other longer term aspects of the role.

The manager can get the short-term benefits of direct billable work and the long-term benefits of growing capacity simply by working longer hours, up to some point. At that point, the manager cannot increase short- and long-term benefits by working harder without burning out, creating family problems, or encountering other constraints on work hours. When that point is reached, the output and profitability of the office tend to stabilize. Attempting to push growth by delegating client work and addressing the support inefficiencies causes a short-term dip in profitability, which pulls the manager back to the short-term loop to prop up profits. The office cannot outgrow the total realistic time commitment of the manager. In order to continue growing, the manager will have to face his or her own personal S-curve, as shown in Figure 2.6.

Let's look now at the personal dynamics driving the manager's behavior. The revenue generated from time in the "player" role not only provides a short-term revenue boost for the office, but it also provides an ego boost for the manager in the form of quick gratifi-

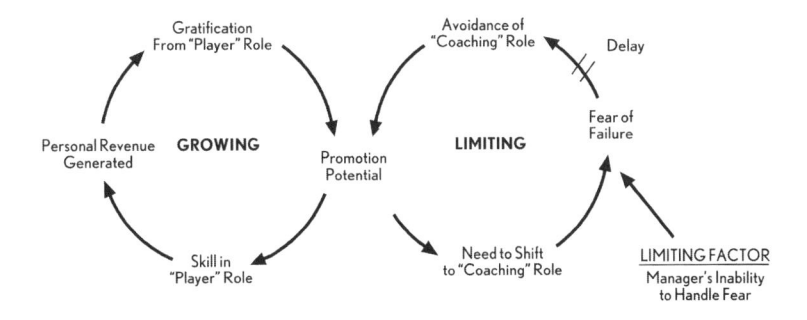

Figure 2.6 - Systems Model of the Personal Challenges at Biggs & Bucks

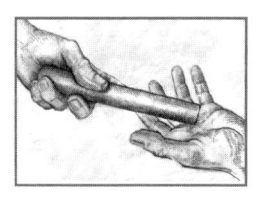

> The more the manager tries out the new role, the greater the fear of failure, and the greater the pull back into the player role. The greater the manager's ability to manage the fear and anxiety of the new role, however, the more of the long-term benefits of coaching he will experience.

cation. In essence, the "player" role of selling and serving clients becomes more and more comfortable, and the skill as a provider grows. Eventually, the manager's productivity and success result in greater promotion potential. Promotion calls for a shift from the player role of direct sales and service to clients to more of a coach role. But this new role is out of the comfortable pattern established early on, and the benefits of the new coaching role are delayed compared with the benefits of the old player role. So the more the manager tries out the new role, the greater the fear of failure, and the greater the pull back into the player role. The greater the manager's ability to manage the fear and anxiety of the new role, however, the more of the long-term benefits of coaching he will experience. The lower the manager's tolerance for anxiety, the quicker he gets pulled back into the player role, reducing the chance to witness the long-term benefits of successful coaching.

In essence, the manager's ability to manage the anxiety and discomfort of the new role shapes success in that role, which affects the degree to which the organization's strategy is executed. In other words, once again the personal ends up in the P&L.

We have taken a high-level look at the first challenge for strategic execution — sizing up the field on which the strategic race will be run. In practice, this means that executives need to understand the stage of growth and the likely systems forces currently working in the organization. These systems forces include those that shape leadership behavior and, ultimately, the comfort of key players with the strategy. This context helps executives anticipate the changes that are most necessary in order to support the execution of strategy. In particular, it is essential to anticipate and prepare for those ways in which the organization will push back or resist role changes or other aspects of the strategy. For example, organizations growing from an entrepreneurial size and scope often encounter resistance to management's efforts to control costs by standardization. We will watch this play out later in our fictional case of Biggs & Bucks.

Our next chapter addresses the second challenge, that of ensuring that the leadership force is in place to drive the strategy. In other words, you have to size up the team and make sure that you have the right runners in the right roles.

Passing the Baton: Winning the Race for Strategic Execution

Chapter 3

The Second Challenge: Sizing Up the Team

Right Runners, Right Roles

In the previous chapter, we discussed how a successful strategy begins with sizing up the field. But this is only the first step in effectively shaping and executing strategy. Of course, having a sound strategy is necessary, but it is not sufficient.[7] Research indicates that CEO failure is not usually attributable to flawed strategy, but to flawed execution. And according to a study cited by Kaplan and Norton, only 10 percent of well-formulated strategies are actually carried out well.[8] Execution is the hard part of strategy, and getting the right people on your team and putting them in the right places are huge steps in the right direction.

---

7 Charan, R. & Colvin, G. (June 21, 1999). "Why CEOs Fail." *Fortune Magazine,* 69-78.

8 Kaplan, R. & Norton, D. (2000). *The Strategy Focused Organization: How Balanced Scorecard Companies Thrive in the New Business Environment.* Boston, MA. Harvard Business School Publishing.

Three Management Levels and Three Handoff Zones

Convention identifies three broad levels of management in which the roles and requirements for success change noticeably, and organizational research has largely confirmed these levels: senior (systems), middle (organizational), and line (operational).[9] In larger organizations, there may be several steps within each of the three levels, but the fundamental three levels are still evident. Think of these levels as the runners assigned each leg of a relay race. All three levels are vital to winning, but they contribute in different ways. We will go more deeply into those roles later, but first we will take a quick look at the three levels and some of the characteristics required for success in each.

Remember that there may not be neat dividing lines between each level. In the end, it will not matter to your success or that of your organization that you fit some formal definition of "senior" or "middle" management. It will matter greatly, however, whether or not your role is properly aligned with corporate or organizational strategy and with other roles around you, and whether or not you have the required skills to succeed in your role. With that caution in mind, let's look at these three levels of management and some of the major responsibilities for success at each level.

Senior or Systems Level

Manage External Boundaries

One way of understanding a managerial role is to look at the boundaries managed by the person in that role. Line managers deal with

---

[9] Zaccaro, S. J. (2001). *The Nature of Executive Leadership: A Conceptual and Empirical Analysis of Success.* Washington, DC. American Psychological Association.

vertical boundaries, up to their boss and down to their work group. Middle managers have these vertical boundaries as well. But they also have a key role in coordinating across horizontal boundaries. Senior managers have these vertical and horizontal boundaries to deal with, but they also have to grapple with the external boundaries of the organization, including financial institutions, political and regulatory bodies, and other forces. We think of the management of external boundaries as a defining characteristic of senior management.

Scan the Environment

The senior role requires strategic skill in order to position the organization to adapt to these external forces. Thus, a skilled senior manager is adept at scanning the environment to anticipate technical developments, customer requirements and changes in customer base, competitive threats, and other challenges and opportunities facing the organization.

Find Causal Patterns

Thorough understanding of the business model and financial drivers of the business is crucial at this level. We think of this understanding as having an accurate "causal map" or mental picture of how things work in the business and in the industry; i.e., a deep understanding of what drives what. Put simply, a successful senior manager

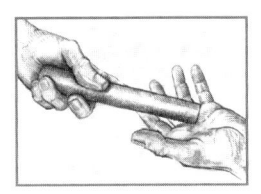

It will matter . . . whether or not your role is properly aligned with corporate or organizational strategy and with other roles around you, and whether or not you have the required skills to succeed in your role.

needs good business sense.

Be a Team Player
Senior managers have to make sense of the complex array of information coming at them from the environmental scanning process. They usually do this interpretation as part of a team of other senior managers, so the ability to work well in a team is often crucial to success at this level. Diplomacy and interpersonal skills, which emerge as important at the middle management level, continue to be critical in senior roles.

Provide Vision and Strategic Positioning
Working from their interpretation of the opportunities and threats in the environment and their knowledge of their own organization, senior managers then create a vision and strategically position the organization within that environment. Does the organization plan to be an innovation leader, a fast second, the lowest-cost provider, or excellent at service and customization? Remember, trying to be all things is a prescription for failure.

Align Structure and Systems
Another major responsibility at the senior level is to align the organization's structure, systems, and activities to support the strategy. These systems include not only the traditional production and administrative systems but also the human system.

Guide Execution
Strategic positioning and alignment require hard decisions and trade-offs, because the organization cannot be equally good at everything.[10,11] Reaching agreement about strategic trade-offs can be

---

10 Porter, M. (November-December, 1996). "What is Strategy?" *Harvard Business Review*, 61-64.

11 Kaplan, R. S. & Norton, D. P. (2004). *Strategy Maps: Converting Intangible Assets into Tangible Outcomes*. Boston, MA. Harvard Business School Publishing Corp.

challenging enough for a senior team whose egos tend toward the large size, but the real challenge is in execution. The strategic position and trade-offs have to be understood and translated into day-to-day decisions, and that begins at the boundary between senior and middle management. A dropped baton here means a loss of competitive focus throughout the organization. A good senior manager guides execution without getting pulled excessively into day-to-day operations.

Measure the Time Horizon in Years

The time horizon for planning at the senior level often extends to multiple years. Even in an unstable market, senior leaders have to grapple with strategic plans and change management efforts that can take several years to execute. The minimum planning time frame we hear in working with senior leaders is three to five years, and it is not uncommon to hear senior executives planning ten years out or more. Managing longer and longer time horizons requires executives to be able to make decisions under conditions of greater complexity and uncertainty. Perseverance, which is a good trait to have under normal circumstances, becomes a vital trait in executing a plan over several years. We will go into much more depth on personal characteristics and their relationship to changing role requirements in Chapter 7.

Middle or Organizational Level: The First Translators of Strategy

Translate Strategy

In a small organization, there may be only three levels, so middle management is easy to identify. In a larger organization, there may be several layers between front-line supervisors and senior managers. The ideal role and required skills for anyone working in the middle will depend in part on the specific organization. Even so, there will be common challenges for those who work between the senior and line levels.

If you work in this broad middle area, you are one of the first translators of strategy. One of the defining characteristics of middle management is having responsibility for some organizational unit or sub-unit, such as a department or a functional area within a department. It is up to you to ensure that the strategic goals of the organization are translated into the specialized language and priorities of your department or functional area.

Work with an Intermediate Time Horizon

Middle managers are involved in forecasting and planning for their unit or sub-unit, so their time horizon is longer than that of line managers. In smaller organizations, this planning horizon might be one year. For example, a director of information systems at a small firm might need to develop a project and staffing plan a year in advance. For larger organizations, the planning horizon might extend to several years.

Create a Functional Vision and Plan

This shift toward the longer time horizon in middle management has an interesting result. We usually think of *vision* as a required characteristic of senior managers, and visionary leadership at the top has been shown to correlate with better long-term organizational results.[12] But the need to plan and set goals in longer time frames suggests that middle managers must have a visionary side as well.[13] The successful middle manager resists the temptation to be the hero — the star player who steps in to solve the myriad technical and oper-

---

12 Collins, J. & Porras, J. (1997). *Built to Last: Successful Habits of Visionary Companies.* New York, NY. Harper Collins Publishers.

13 Katzenbach, J. R. (1995). *Real Change Leaders: How You Can Create Growth and High Performance at Your Company.* New York, NY. Random House.

ational problems that offer themselves on a minute-by-minute basis. Instead, the successful middle manager develops a vision for his or her functional area that aligns with corporate strategy and anticipates the needs of the organization. Part of that vision is the development of a team that solves the technical and operational problems. We will say a lot more about this later.

Another major element of the middle manager's role is translating strategic initiatives into action plans at the tactical and operational level. For example, cost containment objectives have to be broken down into departmental or functional targets and action plans so that line managers have a clear set of boundaries within which to work. This translation role creates a kind of pinch point — the middle manager has to think in terms of long-term execution, but is still very close to the daily firefighting of the front lines.

Manage Internal Boundaries

As we've said, one way of understanding any managerial role is to look at the boundaries that have to be managed as part of the role. Middle managers must successfully negotiate vertical boundaries: getting goals from above and providing direction to the level below. However, one of the biggest challenges for middle managers is managing *horizontal* boundaries with other departments or functions. When there is an issue with another department, a line manager usually can "kick it upstairs" to a middle manager. It then falls to a middle manager to resolve that issue with another middle manager. Success or failure in middle management often depends on skill in handling differences at the boundaries between departments or functions.

Though the idea of middle management typically includes supervision of others within a functional area or department, we also include functional or technical specialists who play a key role in inter-departmental work flows, even if they have no direct reports. For example, we would think of a non-supervisory credit officer or project manager who has to coordinate with other disciplines or de-

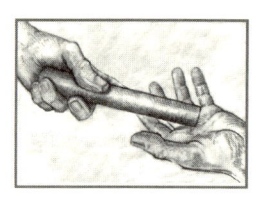

The defining elements here are the need to coordinate horizontally with other disciplines and the need to influence without having formal supervisory authority. If these characteristics apply to your role, you can feel the pinch just thinking about it.

partments as working in middle management.

The defining elements here are the need to coordinate horizontally with other disciplines and the need to influence without having formal supervisory authority. If these characteristics apply to your role, you can feel the pinch just thinking about it.

It is here that a manager moving into the middle ranks first faces a crucial set of challenges. The people you most need to influence don't report to you and often have goals that appear to conflict with yours. If you supervise an operational function, you've got to coordinate with the Marketing Department on a new sales effort. You want as much lead time as possible in order to plan and reduce errors, but Marketing wants to move as fast as possible to try to gain market share. You want it simple so your people can do it efficiently, while Marketing wants it elegant so it will attract more business. Or if you're a project manager for a new product launch, the design engineers want to increase functionality and perfect the design even at the expense of a delay in launch. But your sales team wants to hit the market now and tweak the design later. You are working at the pinch point between quality and speed.

The real grind is that your peers can make persuasive arguments that their point of view is correct. The engineers will argue convincingly that if you launch too soon and have functionality problems, you will damage the customer's trust in you. And the sales team will argue with equal passion that if your competitor gets there first and develops the relationship, then the functionality issues become moot. You probably weren't promoted for your skills in diplomacy, but all of a sudden you've got to start acting like a diplomat. And if you ask your boss whether it is more important to get the product right or to generate some sales revenue now, the answer will probably be "yes."

A related challenge is that you and your peers may speak a different technical language. All of you were promoted to middle management because of your demonstrated skill in your respective areas of expertise, because you spoke the language of your functional areas. Maybe you were promoted because of your engineering skill, so you speak the language of engineers. Or you were promoted to the middle ranks of the finance area because of your performance on the front lines in basic bookkeeping. Just as your native language shapes the way you think, it is this technical language that shapes your view of what is important. And of course your technical language is your primary means for communicating with others. And that's where middle management presents a new set of challenges, because in middle management you must coordinate and often negotiate with people who don't speak your technical language.

Regardless of what technical language got you promoted to middle management, you have to begin speaking the language of your peers to some extent if you are to bridge the gap between departments. If you don't already have it, you must especially develop some familiarity with the language of finance; the financial ratios and metrics of your organization. In many ways, the language of finance will be the common bridge between different technical specialties.

In summary, as a middle manager you have to understand and translate strategy into day-to-day actions, and you have to coordinate your actions with those of peers who have different technical specialties and who often have goals that conflict with yours. You have to balance competing interests while considering both short-term and long-term consequences of your actions. That's why we describe middle management as a pinch point, an intersection between the giant, slow-moving strategic gear above and the smaller, fast-spinning operational gears below.

Develop Line Managers
Another critical responsibility of middle management is the selection and development of line managers. We often see middle managers — who may be in the "sweet spot" of their own technical development — struggle with how to think and act more like a coach than a player. Failure to make this transition, however, can create a dangerous bottleneck at the door of the middle manager who is excessively tied up in technical operations.

Line or Operational Level

Work Planning and Task Assignment
Managers at this level focus primarily on short-term planning and execution of work, usually for a small work team. Line managers translate strategic and tactical goals that have been set at higher levels into immediate production goals. They typically follow and interpret procedures established by others.

Handle Details
Promotion to line manager depends heavily on skill in the technical area to be supervised. Success in the line manager role still depends in large part on this technical skill, because the line manager has to serve as a technical resource for direct reports. For example, a head teller in a bank serves as a resource for tellers who are confronted with unfamiliar tasks or requests from customers. Or an engineer heading up a design team might assist with technical problems faced by a member of the team. Handling of these myriad details typical-

ly falls to the line manager level.

Manage Resources
In addition to technical skill, however, line managers need to be proficient in basic resource planning. Successful line managers need a general understanding of the organization's strategy, mostly in terms of understanding goals, so that work can be planned and line resources allocated appropriately.

Supervise Line Employees
A major task of line managers is supervision of line employees. Line managers are the final translators and ambassadors for strategy. It's sobering to think that the anchor runner in our strategic handoff probably has the least experience and training in this critical part of his role.

Work with a Shorter Time Horizon
The time horizon for a line manager is usually relatively short. That is, a successful line manager may only have to plan in terms of weeks or a few months. For example, a line supervisor in a manufacturing operation may need to plan production runs over the course of a month.

Guaranteeing a Fumble: Failing to Develop Managers for Their Roles

Failure to develop managers as they move from one level to the next is one of the biggest barriers to successful execution of strategy. Probably the most commonly used criterion in selecting candidates for the first step into management is technical skill. Though there are attempts, such as the use of assessment centers, to predict who is more likely to succeed once moved into a management role, most companies still rely on the rearview mirror approach. We look at success in a past role and then hope for success in a new and different role. Either way, we commonly find that managers moving up in the organization tend to underestimate the parts of their role having to do with the translation of strategy and the development of people working under them. In essence, many managers that we have worked with still spend too much time and effort working as they did in their previous role.

We hear many reasons for the failure to prepare and develop managers as they move higher in the organization. The most common reason we hear, of course, is the time constraints of the new managers and their supervisors. Most managers are too busy doing things in the short term to devote much time to preparing someone for the long term. We suspect that a more fundamental reason is that the managers who should be driving the preparation and development probably didn't get much in the way of preparation and development themselves. We see two variations of this line of thinking. One is, "I figured it out and so can you." The other (and, we suspect, the one that is closer to the truth) is, "I wouldn't know where to start."

Whatever the reason, failure to have strong managers at any of the three levels is like having one runner in a relay race wearing snow shoes. The most common responses — running harder or working longer hours — are not likely to make up for the disadvantage to the team.

Now, let's look at some of the possible signs of difficulty in adapting roles at each of the three levels.

Where Senior Managers Drop the Baton

The effects of underperformance by any player in a senior role rolls through the organization like a tsunami. The immediate effects on the senior team may be noticeable, but not necessarily profound.

We have often seen senior teams tolerate or work around questionable performance in a peer for a variety of reasons. But downstream, the effects grow and multiply until they wash over the line level with disastrous effects.

Common reasons that senior managers fail to execute strategy include:

- Failure to appreciate the need for strategic focus and deliberate trade-offs; trying to be all things to all people.
- Assuming that lower levels in the organization understand the practical day-to-day implications of the organization's strategy; failing to set in place the processes to translate strategy all the way to the front lines.
- Not recognizing the difference between delegating and abdicating.
- Paying insufficient attention to the results of growth and demands for new ways of working; staying with approaches that worked at an earlier stage but are inadequate for the current stage of growth.
- Failing to aggressively identify and remove barriers to execution, including technical, structural, systems, and process issues.
- Avoiding (or being slow to) manage painful people issues, such as dealing with a key manager who was a strong contributor at an earlier stage but who cannot step up to new demands.

Where Middle Managers Drop the Baton

As we noted earlier, a dropped baton between the senior and middle levels has ripple effects throughout the entire organization, and the penalties here are steep. Some of the most common reasons that middle managers struggle or fail are:

- Failing to develop a vision for their functional area or department that anticipates the organization's needs and aligns

with the organization's vision and strategy.
- Setting goals instead of creating true functional strategies.
- Not recognizing the need to adapt and grow, especially in response to the new demands that come with organizational growth, reorganization, or other changes.
- Getting pulled into the weeds of technical and operational problems instead of working their way to the hilltop.
- Taking local actions without full consideration of the effects of these actions as they ripple through the larger organization-al system. Though senior managers can also fall into this trap, middle managers seem especially vulnerable in that they make so many day-to-day decisions that affect crossfunctional workflow. Often, these decisions are at a level of detail that keeps them under the radar screen until the problems downstream pile up enough to get noticed.
- Waiting for someone above to resolve cross-functional or other horizontal issues instead of taking the initiative to drive the solution.
- Getting to middle management because of technical competence but failing to manage interpersonal relationships.

Where Line Managers Drop the Baton

The biggest challenge facing line managers is that they were promoted for being technically skilled in some area, but their new role calls on them to manage and lead their work group. Thinking like a manager is different from thinking like an individual contributor. In our experience, the biggest derailers of line managers are:

- Continuing to think and act like one of the team instead of as the leader of the team. We have seen this at its most pronounced when the line manager has been promoted from within a team after a long history as a team member.
- Allowing themselves to be excessively pulled into day-to-day technical or operational problems and losing sight of

the work group's connection with the larger functional strategy. We commonly see managers working on too many projects and tasks, usually in order to fulfill their ego needs for immediate gratification.
- Failing to plan ahead for production, staffing, and resource needs.
- Not getting up to speed with middle management about how to translate the strategic priorities for the function or department into day-to-day priorities and work plans.
- Seeing the line management role as an assigner of tasks instead of as a developer of people.
- Not having or building adequate interpersonal and communication skills.

The Invisible Levels: Three Handoff Zones

For successful execution of organizational strategy, all levels of management must be aligned with the overall strategy and with one another. By "aligned," we simply mean that the three levels should have a shared understanding of the strategy and the priorities as they relate to each level, and that each level focuses on those tasks that are appropriate to its role. If misalignment occurs at any level, there is a loss of focus and a consequent loss of executional effectiveness.

Figure 3.1 provides a summary of the major role requirements and attributes for each level. If you read the countless business research articles on the roles and competencies of managers at these three levels, you will come away with a picture that looks something like the boxes in Figure 3.1. *But what you will not see is much emphasis on the space between the boxes — the handoff zones.* It is here, we believe, that much of the most difficult work of strategic execution occurs. Later, we will offer a brief decision process for identifying performance issues *within* each of these levels. For now, however, let's look at how the three levels have to work together in the handoff zones in order to pass the strategic baton smoothly.

Passing the Baton: Winning the Race for Strategic Execution

```
┌─────────────────────────────────────────────────────────────────┐
│  Core Ideology • Core Purpose and Core Values • Value Proposition Strategy │
└─────────────────────────────────────────────────────────────────┘
                              ↕
┌─────────────────────────────────────────────────────────────────┐
│  Key Internal Processes • Necessary Competencies • Desired Culture │
└─────────────────────────────────────────────────────────────────┘
```

Senior Manager Role
- Manage external boundaries
- Scan the environment
- Find causal patterns
- Be a team player
- Provide vision and strategic positioning
- Align structure and systems
- Guide execution
- Measure the time horizon in years

Key Factors
- Mental complexity
- Strategic thinking
- Business skill
- Interpersonal savvy

Middle Manager Role
- Translate strategy
- Work with an intermediate time horizon
- Create a functional vision and plan
- Manage internal boundaries
- Develop line managers

Key Factors
- Systems thinking
- Basic finance
- Tactical planning
- Resource allocation
- Negotiating
- Role flexibility
- Organizational savvy

Line Manager Role
- Work planning and task assignment
- Handle details
- Manage resources
- Supervise line employees
- Short time horizon

Key Factors
- Technical skill
- Organizational ability
- Work planning

Handoff Zone

Handoff Zone

Handoff Zone

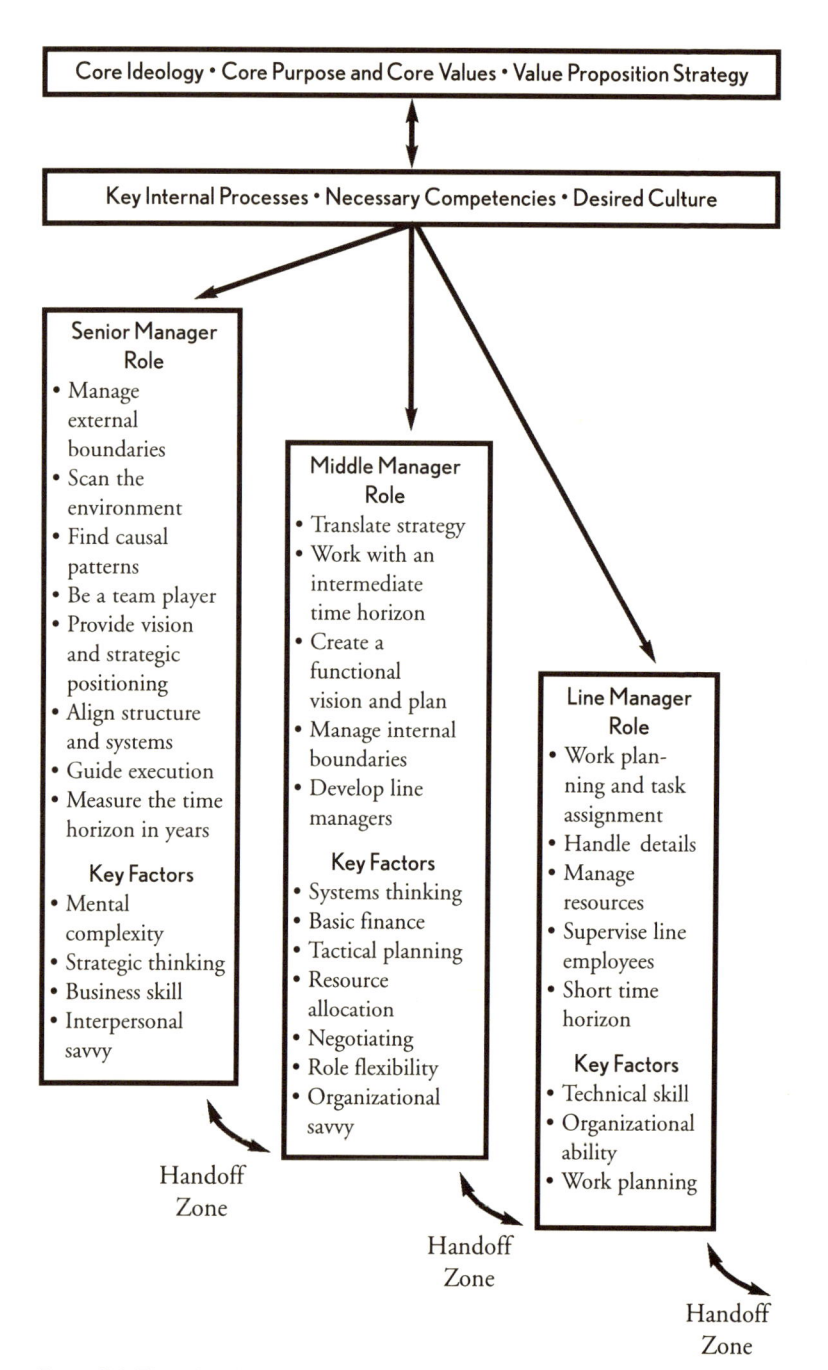

Figure 3.1 - Three Levels and Three Handoff Zones

As we show at the top of Figure 3.1, strategy begins with the organization's core ideology — its unique blend of core purpose and core values.[14] These core characteristics will guide the development of strategy and also create the behavioral boundaries within which people will work. People who are out of alignment with either the core purpose or core values will probably be uncomfortable, at best, working in the organization. If the misalignment is large, the person is simply in the wrong organization.

These questions of fit apply to each level of management. Once we know the size and structure of an organization, the role of each level of management is not difficult to define in the broad terms that we show in Figure 3.1. But the specific ways in which the manager must carry out that role are guided by the organization's values. How much independence is allowed in decision-making? How much tolerance is there for risk and error? How does one handle conflict? Merely understanding your role and having the right skills still are no guarantee of success.

Within the backdrop of core ideology, the strategy is built on the organization's value proposition and its unique blend of internal processes or activities.[15] A strategy map is one of the more practical tools for guiding discussions and decisions about strategy at the senior level and also informing and aligning work throughout the organization. We will not go into detail here about the strategy mapping process, but at this point we will simply note that it produces a visual representation of an organization's financial, customer, operational, and cultural objectives. Looking at a well-developed strategy map, it is possible to see the conections between actions or organizational characteristics at one level and results at another level. These connections then form the handful of strategic themes or battle plans that are crucial to execution.

---

14 Collins, J. & Porras, J. (1997). *Built to Last: Successful Habits of Visionary Companies.* New York, NY. Harper Collins Publishers.

15 Kaplan, R. & Norton, D. (2000). *The Strategy Focused Organization: How Balanced Scorecard Companies Thrive in the New Business Environment.* Boston, MA. Harvard Business School Publishing.

In our work, we have found the strategy mapping process to be indispensable to role definition as well as to strategic execution. In years of working *as* managers ourselves and working *with* managers, we have never heard a complaint of having too little to do or being burdened by excessive resources. Without strategic discipline and focus, managers at each level can be pulled into thousands of activities that may seem important at the time but are not strategically critical. We have seen managers flailing away at tasks even as they get squeezed at the pinch point between strategic intent and daily firefighting. By highlighting the key internal processes needed as they relate to customer experience, managers have a better chance of separating the strategically critical from the nice-to-have. As we will show, a major piece of a successful handoff is the translation of these strategically critical processes into expectations at the functional and, ultimately, the individual level.

The strategy mapping process is useful in other ways. One, as shown in Figure 3.1, is that the identification of key internal processes leads easily into a description of the competencies needed in the organization to drive those processes. For example, as organizations grow in size and develop a larger core of middle managers, those middle managers typically have to be quite skilled in negotiation and problem-solving. Senior managers at this stage usually have to excel at delegating and guiding execution without micromanaging. With the success profile tied back to strategy in a clear visual format, it is easier to then size up the talent in each of the roles. Seeing that the success profile has changed is a powerful motivator for managers whose role demands have shifted. Finally, a strategy map invites attention to the ways in which the culture may need to adapt in order to support the strategy.

The Talent Base at Biggs & Bucks Financial Services

When we left Biggs & Bucks in Chapter Two, the CEO, the board of directors, and the senior team had grappled with some of the challenges of their successful growth. In particular, they had recognized the signs that their earlier approach of allowing local autonomy in systems and processes is showing signs of strain: margins are beginning to be squeezed by duplication, and inefficiencies have developed as each local office carried over the systems and processes that had worked for them in the past.

They recognized the telltale signs of the S-curve of growth beginning to flatten as limiting forces built up. Because they understand their history in systems terms, they are resisting the temptation to bring in another service line to boost further growth. Pushing more volume through a system that has begun to strain would only increase the strain. They know that some degree of consistency in local processes is needed, but they also understand that a major driver of their success is the local ability to adapt to the needs of customers.

At a high level, the Biggs & Bucks strategy calls for targeting key processes for standardization and at the same time leveraging their strong presence in local markets. They developed financial targets for cost management, for deeper penetration of existing accounts, and for new accounts.

As they complete the first draft of their solution path to achieve those financial goals, CEO John Jefferson and his team are beginning to recognize that their new direction depends heavily on having stronger management and leadership talent heading up each of the local offices. Most of the local offices were led by local office directors, who typically managed the office staff and supervised senior financial consultants while also managing their own accounts. The local office directors are drawn from the ranks of the most successful senior financial consultants, who manage teams of account specialists.

The roles most affected by the new direction are the local office directors. As plans to standardize administrative procedures progress, these local office directors should be much more engaged in decision processes that will affect the whole business, not just their local office. Most local office directors see the management aspects of their roles as secondary and believe they should concentrate their efforts on selling financial products and services. But the new financial targets are ambitious. The senior team has a general sense that successful local office directors in the future will develop business and feed their local offices, and that is a far cry from selling and delivering business on their own. Successful local office directors will also have to spend more time planning and managing the boundaries between the consulting and sales functions on the one hand and the growing administrative functions on the other.

Or, as the CEO put it at the end of one strategy session, "Our star players are going to have to start thinking and acting like coaches. I'm not at all comfortable that they're ready to do that."

"Well, we figured it out when we were in their shoes," said one of the senior team. "That's the nature of this business. They'll figure it out, too, or they're in the wrong jobs. We can't get pulled down into the details of 30 local offices. We've just got to set the course and then expect them to do their jobs."

There was a long pause, longer than the senior team was accustomed to and long enough to feel awkward. Finally the CEO answered.

"We're not going to get pulled into the details of 30 local offices. But neither are we going to bet the future of this company on whether 30 local office directors figure this out on their own. We're going to have to start thinking and acting like coaches, too. We aren't going out on the field, but we aren't going to sit in the stands, either."

Chapter 4

The Third Challenge: Anticipating Problems in the Handoff Zone

Understanding the Handoff Process

In the last chapter, we described three levels of management and discussed the importance of alignment among each. We also stressed the importance of the invisible areas — the handoff zones between each of the levels. In this chapter, we will look more closely at these handoff zones, with the goal of helping you anticipate problems that may arise in the handoff process.

Remember: The handoff zone is the space between two management levels, in which the baton of strategy is passed from one level to the next to be translated into specific actions. There is a point in the handoff zone in which two hands are on the baton . . . or at least they should be.

The hardest part of working in the handoff zone is simply realizing that it exists in the first place. Organizational charts (O-charts) give a compelling picture of the structure and roles of each level. But they cannot shed much light on the process needed to pass the strategy through the organization without fumbles. This process is not as clean and well-defined as an O-chart; consequently, much time and energy can be wasted with assumptions and debates about who has the baton or who should have it.

The higher level in the handoff often assumes that the lower level understands or should understand the priorities and how to find the right balance among competing priorities. The higher level often complains that the receiving level is not quick enough in taking the handoff.

The receiving level, on the other hand, often complains of lack of direction (or of micromanagement) from the higher level. We often hear complaints that the senior level has an inadequate appreciation for all that is involved in carrying out the strategy; that the expectations are unrealistic. In essence, the complaint is that senior management *throws* the baton, rather than passing it. Or we hear complaints that senior management never lets go of the baton, that the upper level jumps too quickly into daily operations and tampers with processes that they don't fully understand. We hear all of those complaints as evidence that the two levels do not yet understand the need to coordinate their actions in the handoff zone between their roles.

In brief, then, the handoff zone is the space in which two levels of management meet to ensure that the strategy is translated from the language and priorities of the upper level to the language and priorities of the lower level. It is the space between management levels where a mutual understanding is reached about the strategic baton. The two levels must understand:
- The environmental and business *context* that shaped the strategy;
- A *vision* that describes how the organization will be in the future, given the environmental and business realities facing it;

- The *strategy* itself, including the value proposition for customers, the major trade-offs that will be grappled with, and the internal changes needed;
- The *barriers* to making those changes and the solution paths to address those barriers;
- The personal implications and *performance expectations* for the receiving level and *accountabilities* for both levels;
- The organizational *values* as they apply to actions at the higher level and as those values will get translated into the actions at the receiving level.

We want to emphasize that this process is all about translation from general to specific, from concept to action. So often, failure to fully execute strategy means that something has been lost in translation.

Ideal Alignment and Ideal Handoffs

Now let's see how role alignment and the handoff process look in an ideal case.

Figure 4.1 lists the three broad levels of management on the left, and illustrates the roles *as they are actually carried out* in the ovals to the right. In this example, we are dealing with only one individual at each level, so that we can track the handoff process from one element of strategy through the relevant functional and line translations. In this case, the individuals at all three levels are currently working within the appropriate range, with the senior manager concentrating on the strategic development process, the middle manager translating that strategy into functional and departmental plans, and the line manager handling the work planning process.

The three handoff zones are represented by the arrows. Note that the arrows are two-directional to emphasize that the level mak-

Role Alignment and Handoff Model

Ideal Senior Role	Actual Senior Role		Strategy is developed...
Ideal Middle Role		Actual Middle Role	translated into functional plans...
Ideal Line Role			Actual Line Role	translated into work plans...
			and executed by the organization.

Figure 4.1 - Ideal Alignment and Ideal Handoffs

ing the pass and the level taking the pass both have their hands on the strategic baton. Note also the clear alignment in the handoff process in that the role ovals touch in the handoff zone. There are no gaps between the role ovals, which would indicate dumping or throwing the baton from the higher level without meeting in the handoff zone. And there are no overlaps, which would indicate micromanagement and failing to let go of the baton from the higher level.

Let's illustrate the smooth handoffs of Figure 4.1 with a simple example. Suppose we have a manufacturing company that has grown rapidly because of its innovative product designs. With rapid growth in its product offerings, however, the company has begun to see delays in product launches and more quality problems after launch. Smaller competitors could exploit this trend. Let's say that the company's strategy calls for improvements in the speed and quality of product launches and that there is also a strategic goal to aggressively manage costs.

If the company's management levels are aligned as shown in Figure 4.1, that would mean that senior management is appropriately focused on strategic issues and that middle management is focused on the development and execution of functional plans. Line managers within functional areas would be focused on managing day-to-day tasks in keeping with those functional plans.

So the first thing to notice about Figure 4.1 is that our "runners" are in the right roles. The second is that they are working effectively in the handoff zones between levels, so that the strategic baton is translated from the high-level language of strategy into functional plans and then into work plans at the line level.

To create the alignment depicted in Figure 4.1, all levels of management would need a shared understanding about the elements of the strategic baton.

The Environmental and Business Context of the Strategy

As depicted in Figure 4.1, senior management has done a good job of engaging middle management in understanding the causes and effects of delayed product launches and quality problems. Though middle managers live in the day-to-day world of functional execution in their own technical areas, they need to also have a strong appreciation for the bigger picture, such as the financial impact of delayed launches and quality problems. Middle managers also understand that even highly creative and innovative companies at some point have to rely on standardization to manage costs.

Middle managers have in turn engaged line managers in understanding why there will be a tighter focus on product launches and cost containment. Line managers have kept their teams informed of the overall strategic challenges.

Obviously, each level adapted the degree and depth of information to fit their audience. The result is that all levels in the company have enough information to accurately interpret the initiatives that are coming up.

The Company's Vision

Once again, senior management has driven this discussion. All levels in the company understand that the company intends to grow as the dominant innovator in their market. In other words, the coming focus on standardization and cost management does not indicate a shift in the company's overall direction.

The Strategy

Senior management has driven the creation of the strategic plan with input from the organization, especially middle management. Both levels understand that their strategy will require a balance among increasing the speed of product launches, improving the quality of those launches, and keeping costs within reason. Each functional manager knows how his or her department's actions roll up into one or more of those goals. Each functional manager also has some appreciation of the demands on each of his or her peers.

In turn, those functional managers have engaged line management in understanding the critical priorities in the strategy, so that each line manager can fully appreciate how the work of his or her team rolls up into speed, quality, or cost goals. Those line managers have shared the three big objectives with their teams and then appropriately translated those functional plans into work assignments. With a little imagination, you can envision the myriad of suggestions and problems that might be discussed on a daily basis at the line level. Now imagine the entire team knowing to use "speed, quality, and cost" filters to decide where to focus their time and energy.

Barriers to Execution and Solution Paths

Though both levels still have a hand on our strategic baton, middle management has taken the lead in educating senior management about potential barriers and options for executing the strategy. For example, let's say that middle management in IT argues strongly for conversion to a software package with the potential for greatly improving project management. Middle management in IT also ensures that senior management appreciates the purchase and installation costs, the degree of disruption in the short-term, and other possible barriers to execution. Middle management also suggests different solutions to those barriers, including the pros and cons of simply patching the current system for another year. Senior management then approves the conversion with full appreciation of the disruption to current operations and reasonable expectations for seeing improvement.

Middle and line managers have also met in the handoff zone to ensure that barriers to execution at all levels have been identified and addressed. For example, maybe line managers in IT would have had to push strongly to delay another large project in order to ensure on-time implementation of the new project management system. Without this work in the handoff zone, the new project management system would have had to compete with an existing project, thus increasing the likelihood of a missed deadline. Line managers then carried the baton to their teams. In the case of IT, those employees who were redeployed to get the project management system up and running had a good understanding of why their priorities had shifted. The shift in their work priorities thus appears sensible, rather than a result of poor planning or confusion somewhere upstairs.

Personal Implications, Performance Expectations, and Accountabilities

Figure 4.1 also suggests that each middle manager has a clear understanding of his or her deliverables. Senior and middle levels have agreed on ways to keep senior management informed of the progress and ways in which senior management will need to support the middle managers. Continuing with our example, the IT manager has enlisted and received the support of his senior manager in handling possible resistance to the conversion from R&D, the department that will feel the short-term disruption most keenly. Again, middle managers have engaged line managers in a similar translation of the strategy, and line managers have followed suit with their own teams. A critical point here is that each individual in the organization now sees how his or her work rolls up into the overall strategy. For example, anyone in IT working on the conversion of the project management system knows how his or her daily tasks eventually affect the company's ability to stay competitive with product launches.

The Organizational Values as They Apply at Each Level

Maybe one of this company's formal values is: "Fix the problem, don't fix blame." That is a popular value among many of the companies with which we have worked. But what does that value look like in practice within the different levels of the organization? Figure 4.1 suggests that, as the inevitable conflicts arise, each level of management raises that value to focus their teams on solutions and divert them from the lure of inter-departmental finger-pointing. At the middle level, that could mean resolving resource conflicts with other departments rather than in-fighting. At the line level, that might mean correcting problems as a team rather than shifting blame to a particular worker.

Once again, the critical implication of Figure 4.1 is that each individual in the organization understands where the company is going and how he or she will need to contribute. The strategic goals of improving the speed and quality of product launches while containing costs have been explained and translated into the language and priorities of each individual in the organization.

As you might have noted by now, it takes work to create the alignment shown in Figure 4.1. Usually there are weak points in the handoff that have to be managed or a fumble is inevitable.

Common Problems with the Handoff

That's what strategic execution looks like when managers at all levels are working within their ideal roles and when those levels work effectively in the handoff zone between their levels. If we think of Figure 4.1 as describing a relay race, we would say that we have the right runners in place and they have mastered the challenges of the handoff zone. Now let's look at several potential problem situations that organizations commonly face. Of course, the real world will always be more complex than these examples, but we see the following patterns often enough to call them to your attention. You might find some similarities to your own organization.

Scenario 1: All Levels Working Beneath Ideal Role ... Or Are They?

In Chapter Two we introduced some elementary systems concepts and used them to understand the stages of organizational development. We also noted that strategic execution depends in part on understanding the stages of organizational growth and the systems that drive those stages, because that understanding has to shape the various leadership roles. We have chosen our first scenario to emphasize just how much the alignment in an organization depends on where that organization is going.

In Figure 4.2, we show all levels of management working somewhat beneath their ideal roles. That is, we might say that the senior level is too focused on functional details and not enough on strategic issues, the middle level is pulled too much into day-to-day operations, and the line managers are doing too much fire-fighting and not enough developing of their teams.

But does Figure 4.2 really represent a problem? Look closely at Figure 4.2. Though each level of management is working too much outside of its ideal role, the three levels are actually aligned with one

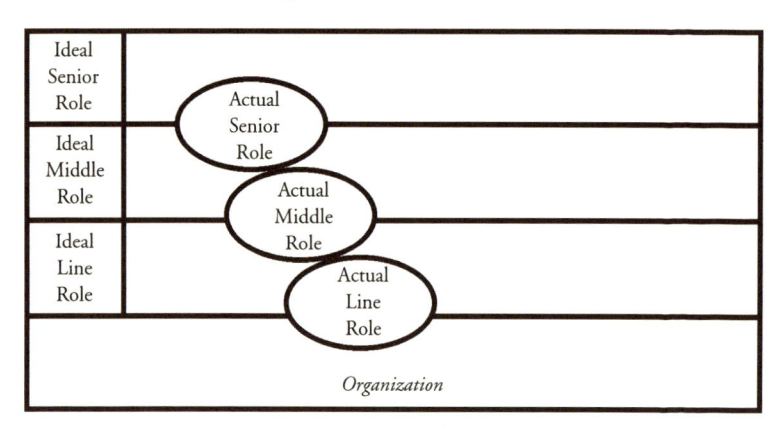

Role Alignment and Handoff Model

[A diagram showing three nested horizontal bands labeled from top to bottom "Ideal Senior Role", "Ideal Middle Role", and "Ideal Line Role", all within a larger box labeled "Organization". Three ovals overlap the band boundaries: "Actual Senior Role" straddles the Senior/Middle boundary, "Actual Middle Role" straddles the Middle/Line boundary, and "Actual Line Role" sits at the Line/Organization boundary.]

Figure 4.2 - All Levels Working Beneath Ideal Role

another. That is, because all three levels are pulled into the level below them, the work of the middle and line levels is actually getting done; it's just getting done by the wrong people as defined by our ideal roles. In reality, that would mean that whatever direction senior management sets, that direction does get translated and carried out by hook or crook all the way down to the line level. The strategic baton is in fact getting passed from level to level. So the only difference between Figure 4.1 that showed ideal alignment and Figure 4.2 showing all levels underperforming is how we define the "ideal roles."

This is far more than an abstract or theoretical point. The ideal role for any level of management is not set in stone. As we showed in Chapter Two with our discussion of organizational systems and stages of growth, the ideal role for a given level depends on where the organization is in its plans and in its growth. Those ideal roles change with growth and complexity. The good alignment in Figure 4.1 can morph into the misalignment of Figure 4.2 simply because the organization has grown and the managers have not grown with the roles. Failure to anticipate the impact of growth in terms of changes in management role can really throw sand into the gears of a thriving organization.

For example, consider a successful company in the Entrepreneurial Stage. If the size and complexity of the organization permits the entrepreneur to keep one hand on the vision and planning while staying involved in day-to-day operations, and each level below the entrepreneur adapts accordingly, we have the ideal alignment of Figure 4.1. It is only when the organization grows to the point that the entrepreneur cannot continue to be the proverbial "chief cook and bottle washer" that we have the risk for the misalignment of Figure 4.2. If the entrepreneur fails to shift to a more strategic role of planning and oversight and fails to develop a stronger bench of managers, then the organization will start to feel like a car that is speeding up but does not make the gear change at the right time.

You can blow an engine that way — in a car or a company. Senior management constantly will be pulled into daily details and away from oversight. Middle managers will start to strain under the pressure to adapt their plans to the growth of the organization and at the same time tend to the myriad of details beneath them. The "midnight oil" that was once rewarded with getting ahead is now burned just to keep from falling behind.

An organization of any size needs skilled managers at all levels right down to the line level, but the scope of the line roles does not change greatly as the company grows. A head teller in a community bank has pretty much the same responsibilities as a head teller in a mega-bank. As we shall see next, the pinch is usually felt at the senior and middle levels.

Scenario 2: Strong Line, but Senior and Middle Management Underperforming

Let's look at another pattern that can accompany growth. Suppose your organization has survived the transition from the Entrepreneurial Stage to the Systems Stage, which requires stronger leadership and more standardization. As your organization grows in size and scope, it will need managers at the middle and line levels who work well within the structure and direction provided from above. We often think of successful managers at these levels as "loyal lieutenants." They are experts in their technical area, and when direction comes from senior management, they execute as directed.

As your organization moves into the Delegation Stage, however, the growing complexity of operations begins to outstrip the ability of senior managers to provide direction. There are simply too many decisions to be made; too much information to be absorbed. It is time for the senior level to begin to function as coaches, making the big decisions but relying more heavily on the middle and line managers to make day-to-day decisions.

If the senior and middle managers fail to make the necessary transition in their roles, the middle ranks may feel constricted by the heavy-handed involvement from above, and in turn become resentful or passive. Your organization will, in all likelihood, become ineffective at responding to the greater array of local needs that come with growth. It will strain to move into the Delegation Stage, where senior managers need to be focusing outward on new business opportunities and delegating more of the internal decisionmaking about functional issues to the middle ranks.

The pressure for change at this point is felt mostly in the senior and middle management levels. Though line managers may feel some role stress as your organization grows, line managers typically interpret and apply decisions made from the levels above regardless of the organization's size. The biggest shifts in role requirements are at the senior level, where managers now need to focus outward on new products and new growth opportunities, and the middle level, where managers now have to take far greater responsibility for running their departments or geographical areas.

It is here that we often see some of the most painful pressures. The senior and middle managers in this kind of scenario have often worked their way up through the ranks of the organization. It is ironic — but very common — that middle managers have helped

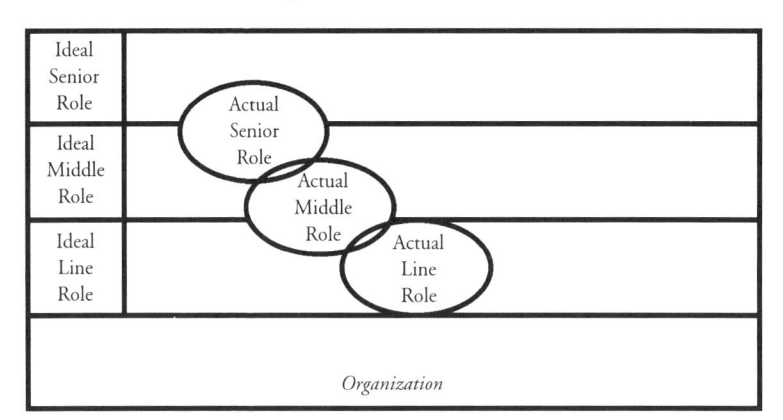

Role Alignment and Handoff Model

Figure 4.3 - Senior and Middle Managers Underperforming in Roles with Strong Line Management

the organization to outgrow their ability to lead it.

When both senior and middle managers are managing beneath the needed level, but line managers are strong performers, we have the misalignment depicted in Figure 4.3.

With this pattern of misalignment, the line level continues to execute as they have done in the past, supervising the production of products and delivery of services just as they did in the previous stage of organizational development. They plan and execute what is delegated from above. Although they may feel the stress of the misalignment above them, and they may complain of various symptoms of the misalignment, it doesn't keep them from carrying out their supervisory responsibilities. Decisions from above will be carried out effectively, even if they are the wrong decisions.

Here are a few common complaints that we have heard from line management in this kind of misalignment scenario:

- "I do my job every day, but I have no idea where we are trying to take this organization. I hear generalities like 'growth' but nobody talks about what kind of growth, where we're going to grow, or how we're going to get there."

- "I'm not sure anybody at the top is really thinking about a strategy. It's like we're just setting all these goals, and trying to do a little of this and a little of that."

- "We get different messages from different managers about our priorities. My boss wants me to resolve customer complaints faster and promises me some resources, but I'm still short of staff and I hear HR is holding off on any new hires until the end of the year. It's hard to plan."

- "We keep hearing about systems improvements and training initiatives, but they're a day late and a dollar short if they happen at all."

- "On their own initiative, my team came up with a way to deal with a part on this transmission that doesn't seat properly during production. Then we find out months later that Quality had decided that the part settles during shipping and seats itself, so that it wasn't a problem. Couldn't somebody have taken the time to tell us? What message does that send my team about taking initiative?"

Scenario 3: Fumbling in the Middle Ranks

In the scenario we just described, who usually feels the pinch first? Often, change first occurs at the senior level for a number of reasons. Obviously, if the organization flounders, the most visible targets are the ones at the top. Just as senior leaders reap the rewards of success, they are also the ones most exposed when growth is slow or targets are missed. It is also easier for owners and stockholders to take action at the senior level. Sometimes the people at the top grow into their roles, and sometimes different people are put into those roles. Either way, change often occurs at the senior level first, and we see a pattern like that of Figure 4.4.

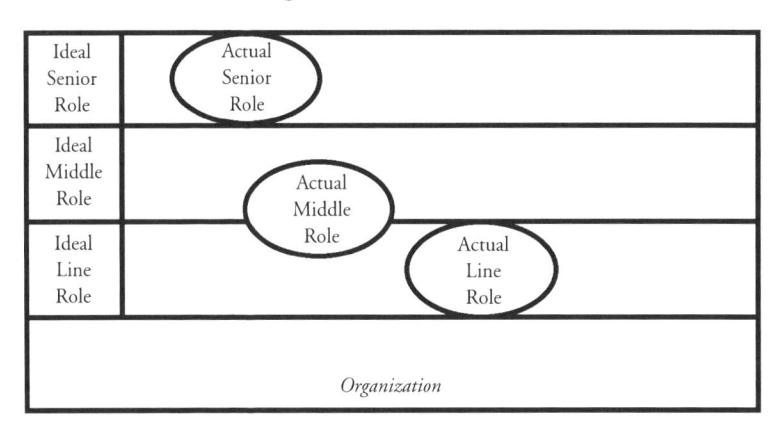

Role Alignment and Handoff Model

Ideal Senior Role	Actual Senior Role		
Ideal Middle Role	Actual Middle Role		
Ideal Line Role		Actual Line Role	
Organization			

Figure 4.4 - Fumbling in the Middle Ranks

Though we could see this pattern in a number of situations, we see it frequently as organizations move into the Delegation Stage and beyond. In the Delegation Stage, for example, the scope of the middle management role has increased far beyond that carried out by the "loyal lieutenants" who thrived under strong top-down management in the Systems Stage. The middle management ranks now need strong leadership skills to envision, engage, plan, and execute a larger scope of responsibility for their functional or geographic area. They have to begin to think like businesspeople and not just technical or functional people. They have to actively identify and address problems in execution, and that usually includes working effectively with multiple cross-functional challenges.

If the middle managers supervise a field office or group, they have to in many ways think like entrepreneurs in terms of vision, initiative, and taking ownership for their office or group. In addition to thinking like businesspeople, however, they also need corporate savvy. They have to ensure alignment of their group's work with the larger strategic plan. They have to understand that the corporate office has many mouths to feed in terms of resource allocation, so they have to approach Corporate the way entrepreneurs approach venture capitalists: develop a vision and a business plan, and show the return on investment. Complaining about being under-capitalized takes the group nowhere.

Here are a few representative complaints that we have heard from senior management regarding their observations of a misaligned middle management:

- "We've got a solid strategy. We know what we want to do. But we can't seem to get our ducks in a row about how we're going to do it. We've got a lot of projects and initiatives going, but they don't seem to be coordinated. I want to see more things finished, not just in the works."

- "What's keeping me awake at night is my bench strength. I've got good people who helped us to build this organization, but it seems like some of them have just stalled. We're bigger now, a lot bigger. There's too much that doesn't happen inside this organization unless I get involved and make it happen. I need to be thinking about what happens next, not why something didn't happen yesterday."

- "I've got some great technical people under me, but they're still thinking like technical people. I need them to start thinking like they're running a business. I need to be able to rely on somebody to take their area, figure out what needs to be done, and then go and do it."

Here are a few examples of what we've heard from the line level regarding what misalignment at the middle level often looks like to them:

- "We just have too many issues between departments that aren't getting resolved. Who is driving the product launch? Is it Marketing? Is it Production? It's like the right hand and the left hand aren't communicating. So I end up waiting for the go-ahead on my piece of it."

- "There are things that would make our life so much easier, and it shouldn't be hard to do it. There are things we ought to be able to access on the network, and I know somebody can make that happen. I'm just not sure who could get it done or who should go to that person."

- "We're in constant firefighting mode. We're short of parts, then we're trying to cut back on inventory. We fill out urgent reports to send upstairs, then we hear nothing about it. What's that all about?"

- "Training? What's that? We used to do a better job of that, but now it's a matter of getting a body into the position and doing the best we can. It's not efficient or effective, but that's how we do it."

Defining the Handoff Zone at Biggs & Bucks

We can look at role misalignment like that of Figure 4.4 in a couple of ways. As we have used it so far, it can represent alignment or misalignment with three individual managers in a vertical chain of command. But suppose the pattern depicted in Figure 4.4 is a common one in the organization, with numerous middle managers in different departments underperforming in their roles. Perhaps the organization has grown to the point that senior managers can no longer be involved in day-to-day decisions, and the organization needs a strong rank of middle managers to step up and lead their areas. In that case, Figure 4.4 would represent an average of the individual alignment issues. At a glance, we would be able to predict that the

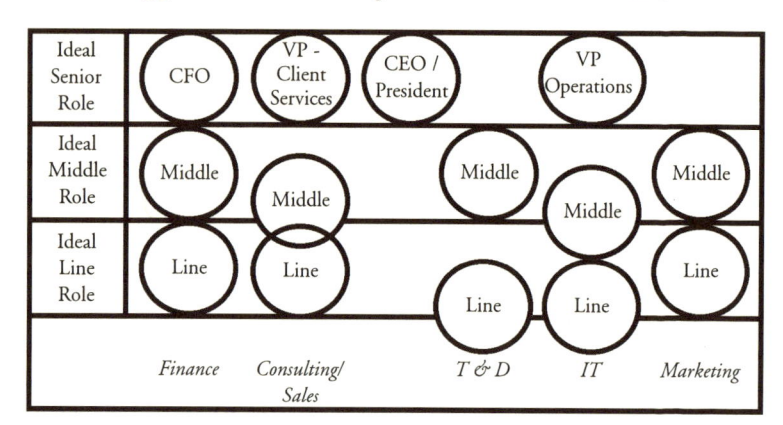

Biggs & Bucks Role Alignment and Handoff Model

Ideal Senior Role	CFO	VP - Client Services	CEO / President	VP Operations
Ideal Middle Role	Middle	Middle / Middle	Middle / Middle	Middle
Ideal Line Role	Line	Line	Line / Line	Line
	Finance	*Consulting/ Sales*	*T & D IT*	*Marketing*

Figure 4.5 - The Talent Bench at Biggs & Bucks

organization's strategy would probably not be translated into functional plans and that problems would pile up at the boundaries between departments because of misalignment in the middle level. After all, these are critical aspects of the middle management role.

If we expand Figure 4.4 to look at alignment across several departments, we would finally have a picture that looks like Figure 4.5, which depicts Biggs & Bucks.

At a glance, we see places of concern, where a dropped strategic baton is likely unless the handoff process is managed well. Recall that the Biggs & Bucks strategic direction involves greater continuity in product and service offerings across offices, more standardization of processes to reduce costs, and creating more of a "one company" brand. In Figure 4.5, we see the senior team comprising the CEO/president, the CFO, the vice president of client services, and the vice president of operations. Let's assume that each member of the senior team works or is capable of working well within the requirements of their role in the new strategy. That is, they spend an appropriate amount of time scanning the external environment for threats and opportunities, and they focus on a handful of strategic goals. They have assessed the internal strengths and weaknesses of the organization, and they have developed a plan to leverage the strengths and address the weaknesses. Each is willing to delegate functional details to the next level.

The CFO supervises two accounting managers, each of whom in turn supervises line supervisors who head up Accounts Receivable, Accounts Payable, and other functions in the Finance Department. As Figure 4.5 shows, managers at each level are working within their appropriate roles, so there is good role alignment in the Finance Department. We would predict open communication up and down the line, and relatively smooth translation of financial goals into actions and priorities fitting for each level as the new strategy is rolled out.

The picture in Consulting and Sales is a little more difficult. The vice president of client services has the skills and willingness to work at a strategic level. This vice president, however, supervises a group of local office directors at the middle level, most of whom are currently tied up in the details of selling services and taking care of clients. In the past, the high degree of local autonomy has allowed local office directors to gloss over the planning and development aspects of their roles and concentrate on personally generating revenue. Local office directors have been able to rely on Operations staff to patch together a workable set of forms, processes, and other backroom functions. The new strategy, however, will put considerable pressure on the local office directors to work with Corporate on the standardization of processes to reduce costs. They will also be the point positions for planning the change internally, communicating the change to their offices, dealing with the resistance that will likely occur, and managing the performance of staff under the new processes. Though a few local office directors may be further up the curve, Figure 4.5 represents a rough average ... and the average local office director is still working much like a financial consultant.

Moving over to Operations, the picture is still more complicated. There is a director of training and development (T&D) who reports directly to the vice president of operations and who is well-suited to the role requirements presented by the new strategy. As depicted, we would expect this manager to translate the strategy into a functional training plan and to coordinate with peers to ensure that the training plan meets their needs. The line managers in T&D, however, are not currently working at the level that will be required to carry out the strategy. As depicted in Figure 4.5, these supervisors would likely be too tied up in day-to-day training to take the handoff effectively from the director of T&D. Thus, the translation of the functional training plan into detailed tasks and timelines for non-management employees could be delayed or jeopardized.

Further over in Operations, we see the weakest link in whole field. The vice president of operations also supervises an information technology (IT) director, who in turn supervises line managers who lead various information services at Corporate Headquarters and at local offices. The IT director is good with computers and networks, and he moved up in the management ranks when the company was small but growing. In the recent past, this manager has developed a good reputation as the "go-to" person if a team runs into a particularly tough systems problem.

He has hired good technicians and promoted some of them to line management. But the new strategy will depend heavily on having a change agent in this role — someone who can work comfortably in the handoff zone with the senior team and then translate the strategic goals into a workable plan for IT. This manager will also carry much of the weight for coordinating with local offices and with other functions to ensure that the standardization efforts deliver cost savings without unduly limiting the local office's ability to adapt to local markets. Adding to the coming role pressure, this manager has hired and promoted talented technicians but he has not developed his supervisors as supervisors. His skill in fixing technical problems will be of little help in the new Biggs & Bucks.

The vice president of operations also has responsibility for marketing, and luckily for him, he can count on middle and line managers who work at the right level. Thus, we would expect few problems in the handoff and translation of strategy into marketing activities.

Your Execution Is Only as Good as Your Weakest Links

Even with our hypothetical Biggs & Bucks example, we can see predictable challenges in the execution of strategy. We would expect the company's Finance and Marketing Departments to run smoothly when we look at those departments vertically. But the Biggs & Bucks strategy map requires a more horizontal perspective, and that is where we see the impact of the weakest link. Suppose the CFO of Biggs & Bucks wants to standardize expense tracking as a way of driving down costs and reducing margin pressure. Or the middle manager in Marketing lobbies for a three-tiered client segmentation, so that products and services could be more efficiently geared to the needs of the client. Both of those efforts would address some of the challenges faced by Biggs & Bucks, and both of those efforts would depend heavily on the middle manager in IT to make the translation from the languages of Finance and Marketing into the language and priorities of IT. Based on Figure 4.5, we would expect both efforts to be delayed or possibly fumbled in the handoff to IT middle management. Having fast runners in Marketing and Finance is not enough if IT can't take the baton and run with it.

We also see that Consulting and Sales has a weak link at the middle level. We have described local office directors for the most part as working like financial consultants; too tied up in taking care of clients to take on the planning and coaching demands of their role as middle managers. But the standardization efforts pushed by Finance and the segmentation approach pushed by Marketing would both require careful and thoughtful input from local office directors. If those local office directors, however, are so focused on their vertical roles that they fail to coordinate adequately with their peers in Marketing and Finance, we would expect more fumbling of the baton.

It almost goes without saying that we would predict the need for close coordination between local office directors and IT groups — that they would most need to think strategically in order to ensure that the standardization efforts do not adversely affect client experience. We can almost feel the pull acting upon the vice presidents of client services and operations as they see the bobbling of the baton at the level below them.

In coming chapters, we will continue to use examples from different Biggs & Bucks departments, but we will focus particularly on the Training and Development Department to illustrate our approach to managing the handoff all the way to the front lines. We have chosen this department for a detailed example for two reasons. First, given what we know of the coming change in direction for Biggs & Bucks, we would expect the training effort to be critical to good execution of strategy. Second, by following the strategic handoff through the Training and Development Department, we can go into the level of detail necessary to illustrate the handoff process without getting pulled into the technical jargon of IT, Finance, or Marketing.

In the next chapter, we look at the development of the strategic baton, and from there we will follow the handoff process through Training and Development all the way down to the work of a single trainer.

A Brief Preview of the Players

In the following chapters, you will meet the individuals who are responsible for the handoff of one critical piece of the Biggs & Bucks strategy: a series of training events designed to enhance the product knowledge of financial consultants across all of the local offices. The key players are:

- **Jim Newman, director of training and development:** Jim is an experienced middle manager who reports to the vice president of operations, a member of the senior management team. The first pass of the strategic baton for the staff development portions of the strategy will occur between Jim and this vice president.

- **Jamie Eldridge, local office director:** Jamie is a peer of Jim Newman's. She has a strong background in financial consulting, and she has risen through the ranks to run a local office. She has enjoyed the relative autonomy of the local offices and views with suspicion and concern the talk about increasing the consistency of the local offices in terms of product offerings and internal operations. But because of her strong background in consulting and her deep knowledge of financial products, she will be the logical choice to provide technical support to the Training and Development staff on this critical project.

- **Myra Bennis, supervisor of training and development:** Myra is the line supervisor who reports to Jim Newman. She has experience in developing training, but as a relatively new supervisor she is not yet experienced in the finer networking and negotiating skills that will be needed for the cross-functional aspects of a training initiative of this size and strategic importance. The second pass of the baton will occur between Jim Newman and Myra Bennis.

- **Tracey Collins, staff trainer:** Tracey is a new hire with Biggs & Bucks. She was hired in large part because of her strong skills in materials design. She does not have a strong network yet, and she is still learning the ins and outs of the Biggs & Bucks culture. She will be the anchor runner who takes the final handoff of the strategic baton from Myra Bennis.

Chapter 5

The Fourth Challenge: Defining the Strategic Baton

Seven Elements of Strategy

In this chapter, we will discuss at length seven elements of the business strategy that must be passed and translated from senior management through middle management to the front lines. We think of these seven elements as comprising the strategic baton. We will also

> **Seven Elements of the Strategic Baton**
> - The Business Context – What are we facing?
> - Organizational Vision – Where are we going?
> - The Strategy – What is our path?
> - Organizational Value Proposition and Major Trade-offs – How will we differentiate ourselves?
> - Barriers to Execution and Solution Paths – What could stop us?
> - Personal Implications and Performance Expectations – What does this mean for me?
> - Organizational Values and Team Agreements – How will we get there?

show, by way of our Biggs & Bucks case study, how each element might be applied.

The Business Context: What Are We Facing?

The first element of the baton has to do not with the strategy itself, but with the environmental and organizational conditions that led to the strategy. This context includes an environmental scan, the business case for the strategy, and the organizational history and stage of growth for the company. Without this business context, the changes required by a new strategy will seem to be arbitrary and disconnected from previous methods of operation.

Environmental Scan

We are assuming that senior management has led the organization through a process of strategic planning. In many organizations, what is called strategic planning is actually goal-setting — simply taking previous results and adding a certain percentage. But true strategic planning begins with environmental scanning and develops a comprehensive picture of the opportunities and threats facing the organization. This process includes assessment of:

- Competitive threats in terms of technological, financial, and market changes.
- Customer expectations, buying patterns, and potential changes because of technology, demographics, or other forces. This involves the identification of barriers and opportunities to increased penetration with existing customers as well as new customers within existing markets.
- New or untapped markets, including selling existing products and services to new markets and the potential for expanded offerings.
- Economic forces acting on customers, competitors, suppliers, and distributors. For example, how would changes in interest rates or oil prices affect each of these?

- What kinds of events could threaten supplies of needed resources for the organization?
- Identifying the range of strategic options available to the organization. Is the environment stable and predictable, so that long-term forecasting is possible? Or is the environment turbulent and unpredictable, so that flexibility has to be built into the strategy and the culture? Is the environment rich in resources so that many options are possible, or does the resource picture demand tighter focus?

We should note that environmental scanning is an essential competency at the senior level, but it is not always limited to that level. As an organization grows into the Delegation Stage and beyond, this competency becomes more critical to success in the middle ranks. Middle managers in these stages have increased responsibility for forecasting and shaping the direction of their functional or business areas of responsibility. Especially when these managers supervise business units with P&L responsibility, more of the weight for understanding their local markets and finding new opportunities falls upon them.

Environmental Scanning at Biggs & Bucks

Among other things, the environmental scan at Biggs & Bucks revealed customer loyalty and trust that seemed stronger than that usually found in the financial services industry. Many of the branch offices had successfully established themselves as insurance firms or financial planning firms before becoming part of Biggs & Bucks. Customers valued the quick response and personal service. One of the biggest threats seen in the scan, however, involved the rising expectations of customers. Local offices had somewhat varied product and service portfolios that depended on their early history. For example, some had strong in-house legal resources for estate planning, while others simply offered referrals to local attorneys. A few had branched into financial consulting with small businesses, while others had not explored this possibility.

A second major threat was the rising cost of local autonomy and the myriad databases, forms, reports, and procedures inherited or developed in the local offices. specially with the smaller average accounts in some newer markets, the high level of personal service created a serious drain on the profitability of those accounts. Though Biggs & Bucks was still profitable, many of the very approaches that drove customer loyalty were reaching the point of diminishing returns.

With considerable anxiety, the senior team realized that the firm faced difficult trade-offs between the entrepreneurial freedom that drove its early success and the realities of running a larger company. With its long history as a loose federation of successful local offices, Biggs & Bucks needed to look and act like one company if it was to continue to grow.

The Business Case

So far we have described the baton to be passed in terms of a general vision and perspective based on organizational development stages. Now we turn to the heavy lifting — the need to make the business case for the strategy that is about to follow.

People need to understand why they are asked to do what they do. Managers usually understand this need when it comes to specific tasks, but they often miss powerful opportunities to educate the organization about the market in terms of customer trends, competitor strategies, financial pressures, and other drivers of strategy and organizational change. Educating their teams about market realities is one of the best practices of managers down in the ranks who make change happen.[16]

In our experience, managers who find the opportunity to enlist their teams in understanding and evaluating these market forces reap several benefits:

- **People understand the potential opportunities and threats in the marketplace that the organization has to face.** Thus, they understand the changes they see as coming from external forces and not from the whim or personal preferences of management.
- **They can see the personal implications of the opportunities and threats facing the organization.** Both opportunities and threats give people good personal reasons to commit to achieving their goals.
- **Better informed people are better able to participate.** They can offer ideas for improving the processes around them when they understand those processes in the larger business context.
- **By teaching employees more about the market and about the business, managers are preparing people for the next step in their own career progression.** Some people will grasp these trends and their implications quickly, while others will lose interest after the immediate gratification of "What's in it for me?" Managers who pay attention to these reactions have valuable information about who has potential to move up.
- **The fact that someone has taken the time to provide background information often increases respect for and trust in the manager.**

How you do the educating depends on your team, their backgrounds, their preferences, and your own preferred approach. You

---

16 Katzenbach, J. R. (1995). *Real Change Leaders: How You Can Create Growth and High Performance at Your Company.* New York, NY. Random House.

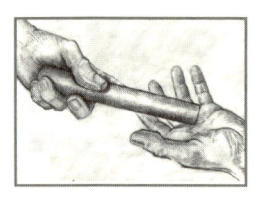

> Educating their teams about market realities is one of the best practices of managers down in the ranks who make change happen.

can use a mixture of formal presentations and informal discussions. We have seen good results when managers invited someone from the marketing team to do a brief overview of customer feedback, market opportunities, and actions by competitors. In addition to providing information to the team, there was the added benefit of building a good relationship with another department. Some managers we know have done excellent presentations at a white board, making notes and visually highlighting important connections on the spot. You can also be on the lookout for articles and internal reports that you can circulate to educate your team about important developments in your industry.

One subtle but important point: tell people why you are providing this information so that they have an accurate context for it and don't jump to conclusions. A manager with one of our clients was concerned about the lack of response when she tried to engage her team in understanding the importance of driving down costs as part of a strategic process. Then one person broke the cold silence with, "Can you just tell us when the layoffs start?" Many of the people in the room had only heard managers talk about cost reductions when there were problems. Imagine the relief when people realized that there were no layoffs in the works and that their manager was just committed to their development and involving them fully in the business.

Let's keep up with the process at Biggs & Bucks. Note, especially, the key points that the senior team decided most needed to be made to the organization.

Defining the Business Case at Biggs & Bucks

The senior team had at its disposal reams of data about customers, competitors, and internal processes. They were not naive about the difficulty of the direction they had chosen, but they were convinced that was the right direction and that the time to start was while they were still successful. The problem was how to convince a successful organization that change was needed.

After wrestling with so much information, they finally distilled the business case for their strategy to the following:

- Comparisons across offices showed huge variation in number and type of services provided to the wealthiest clients. Though their systems did not allow consistent comparisons, the CFO was able to pull together strong indications that those offices with the deepest penetration in these accounts had the best profitability. He was also able to show the particular mix of products and services that seemed to provide the biggest jump in profitability. The projections from selling one additional product for each client in this group were stunning. One observer summed up the challenge as, "Would you like an estate plan with that?"

- *Having a more consistent product and service portfolio across the company was the key to a deeper penetration of the wealthiest client accounts. Industry data showed strong client preference for one-stop providers. A simple spreadsheet of products by office showed so many holes that one executive compared it to Swiss cheese. The comparison stuck, and the team began to talk about the need for "more cheese and fewer holes."*
- *Though the core of the business had been built on upper middle class and wealthier clients, many of the offices had attracted younger clients with more basic financial needs. These were, on the average, the least profitable clients. An hour of consulting or sales time was likely to yield a much smaller investment in a fairly predictable array of products. Those offices with the highest percentage of these accounts typically had the lowest margins. Simple calculations showed that those accounts below a certain size cost more to service than the company made. Simple calculations also made two easy points: when an office sold a basic package of mutual funds, life and disability insurance, and wills to these smaller accounts, margins were better and servicing was simpler because less-experienced consultants or administrative staff could handle inquiries.*
- *Over the last few years, the number of different forms, databases, and procedures had become a nightmare, and a costly one at that. Another spreadsheet showed the number of different forms used to gather basic client information,*

and from there it was fairly easy to estimate the number of hours spent in converting this information to a standard format at Corporate, and from there it was possible to estimate the financial impact of the duplication.

Armed with this information, as well as a handful of other key points from the environmental scan, the senior team at Biggs & Bucks ensured that they delivered a consistent message about the background of the strategic direction they had chosen. They knew that making the business case would not make change easier, but it would make change more sensible.

Stages of Growth and Organizational History

One element of the strategic baton that is often overlooked is the importance of perspective. History provides a framework and perspective, and it gives meaning to the present, whether for a nation, an organization, or an individual. Without this, it is harder to make sense of what we see around us.

In the case of an organization, where it is headed depends in part of where it has been and what has to change to be successful in the future. In particular, understanding growth from a systems perspective helps people to value the successes of the past while realizing the need for change. Indeed, all successful organizations go through developmental stages, and each developmental stage has its own requirements for organizational systemic change. If it fails to meet those requirements, it will no longer be successful.

We have often interviewed people in growing organizations who understand the strategic direction but who, at the same time, question it: "Why do we have to change what's working? I'm afraid we're getting away from who we are." We are especially likely to get these

> The problem was how to convince a successful organization that a change was needed.

questions from people in organizations that have a strong history of success. These kinds of questions illustrate the need to position strategy in terms of history.

Our hypothetical case of Biggs & Bucks highlights the importance of understanding and presenting the strategy in light of the organization's history. Here is part of the story of Biggs & Bucks that was passed through the organization — sometimes in formal meetings, sometimes in written form, sometimes in one-on-one discussions, but always there. Note the rough outlines of the stages of organizational development in the history of Biggs & Bucks.

Stages of Growth and Organizational History at Biggs & Bucks

In the founding days of the company, Mr. Biggs and Mr. Bucks personally sold insurance products and serviced their own customers. Both had a strong commitment to their sales and service model — build a relationship with your client by understanding what the client needs and then help them meet that need. Mr. Biggs often said, "Selling is easy. If the customer doesn't need it, don't push it. If they do need it, you're serving them by selling it to them. And the only way you'll find out if they need it or not is to shut up and listen to the customer."

That approach seemed to work especially well with upper middle class wealthy clients whose financial situations were more complex. As their reputation with these clients grew, Biggs & Bucks began adding salespeople, but they kept a personal hand in the majority of their client's services. There were no quotas or hard-sell approaches. In addition to personally serving clients and overseeing the work of more junior consultants, they divided up the oversight responsibilities of the administrative staff. Though the hours were long, the two founders had the reputation of doing whatever it took to provide the highest quality of service to their clients.

One story had circulated for years that Mr. Biggs often surprised employees by asking about family members by name. A favorite photograph in the company album showed Mr. Bucks grinning with ink stains on his hands and white shirt. He had been caught in the act of helping to service an early photocopier. Mr. Bucks also had a penchant for restoring sports cars, and he often used automotive metaphors in describing the company. Those early years were marked by steady growth and profitability, or "first gear," as the early phase became known.

With new offices and a much greater client list, however, Mr. Biggs and Mr. Bucks strained to keep up, and occasionally the business suffered because there was only so much of the two men to go around. Eventually they created a position for an office manager to oversee the backroom functions and bring some order to the growing administrative chaos. After two false starts, they finally hired an office manager with the skill to bring much-needed standard procedures to the backroom functions and a strong enough person-

ality to handle the complaints about the "growing bureaucracy."

The next major change was when Jean Lee became the first consultant to have an ownership position with the firm. Long-timers who worked with Mr. Bucks often referred to this period as "second gear." As Mr. Bucks approached retirement and began to reduce his time in the office, Jean Lee was able to use her considerable organizational skills to establish a line of reporting authority to speed up response to clients. She had a strong background in insurance, but also had developed a following as a financial planner. Over time, she recruited from her network of financial specialists and Biggs & Bucks began to offer a more diversified portfolio of products and services.

Jean Lee and Mr. Biggs continued to personally oversee the largest accounts, but eventually the bulk of the company's accounts were overseen by two new partners: John Jefferson and Lilly Barstow. Jefferson had a strong background in securities, and Barstow was an attorney. Between the two of them and the consultants they brought in, Biggs & Bucks developed a statewide reputation for sound financial planning and investment strategies. They had also developed a financial consulting and planning model that worked. They had tier one products that attracted clients, and they knew the signs that clients were ready for the bigger commitment (and margins) from tiers two and three. If you worked at Biggs & Bucks, you followed this approach.

By the time Biggs, Bucks, and Lee had retired and Lilly Barstow had become the next CEO, the company had made its first two acquisitions: one a small but thriving insurance agency specializing in

The Fourth Challenge: Defining the Strategic Baton

small business, and the other a small but promising securities firm catering to wealthy retirees. With expanding markets and new acquisitions, Barstow realized that the three-tiered approach that worked so well for their own offices did not seem to fit as well with the new acquisitions. Barstow wisely decided to allow these acquisitions to work fairly independently and they rewarded her trust by leveraging the Biggs & Bucks reputation into phenomenal growth and return.

By the time John Jefferson succeeded Barstow as CEO, the company had continued this practice of acquiring small companies in niche markets, leveraging the Biggs & Bucks reputation and allowing a fair amount of autonomy in growing those niche markets. Even some of the original Biggs & Bucks offices had found the three-tiered approach cumbersome, and they had developed their own approaches that fit the unique demands of their local markets. Thus, the company had shifted into "third gear" by the time Jefferson had been CEO for five years.

Though this process had driven several years of outstanding growth, the company was beginning to feel like a car that has run all it can out of third gear. Margins had dropped off, largely because of duplication and inconsistency in processes and procedures. One local office director had been sued by a former employee for wrongful discharge, and the home office had been taken by surprise at the diversity of employment practices in the local offices. Though overall client satisfaction was high, two offices had narrowly escaped lawsuits by clients over processing delays that cost the clients money. Biggs & Bucks made up the losses to the clients, but it was becoming clearer that local autonomy was getting expensive.

> The long-timers felt that a *"shift into fourth gear"* was needed and was imminent, as the local autonomy that had driven growth was starting to strain. The company needed to pay more attention to those areas that could be standardized without hurting customer experience. They had seen the company shift as its conditions changed.
>
> Almost half of the company, however, had come in under Barstow or Jefferson, and they had only known the relative autonomy of third gear.

Now put yourself in the place of one of those people who came in under Barstow or Jefferson. Without the historical context, and especially without understanding the forces driving the S-curve, the language of "gear shifting" would mean little, and the coming changes could seem arbitrary or even wrong-headed. After all, most people worked in local offices that had not had potential legal problems arising out of inconsistent HR practices or systems problems. For them, the need for change would be far less evident. This is especially true when senior executives recognize signs that the company is approaching the point of diminishing returns with their current approach and are proactive in preparing for the next phase. At that point on the S-curve, the restraining forces are still growing but the effects are not fully felt yet. With the historical context, however, the changes seem to fit within a much larger pattern. Leaders can draw attention to the early indicators of trends and help the organization understand the significance of what they're seeing. With that context, people might still be anxious or uncomfortable about their ability to make the needed changes but at least those changes won't seem arbitrary or ill-founded.

Organizational Vision: Where Are We Going?

We now turn to the second element of the baton: the organizational vision. The ability to generate and articulate a vision for an organization is widely considered a necessary competency for leadership.[17,18] In their classic study, Collins and Porras demonstrated the considerable financial benefits that accrue to companies guided by visionary leadership.[19]

In our work with leaders, we find that visioning too often takes on a mystical aura, as if only a select few have the rare qualities to be visionaries. We would not argue that there are leaders who seem to have innate gifts for envisioning a better future and inspiring others to help them get there. In fact, we have worked with our share of such leaders and found them impressive and inspiring. But the elements of good organizational vision have many practical components that should be possible for leaders at all levels of an organization to comprehend and communicate. In fact, leaders at all levels need to be able to formulate and share a vision that is appropriate for their level.

Of course, we would not say that a middle manager in IT or a line supervisor of an operations team needs to have a 10- or 20-year vision for the organization. But people in IT and on the line in Operations need to understand not only where the organization is going, but also where their part of the organization is going. Vision sets the stage for strategy, and that is true to some extent throughout the organization.

---

17 Kouzes, J. M. & Posner, B. Z. (1987). *The Leadership Challenge: How to Get Extraordinary Things Done in Organizations.* San Francisco, CA. Jossey-Bass.

18 Zaccaro, S. J. (2001). *The Nature of Executive Leadership: A Conceptual and Empirical Analysis of Success.* Washington, DC. American Psychological Association.

19 Collins, J. & Porras, J. (1997). *Built to Last: Successful Habits of Visionary Companies.* New York, NY. Harper Collins Publishers.

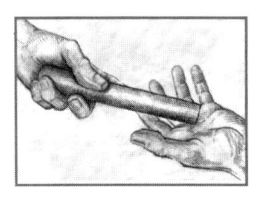

> If the language of the vision provides direction, helps people to understand where the organization is going, provides a reference point for planning, engages and inspires people, then it does all a vision can do.

Elements of Vision

There are many definitions of vision as it relates to leadership. Writers in the field and executives in practice each usually emphasize a slightly different aspect of vision in their own definitions, but here are some common factors that we encounter and use in our own work:

- Vision is *a mental picture or description* of a desired or ideal future. Though it is an ideal, the vision needs to represent an ideal that is possible to achieve.
- Vision often includes, explicitly or implicitly, the *values* that make the vision ideal and that guide the organization in pursuit of the vision.
- A vision provides a *reference point* from which people view the current state of the organization. The gap between the current situation and the desired future should serve as a motivator for people in the organization.
- Statements of vision help to give *meaning* to organizational changes that people see around them. Thus, vision can help people see constancy in the middle of organizational change, so that the changes do not appear arbitrary. Constancy and predictability in the midst of change can help peo-

ple manage the stress that inev-itably comes with change.
- The vision should carry strong implications for the high-level *goals and objectives* that would need to be met in order to achieve the vision. Visioning begins the strategic planning process in general, providing memorable language that serves as a rallying point. Because the vision is high level, it leaves room for maneuvering as circumstances dictate. Visioning then is a bridge into the detailed planning process.

About Vision Statements

There is no doubt that there can be value in having a simple, compelling statement that is written down, especially if it is actually used by people in the organization. Over the years, we have become a little less concerned about what the vision says and more focused on what the vision does. If the language of the vision provides direction, helps people to understand where the organization is going, provides a reference point for planning, engages and inspires people, then it does all a vision can do.

If the vision does these things, we are not concerned with whether it has been transformed into a formal statement that people memorize. We are even less concerned with whether the vision is written on laminated cards carried in every wallet or purse in the organization. We have participated in too many discussions about organization direction in which someone had to pull out the card to tell us the vision. If you have to pull it out and read it, it probably hasn't been an important part of your decision making. In gauging the effectiveness of a vision, we listen for whether different people zero in on a similar picture and a shared meaning, even if they use somewhat different language to describe it. That kind of consistency comes from a communication process, not a printing process.

Of course, the development of vision begins at the senior level, and the senior level bears much of the responsibility for ensuring the communication of the vision. We should note, however, that teams at the middle and line levels also need to be guided by a vision, and the development of that vision is part of the handoff process we will cover in the next chapter.

The Relevance of Vision at Biggs & Bucks

John Jefferson, now the CEO of Biggs & Bucks, was a skeptic when it came to formal vision statements. He had seen too many times in his career that senior teams spent hours crafting language that graced the annual report but did little beyond that. "Ask the average employee about the vision statement," he says, "and you'll either get a blank look or they'll have to pull out a card and read it to you." Consequently, he resisted suggestions from his team that the organization develop a vision in the sense of a formal statement developed in a structured process.

On the other hand, Jefferson was a strong believer that organizations needed vision — a general sense of where they were headed that could be communicated easily and offer inspiration and perspective to people in the organization. Over a period of months, the senior team at Biggs & Bucks grappled with where they wanted to take the company. Some conversations were over lunch, some were over drinks, and some were in team meetings. They also talked with others in the organization and spent a lot of time listening. Though they never crafted a formal statement, they began to see that their hopes for the future of the company converged around several points. Though each of them described those points in different language and using different imagery, each conveyed the same ideas:

- *Biggs & Bucks had established a foothold in their region of the country, and had the poten-*

tial to dominate the market in their region. They also believed that the company had the potential to grow to a national presence if they could continue to build strong, trusting relationships with their clients and to focus on client needs.

- *In order to be able to meet the needs of their upper-end clientele, they needed to offer a more complex array of financial products and services. They also needed financial consultants who were true consultants and not just product-pushers. Finally, they needed to have administrative systems that helped the company meet client needs and keep costs down, but the team was very clear that those systems should never take on a life of their own.*

- *An interesting discovery for the team was that they all had some interest in developing the lower end of their market, especially people just starting out with careers and families. From a business perspective, many of these less profitable clients could become more profitable in the future, so it made sense to start the relationship now. Beyond that, however, the team just liked the idea of making quality financial planning available to people who had not yet amassed substantial wealth. Mr. Biggs and Mr. Bucks both started out at the low end of the economic scale and built quite a business. Nobody on the team had been born with the proverbial silver spoon, and they all were doing well financially. So in addition to building a base of loyal clients for the future, it just seemed like the right thing to do.*

Strategy: What Is Our Path?

Mapping the Path

The planning process lays out the organization's strategic adaptation to the forces identified in the environmental scan. In our experience, the strategic planning process is greatly enhanced by the development of a strategy map describing not only the financial goals but also the drivers of these goals from the organization's talent base, internal processes, and customer experience. There are many ways of creating such a map, and many of our clients have created their own visual representations of their strategies; the important point is that they took the time to do it. First, the discipline of mapping the strategy forces management to tackle hard questions about trade-offs and priorities. Second, the resulting map is a powerful education and accountability tool.

A Strategy Map Prototype

Figure 5.1 shows what a strategy map for Biggs & Bucks might look like. This map is representative of those we have developed in working with our clients, though the final product for each client is customized to that individual client's needs. We have simplified the map for ease of presentation and discussion.

The map is laid out in four large segments identified down the left side of the map in bold:

1. **Financial goals**
2. **Customer goals**
3. **Internal process goals**
4. **Culture and competency goals**

The map begins with the organization's vision and high-level financial goals in the top section. Following the model, we have broken the financial goals into those having to do with cost management and those having to do with revenue growth. Subsequent sec-

The Fourth Challenge: Defining the Strategic Baton

Strategy Map
Lasting Value for Clients and Shareholders

Financial Goals

Cost Management Goals
Overhead expenses at or below x%

Revenue Goals
$xxx in total sales by 20xx

| Productivity $xxx revenue per FTE by 20xx | Improve Profit per Location x% profit per office by 20xx | Current Accounts Increase revenue from current accounts to $xxx by 20xx | New Accounts $xxx from new accounts by 20xx |

Customer Goals

Convert the unprofitable | Expand the profitable

Relationship Strategy

Trusted advisor for tiers two and three

Core portfolio for tier one accounts

| Provide a full array of self-help on-line options | Charge fair fees for value-added services | "One company" products and services | Valued for our product knowledge |

Service Strategy | *Sales Strategy*

Internal Process Goals

| Channel clients to right product / service mix | Establish accurate costing and pricing processes | Segment client acquisition activities | Develop one-client management system |
| Standardize administrative processes | Establish uniform compensation and HR systems | Excel in product and sales training | Create strong product research and selection |

Culture and Competency Goals

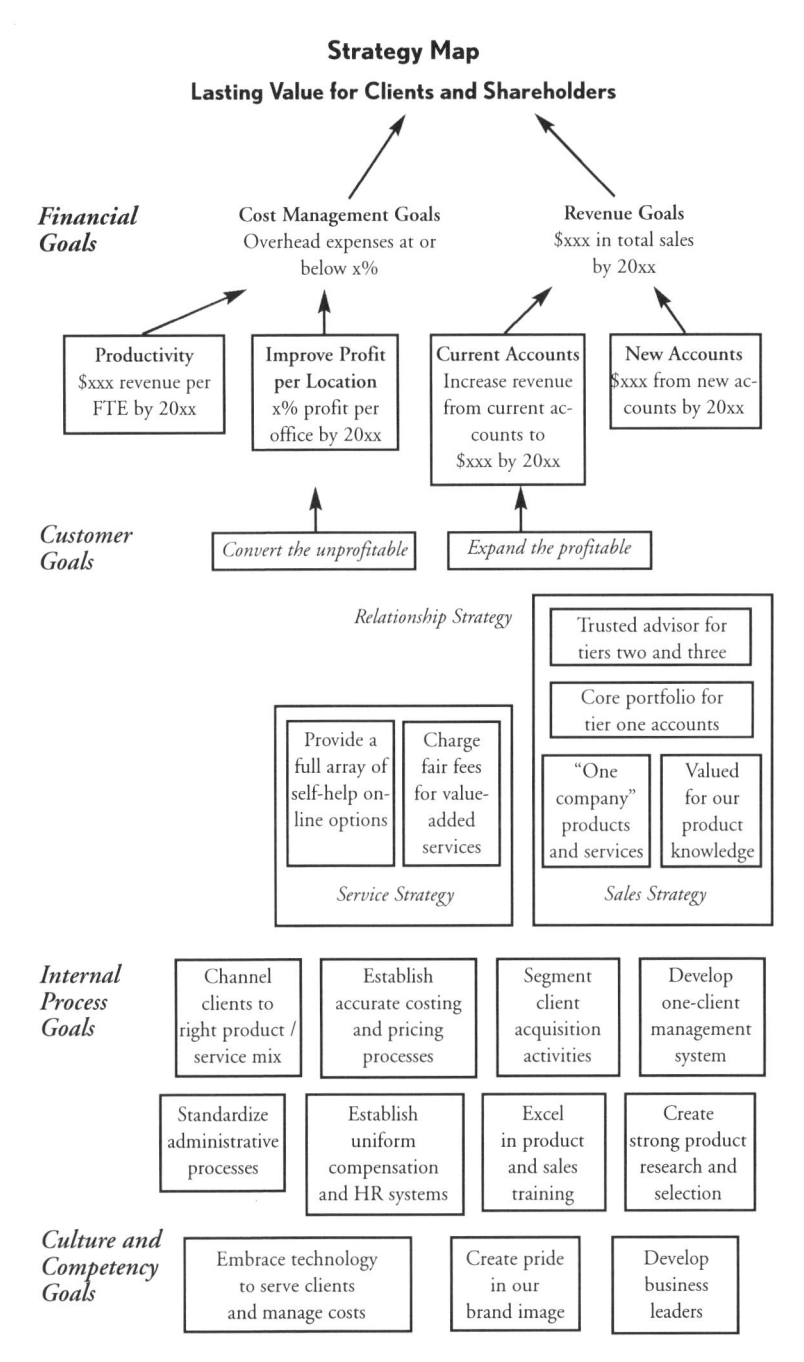

| Embrace technology to serve clients and manage costs | Create pride in our brand image | Develop business leaders |

Figure 5.1 - Strategy Map for Biggs & Bucks

109

tions of the map should roll up into one or more aspects of the financial goals. The next segment defines goals relating to customer experience: the organization's value proposition. These in turn are driven by goals for the key internal processes that support the customer's experience and manage costs. Finally, the map lays out the cultural and competency foundations that support those internal processes, the customer experience, and ultimately, the financial goals. The map gives an overview not only of the goals but also how those goals work in relationship with one another.

A Strategy Map for Biggs & Bucks

Biggs & Bucks has addressed its rising overhead and tighter margins through cost management and revenue goals. By setting targets for revenue per full time equivalent (FTE) position and for profitability per location, the map draws immediate attention to margins. The cost management targets should show the quickest returns. Expanding revenue by selling deeper with current clients should yield results in the intermediate term, while expanding revenue from new clients takes longer.

Following the map from right to left, you see the firm's overall strategy for steady growth. They plan to keep a feeder system of new clients, who will probably be less profitable at first. By selling deeper into those clients over time, the profitability should improve. Finally, finding ways to drive costs out of the process keeps margins within range. Biggs & Bucks captured their approach in two simple goals: convert the unprofitable to profitable, and expand relationships with the profitable. At any point in time, Biggs & Bucks wants to have clients at each stage of the profitability curve, thereby creating relatively smooth growth well into the future.

Moving down to the Customer Goals segment of the map we see goals reflecting the Biggs & Bucks hope of being the single source for financial planning needs for their clients. That is, their value proposition focuses more on customer intimacy than on being the lowest-cost provider of these services or being on the leading edge of financial consulting. Their goals in this segment of the map clearly roll up into the financial strategy just described.

First, look at the sales strategy: ensure that tier one clients — those with fewer current resources but good potential for the future — have a core set of products and services that gives them a good foundation and improves the margins for Biggs & Bucks. These are often young professionals with a fairly basic set of financial needs. By developing strong relationships, the company also wants to become trusted financial advisors for tiers two and three, those upper-middle income and upper income clients with larger accounts and better margins. Biggs & Bucks also wants to offer their clients a more consistent array of products and services, thereby addressing the holes in their "Swiss cheese" offerings. Thus, a customer objective is to create a "one company" look in products and services. In keeping with their desire to be trusted financial advisors, they will need consultants who are valued by clients for having strong product knowledge.

Achievement of these goals should drive the formation of deeper relationships with profitable clients, in turn increasing revenue from existing clients. By making sure that the tier one clients have the core package of products and services, more clients should be converted from unprofitable to profitable. The service strategy supports this conversion process. By having a full array of self-help options, clients (especially those in tier one) can be encouraged to use these less-costly alternatives rather than calling a consultant. By introducing a reasonable fee structure for some services, the company ensures that the cost is then offset by revenue. Again, the senior team made sure that customer experience was valued and promoted while at the same time addressing concerns regarding margins.

With the financial and customer goals in place, the remainder of the map focuses on the internal processes that Biggs & Bucks needs to do well in order to meet those goals. With a strong push to work with a different approach for each of the three tiers, there is a cluster of internal process objectives that focus effort and resources on client segmentation. First, it becomes essential to have internal processes to channel clients to the right mix of products and services. Second, the costing and pricing processes that determine client profitability need to be accurate. Third, client acquisition activities need to recognize the fact that the three tiers probably come into the company through different channels. Next, there is a cluster of objectives dealing with the company's inefficient and costly patchwork of systems: converting to a one-client management system, standardizing administrative processes, and having uniform compensation and human resources practices. Finally, in order to create the desired customer experience, Biggs & Bucks must excel in supporting and developing its financial consultants. Hence, we have the internal process objectives to excel in product and sales training and to provide strong product research and selection.

The senior team then dove deeper into the requirements for executing the strategy. Instead of treating technology as a necessary evil, it will be essential for the culture to embrace technology as a tool for serving clients and managing costs. Given the history of local autonomy, it will be important to create pride in the brand image for the entire company. Finally, growth will not be possible without a solid base of business leaders, so the final objective is to devote resources and efforts to developing these key employees.

Figure 5.1 shows the benefits of creating a visual map for a strategy. Goals higher in the map should be supported by one or more goals lower in the map. It is hard to imagine a better depiction for the notion of alignment than the line-of-sight relationships of goals throughout the map. Activities that do not roll up through the map are probably out of alignment with strategy, or at least not high priorities. Failure to achieve any of the goals lower in the map grossly weakens attainment of customer and financial goals. On the other hand, activities that lead to goal attainment lower in the map should enable goal attainment higher in the map.

In their book, *Strategy Maps*, Kaplan and Norton describe a series of vertically aligned goals in a strategy map as strategic themes. To identify these broad themes, it is best to start at the internal process level, as these are the drivers of the customer and financial goals. Tracing upward from each internal process goal, we see the customer and financial goals that depend upon strong execution of that internal process. Looking downward from an internal process goal, we see the cultural characteristics and competencies needed for skilled execution of that process.

Now imagine for a moment that you are the director of training and development for Biggs & Bucks. Could you imagine a more potent demonstration of your strategic priorities? With all the potential demands on a manager's time, few things could help more in prioritizing and executing projects relating to training and development than this one-page picture.

For each of the internal process goals, we can trace upward and downward to clarify the pathway or theme that leads to financial success. For example, channeling clients to the right product and service mix is a critical process if Biggs & Bucks is to convert unprofitable clients and expand profitable relationships. This portion of the map should stand out for anyone in marketing whose job relates to segmentation. For each of the internal process goals, you should be able to track upward to see the customer and financial goals that are driven by that internal process.

After developing a first draft of a strategy map with clients, we challenge them to review the map for "floating" goals or activities — those that do not fall along the path to critical objectives in other areas. If the goal or activity is important, then we modify the map to capture the results of its achievement. If the goal or activity turns out to be less critical, we drop it from the map. Dropping an item from the map does not mean that someone should not get to that item at some time, but it does mean that the item is not critical to strategic execution.

This is the model we have used. But if our clients have worked successfully with another method, we adapt our processes to that. The important point, we believe, is to develop a visual model that facilitates the strategic handoff by educating the organization and setting the stage for accountability planning.

Organizational Value Proposition and Major Trade-offs: How Will We Differentiate Ourselves?

Strategic thinking is one leadership ability that becomes more and more important as one moves higher in the organizational hierarchy. It is also one of the most challenging sets of competencies for many leaders. The challenge is not made easier by the fact that there are numerous experts who have their own approaches to strategy, making it hard to find true best practices.

Organizations cannot offer everything to everybody, so the essence of strategy is managing the trade-offs between various things that customers might value. You can think of these trade-offs in two ways. First, there is a trade-off in what the customer experiences. If the customer wants lower cost for a product or service, that customer gives up, to some extent, special features and customer support that would come at a higher price point. Conversely, if you as the customer want the latest features and functions, you expect to pay more. If you want the convenience of having products and services customized to your particular needs, then you expect to pay more for that personalized service. Kaplan and Norton describe these approaches as the Low Total Cost, Innovation, and Customer Intimacy value propositions.[20]

Your organization's value proposition is your particular blend of elements of each of these, realizing that you cannot be equally good at all of them. To fully understand your value proposition, you have

---

20 Kaplan, R. S. & Norton, D. P. (2004). *Strategy Maps: Converting Intangible Assets into Tangible Outcomes.* Boston, MA. Harvard Business School Publishing Corp.

to determine in which of those elements you will strive to be different from the competition in the customer's eyes and in which of those elements you will strive to be merely acceptable. For example, though Biggs & Bucks showed interest in cost containment, as most companies do, even a cursory look at their strategy map shows that they do not differentiate themselves in the customer's mind based on providing the lowest-cost products and services. And their innovation goals are modest, essentially targeting the innovation of their internal processes to manage costs and better serve customers. That is, clients would not think of latest technology or breakthrough financial products when they think of Biggs & Bucks. In our example, Biggs & Bucks strives to differentiate itself by developing an intimate understanding of the financial needs of their customers, with cost containment and innovation as secondary considerations.

The second trade-off is in the internal activities and processes that the organization uses to deliver on its value proposition. Once again, you can't be equally good at production, distribution, purchasing, product development, customer service, and a host of other internal activities and processes. So again you make a trade-off as you focus your resources on those particular activities and processes that are most critical to your value proposition. If you want to differentiate on low total cost, for example, you focus on purchasing, production, and distribution. You may offer basic service, but it is not highly personalized because personalization drives up costs. In a similar vein, if you want to offer the customer the latest and most innovative product features, you devote your limited resources to research and development and managing the product pipeline. You've got to manage cost within reason, but not to the same extent as a company that lives or dies by having the lowest cost. Here is the essence of what we mean by alignment: the trade-offs in your activities and processes should line up sensibly with the trade-offs in your value proposition.

As shown in Figure 5.1, the internal process goals at Biggs & Bucks align tightly with their customer-focused value proposition.

Having a one-client management system is essential to having a "one company" look to products and services. Other IT projects become "nice-to-haves" if they conflict with the "must-have" goal of converting all of the local offices to a single client management system.

A strategy map can also call attention to a common challenge: having departmental or functional goals that could be in conflict with one another. For example, a manufacturing manager's goal of reducing changeover costs might conflict with a sales manager's goal of responding quickly to customer requests for changes. A strategy map can show, at a glance, the areas where potential goal conflicts can occur.

Let us go back to Biggs & Bucks for an illustration. Imagine that you are the head of Marketing looking at the map in Figure 5.1. You can quickly see the focus on segmentation of clients into tiers, channeling clients into the right product and service mix, and segmenting client acquisition activities. It is clear that your department owns a major piece of the map. You have the technical know-how to data-mine the company's clients and offer a sensible approach to segmenting levels of product and service to the three tiers of clients. You and your team can figure out the product and service mix that best fits the needs of the three tiers of clients and is also most profitable for Biggs & Bucks. You can also figure out the most likely avenues for attracting clients in those three tiers. But you also see the goal of having a "one company" look to the product and service offerings, even though these are targeted to three different tiers of clients. So you and your team know to search for ways to ensure that each of those three tiers gets the products and services that best fit their tier, but also that the whole experience has a Biggs & Bucks look and feel. In essence, you and your team have been given the task of finding the right trade-off between treating clients differently based on their profitability and treating them all the same as clients of Biggs & Bucks. The ideal trade-off might not be easy to find but it would be hard to recognize the need without a map such as that in Figure 5.1.

If you create a visual representation of your customer goals and your key process goals, you have the beginnings of a strategy map. If you track these objectives to their financial impact, especially on cost management and revenue growth, you have a clearer picture of the drivers and the results of your strategy. If you go so far as to identify the skill sets, informational supports, and cultural characteristics needed to accomplish all of the above, you have everything you need for a strategy map. The discipline of developing the map helps to challenge the senior level to make deliberate and informed trade-offs. The resulting visual map gives you a powerful accountability and teaching tool for passing the strategic baton.

So how does all of this relate to the baton that is getting passed through the organization? Simply put, at each pass of the strategic baton, it is critical that each of the following be translated into the departmental specialties and, ultimately, into individual work priorities:

- What is our department's contribution (and what is my individual contribution) to each of the following?
    - Our financial targets for cost containment and revenue growth?
    - Our desired customer experience?
    - Our key internal processes?
- How do we need to change our behavior in order to accomplish the above?

Once again, whether you use formal presentations with fancy graphics or informal presentations on a white board, your chances of good execution begin with an understanding of what is to be executed. After a series of such presentations were rolled out in one of our client organizations, the most encouraging feedback from a line manager was that his team now understood the strategy and that "the strategy map has become a part of our daily life."

The Barriers to Execution and Solution Paths: What Could Stop Us?

By now the strategic baton looks both comprehensible and exciting. We have created a context by looking at market conditions and stages of organizational growth The organization's vision is then cast in the light of those conditions, and the strategy has given us a coordinated set of pathways to reach the vision. If we have done our work well, we should have a picture that makes sense and inspires.

All that remains now is to carry out the strategy, and that is where our beautifully conceived plan faces the brick wall of reality. The strategy describes what *should* happen, but it is critical also to address what *will* happen. Because the organization does not start afresh each day, there are legacy systems and procedures, some of which will support execution and some of which will hamper execution. Those legacy systems include the human system. We start with the talent base that we have, and that talent base may have gaps in light of our intended direction. There are also resource constraints and countless other potential barriers to execution that have to be identified and addressed. Otherwise, our strategic planning has been a paper exercise.

If the organization is in a stable stage of growth, then the barriers to execution usually will take the form of resource constraints. The solution path will involve squeezing more out of existing systems and resources by being more efficient or bringing in more resources similar to the existing ones. But if the organization is close to the point of diminishing returns for its current stage of growth, the barriers will have a different look and feel. As the top of the S-curve is approached, doing more of what has been done in the past will simply exacerbate the resistance from the limiting cycles.

For example, if the company is straining to move from the Systems Stage to the Delegation Stage, the driving forces that have grown the organization so far were probably the efforts to standardize processes during the Systems Stage. But the resistance would be felt in the form of those standardized processes starting to limit the ability of local managers to respond to their local market conditions. If the strategic planning process has correctly identified the needs, then the strategy probably has recognized the need to decentralize somewhat and push decisions down to the level of local markets. But these efforts to delegate more would reveal another possible limiting factor, the talent bench. Some managers will take the delegation and run with it, while some managers likely will struggle to step up to the new demands for independent decision-making. In managing the strategic handoff, it is essential to anticipate and plan for such potential barriers. Failure to anticipate means lost time and wasted effort. In this case, potential solution paths might include a more active leadership development process, mentoring arrangements, competency profiling and assessment, or any number of efforts designed to ensure that the bench is deep enough to execute the strategy.

When it comes to actually executing strategy, the identification and removal of potential barriers to execution is probably the most difficult work that you will face. In the movies, the charismatic leader often handles potential barriers by telling some poor underling to "just make it happen or I'll find somebody who will!" That may sound impressive, and there are occasionally times that the tough approach may work. But in the real world, execution is usually not quite so simple or heart-stirring. What if the problem isn't the person taking the handoff? After all, maybe there's somebody else out there who can make it happen and maybe there isn't. Or maybe someone can make it happen but not with the resources they've got or within the time allotted. Or maybe they can make it happen, but at the cost of not making something else happen that you also want. ("I can give you the speed you want, but the quality may suffer.")

The reality is that the responsibility for identifying and addressing barriers often does not lie so clearly with the level taking the handoff, but neither does it clearly lie with the level making the handoff. When it comes to identifying and removing barriers to execution, both hands are on the strategic baton until a solution path is found. In this crucial handoff zone, managers at each level will have to find the right balance between micromanaging and dumping.

An Assessment of Barriers to Execution at Biggs & Bucks

The first barrier to strategic execution at Biggs & Bucks is a cultural one. The strategy calls for creating a "one company" look and feel in products and services. These efforts would include, for example, the standardization of forms and processes as well as the emphasis on a core set of products and services for tier one clients. In a culture that sees autonomy as the norm, these changes will probably be met with skepticism at best and resistance at worst. Hence, the senior team explicitly set a goal to create pride in the brand image for Biggs & Bucks.

The second barrier has to do with likely limitations of the legacy talent in the local office director roles. Most of these people have built successful careers thus far by providing direct service to clients during a stage of growth in which staff at Corporate adapted to and accommodated the different approaches of the local offices. These are the same local office directors who will now carry much of the burden for driving the changes mandated by the strategy, which means that they will have to work more as business leaders than as service providers. Recognizing how much their strategy depended on changing the behavior of these local office directors, the senior team explicitly set a goal to develop them as business leaders.

At this stage in its growth as an organization, the successful execution of strategy at Biggs & Bucks rests largely on the shoulders of people who will probably find the new direction constraining and threatening in varying degrees. Success or failure will depend on enlisting the understanding, commitment, and skill of each person in the organization.

Personal Implications and Performance Expectations: What Does This Mean for Me?

No handoff of the baton can be successful unless the recipient knows what to do with the baton. Armed with an understanding of the business context, the vision, and important elements of the strategy, each level in the organization should now be able to begin the translation process. We often tell senior managers that their strategy, no matter how elegant and carefully crafted, will go nowhere until it is understood at a personal level right down to the line level. We think of this personal translation as having two components:

What Is Expected of Me?

At a minimum, each person in the organization needs to understand what is expected of them in light of the strategy. This understanding includes their priorities, their deliverables in terms of work products, and the ways in which they should work with others.

What's in It for Me?

Making sure they understand the baton that has been passed to them is only the first step. Next you have to make them want to run with it. That is, you have to help them find the answer to the question, "What is the payoff for me if I deliver?" By this we mean far more than the obvious, "You get to keep your job." Tapping into each individual's motivational style is a powerful skill for managers at all levels. Especially in the middle and senior ranks, however, where so much of the action is across departmental lines, the ability to appeal to individual needs can make the difference in where your request ends up in a peer's to-do list. Some people are motivated by upward mobility, some by being valued as a team player, some by public recognition, and on and on. If someone's personal payoff can be aligned with what the organization needs from them, you'll have alignment right down to the visceral level, and that is where the energy for execution comes from.

For the middle ranks, the translation is into the language of functional and departmental goals and accountabilities. It is here that people in the middle come to understand through the handoff process what their personal priorities are. There are numerous trade-offs that a middle manager can make in translating strategy into functional or departmental priorities.

Look at the Biggs & Bucks strategy map in Figure 5.1 in the mid-section of the map for Customer Goals, where we have the goals for tier one clients and then for tiers two and three. A Marketing manager can produce a finer-grained segmentation of customers and products that will take more time and be more complex to work with, or he can produce a rougher segmentation more quickly that can be easier to teach to the consultants and easier for Operations to implement. The finer-grained approach may be more effective in the long run because of its tighter focus on the needs of clients in each segment. But will it be worth the trade-off in time, cost, and complexity? Both can be done technically, but which aligns better with strategy?

Even with that question answered, there are personal implications lurking in the social network. Let's say the decision is to stay with a three-tier segmentation approach and, at the same time, to go for faster implementation. The Marketing manager will have to work with counterparts in IT and in the Consulting and Sales ranks in order to get good data, and with HR in order to ensure that training about the three-tiered approach is successful. But what if the counterpart in HR has differing priorities such as managing the conversion to uniform compensation and HR systems? The personal implication for the Marketing manager is that his ability to negotiate with HR will have a large impact on the ultimate success of his segmentation efforts. In fact, horizontal relationships will be as much a factor in the Marketing manager's success as will the vertical relationships. Middle managers have to understand personal implications of strategy not only in terms of technical priorities, but also in terms of how they will have to manage key relationships with peers.

If there has been a fumble above them, there is little that line managers can do to save the day. But even if the first handoff from the senior to the middle ranks was successful, execution still rests on the final handoff to the line level as managers there make the final translation into daily work priorities for each individual contributor in the organization. It is a sobering thought that these line managers are often the least trained and experienced, and yet they are the final translators of strategy into personal expectations for individual contributors on the line!

The baton now includes the strategic context, the vision, core elements of the strategy, and personal accountabilities. If the strategy has been translated appropriately for each level, people now know what they are to do. The final element of the baton describes how they should do it.

Organizational Values and Team Agreements: How Will We Get There?

Evidence suggests that companies with strongly shared values tend to outperform companies with less strongly shared values.[21] This finding makes sense when one considers the way values contribute to cultural fit. Values are at the core of how human beings behave as individuals and in organizations. They energize and motivate us toward some actions and away from others. Without these powerful behavioral guidelines, we may find that we have hit our targets but have done so in a way that is unacceptable in the culture.

In some companies, for example, a team leader wouldn't raise any eyebrows by taking a controlling and dominant approach with team members to deliver a project on time. Like it or not, that might just be the reality of how people work in this particular company. In other companies, a team leader who takes such an approach could be seen as a poor leader, as stifling input and creativity, while some-

---

21 Kotter, J. P. & Heskett, J. L. (1992). *Corporate Culture and Performance.* New York, NY. Free Press.

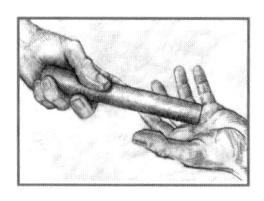

> If someone's personal payoff can be aligned with what the organization needs from them, you'll have alignment right down to the visceral level, and that is where the energy for execution comes from.

one with a more subtle influence style might be seen as a rising star. People who have worked in companies with very different cultures would not be surprised to see similar behavior producing very different responses. What might be more surprising and confusing, though, is that both companies might have values statements that include valuing people, and both could be adamant that they live by that statement. An identical statement is often interpreted differently in different corporate cultures. In turn, the way in which people actually behave in accordance with that statement will look very different.

The importance of translating values into more specific expectations becomes clearer when one considers the broad and general language of most values (e.g., integrity or quality). And, in fact, we find considerable overlap between companies in their expressed values. In public programs having executives from a variety of companies, we often have participants describe their company's values and find a handful of typical themes. Quality, integrity, concern for people, treating people with respect, doing the right thing, and other high-level values are quite common. In years of doing this exercise, we've never seen a values statement that says, "We treat people like dirt." Consequently, many executives content themselves with developing a values statement that, like the vision statement, goes on to laminated cards for everyone's wallet or purse. As with performance expectations, however, the translation job is not finished until people understand what those words mean in day-to-day practice at their level in the organization.

A simple exercise that we have found useful in making the values statements real and useful is to have people generate behavioral examples for each value that fits their daily work situations. For example, "What are some examples of integrity in our corporate Finance Department?" "What are examples of integrity out on the production line?" "What do we mean by 'focus on the customer' in Accounts Receivable?" At different levels in the organization and in different functions, the specific ways in which these values are expressed may be quite different, though they share the same flavor. Sharing these examples around the organization from different levels and functions helps people see the values as they are put into practice.

It is equally important to evoke examples of behaviors that do not fit the values. For example, "delight the customer" may not mean "losing our shirt to keep a fussy customer happy." People need to know where the lines are drawn.

From this simple process, the team can then reach agreements about how they will work together in their local work en-

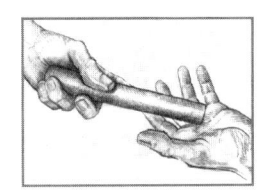

> It is a sobering thought that these line managers are often the least trained and experienced, and yet they are the final translators of strategy into personal expectations for individual contributors on the line!

vironment. The team can also add specific agreements that may not be covered in the organization's values but that have special significance to the team. These agreements then provide guidance and boundaries for behavior that come from the organization's social system itself and not from formal policies.

In this chapter, we have considered the fourth challenge of passing the strategic baton, that of defining the baton in terms specific to the organization. We now turn to the fifth challenge, that of actually making the handoff.

Chapter 6

The Fifth Challenge: Translating Strategy into Expectations

Now that we have covered the components of the strategy and the strategy mapping process, let's discuss communicating that strategy to the local management level. How do you translate strategy into performance expectations as the baton gets passed?

Because of its unique role, the senior level actually performs two passes of the baton. The first pass is to the entire organization, painting the strategic picture in fairly broad brush strokes. The second pass of the baton is the handoff down to the middle level, which involves a greater level of detail. Because these two passes differ in purpose and method, we will look at each separately.

Translation of Strategy: Senior Management to the Organization

The first handoff of strategy that senior leadership makes is in the form of communication with the entire organization. People want to hear straight from the top where they're going and why they're going there.

Communication to the whole organization must be tailored to the size and culture of the company. We have seen this process handled well in a combination of large forums, senior executive visits to team meetings, video presentations, material for new employee communication, and the traditional walking around approach. These organization-wide communications are a good opportunity for senior management to address the first two elements of the strategic baton:

- **The Business Context:** Where have we come from? What stages and defining events have we seen in our history? What practices caused our success in those earlier stages? What are the customer, competitive, and other environmental factors that have shaped our plans for the future?

- **Vision and Strategy:** How do we need to change in order to thrive in the future as we anticipate it? What is our value proposition — i.e., what we hope to create for ourselves and for our customers? What are our strategic goals? What are the major themes in our strategy?

Think about what happens when this business and strategic context is not provided. Highly engaged people are likely to look for ways to improve what they see going on around them. Without context, however, those well-meaning ideas for improvement may be wasted. For example, someone may express concerns that the organization should invest more heavily in product development in order to catch up with a familiar competitor. But if the strategy is to be a fast second in the market and not to be the first with new products, then "first to market" or "catching up" are not goals in the first place. But without this context, people are left wondering why the organization does not address things they see as barriers.

Without the strategic context coming straight from the top, a concerned employee might wonder if senior management has its act together. The result, of course, is a sense that the organization is failing somehow, and that suggestions for improvement go unheeded. And the most enthusiastic employees are the ones most likely to have this demotivating kind of experience.

On the other hand, if the strategic context is communicated effectively by senior management, the same employees can more accurately interpret what they see around them. And employees will perceive that the executive leadership team has their hands on the wheel and are in control. In turn, employees feel secure and confident about their own personal future. This is a powerful way to induce followership. That's not a bad return on a little personal communication.

A key piece of this communication process is the must-haves of the strategy, the critical elements on which the strategy hinges. Often, these must-haves are the key process goals at the heart of strategic themes. For example, completion of any project relating to "developing a one-client management system" – one of the Internal Process Goals in our Biggs & Bucks Strategy Map (see Figure 5.1 or Figure 6.1) – would be a must-have at Biggs & Bucks.

We see the power of something as simple as communicating the must-haves in a number of our client companies. In these organizations, the must-haves figure prominently in decision making in the middle ranks. When this communication works down through levels of management, it is quite common for us to talk with people at the line level who know the must-haves and are therefore in a better position to understand the decisions they see around them.

Now let's look at the second piece of strategy translation that senior management must do: communicate with and engage middle management.

Translation of Strategy: Senior Management to Middle Management

The essence of strategy is trade-offs — defining those areas that will competitively differentiate the organization in the eyes of customers and those areas in which the organization will compromise in order to obtain that differentiation. Once you have that defined, you will need to be sure that a system of activities is aligned to make it all work.[22,23] Senior management still has the baton until those trade-offs have been understood and translated into functional plans by the middle managers who supervise those functions. For our purposes, we will define middle managers as those having responsibility for functional units such as Marketing, IT, and HR.

A common problem in execution is that senior management's understanding of those trade-offs is at a general level, but middle management has to apply those general concepts to specific functional decisions. Unless both levels are on the same page, the execution of strategy can drift from the original intentions. A further difficulty is that the trade-offs are rarely of the either/or variety; they are much more likely to be of the more here/less there type. Finding the right balance is, at best, one of the biggest sources of frustration and, at worst, a fumbled baton. Senior management's attempts to delegate the details of execution often look like evasion and unrealistic expectations to those taking the handoff.

Both levels are in a potential bind at this point. Senior managers must walk the tightrope between getting pulled into the details of execution on the one hand and not fully appreciating the challenges of execution on the other. For middle managers, pushing too hard

---

22 Kaplan, R. S. & Norton, D. P. (2004). *Strategy Maps: Converting Intangible Assets into Tangible Outcomes.* Boston, MA. Harvard Business School Publishing Corp.

23 Porter, M. (November-December, 1996). "What is Strategy?" *Harvard Business Review,* 61-64.

for clarity or informing senior managers about potential barriers to execution may come across as uncertainty, failure to take initiative, or other career-limiting characteristics. However, unless middle managers make sure that senior management fully appreciates the functional challenges down in the organization, then senior managers form unrealistic expectations.

How often have you heard an exchange like the following?

Senior Manager:
"We are known for our ability to customize in order to meet the customer's needs. We are hard to beat in that area. It's in our DNA. We know we can't compete purely on price, so we will rarely be the lowest-cost provider. But let's not forget that we just can't let our prices get out of hand."

Middle Manager:
"I agree. But the more we customize, the more our customers expect from us. And our biggest customers can act like the proverbial 800-pound gorilla sometimes. They throw their weight around. They know we can't afford to lose them, but being so responsive and flexible runs up our costs. So just how far do we want to bend for our customers?"

Senior Manager:
"That's a tough one. But we survive in this business because of our relationships with our customers, so we'll do what we have to in order to keep them happy. You'll just have to find a way to keep your costs down."

In situations such as this, the generalities coming from senior management may look like evasion to those in middle management who want more clarity, but often that is not the case. Senior management may not be able to be more specific because of the normal

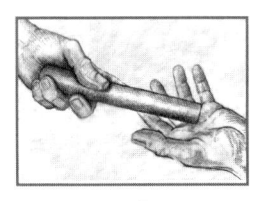

> ... clear translation of strategic trade-offs into good decisions in the middle ranks is a shared responsibility of senior and middle management.

uncertainties in business planning. And they run the risk of micromanagement if they delve too deeply into the specifics of execution. On the other hand, it is not realistic for middle management to take those generalities and make good decisions completely on their own.

Our point here is that clear translation of strategic trade-offs into good decisions in the middle ranks is a shared responsibility of senior and middle management. Answers to difficult questions about priorities lie in the handoff zone between the senior and middle management levels — both hands should stay on the baton until the strategic trade-offs have been reasonably clarified and translated. There is no precise role boundary here. Instead, there is a set of challenges that have to be met by both levels working in the handoff zone.

For example, senior management might identify the need to improve the company's client management system, and they may want certain capabilities such as using caller identification technology to speed access to a client's account information when the client calls with a question. Senior management would, of course, understand the link between these technical features and business outcomes such as faster customer service and using such calls as an opportunity to suggest other products or services not currently shown in the client's account.

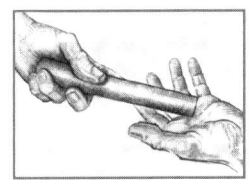

Beyond that level of understanding, however, senior managers other than those who came up through the IT ranks would usually be lost. It is middle management in IT who would identify specific technological options for achieving those goals. The level of technical knowledge here greatly outstrips that of the level above, as it should. The challenge at this point is making sure that both levels reach agreement about the plan without pulling the senior managers to an inappropriate level of detail or leaving the middle managers wondering about what is expected of them. There is indeed a narrow path between micromanaging and dumping, which is why we believe that the risk of a significant fumble is greatest in this first handoff zone.

> There is indeed a narrow path between micromanaging and dumping, which is why we believe that the risk of a significant fumble is greatest in this first handoff zone.

A General Process for Managing the Handoff

1. Here's How We Do It

How you manage the handoff from senior to middle management obviously depends on the circumstances at your organization. Furthermore, it would be a mistake to rely on a single method or approach for managing the challenges of the first handoff.

Even so, we have had good results facilitating a structured hand-off process in which senior officers review the organization's strategy and guide a discussion of it with teams of middle managers, preferably using a strategy map to lay out the broad outlines of strategy. Teams of middle managers are then given the task of using a simple force field process or other method to identify the conditions working toward success as well as the restrainers of success for customer and process goals. Each team of middle managers then presents its findings and leads the full group, along with senior managers, in a discussion of potential solution paths. Typically, the process spans several days. The process is always a little different with each client, and we often incorporate leadership development activities such as 360-degree feedback and personality assessments as part of the process. But the following should give an idea of the parts of the process that are designed to manage the handoff:

Preparation for the Handoff

Each senior manager and his or her direct reports meet one-on-one to prepare for the group session. In particular, the meeting focuses on the contribution that will be needed from each direct report for the strategy to succeed. Ideally, each direct report can draw a connection between the priorities for his or her team and some aspect of customer experience, cost management, or revenue growth. There is also a preliminary discussion of the key links with other departments or functions and an assessment of how those links need to work in order to carry out the strategy.

Multi-level Workshop

Next, we recommend organizing a workshop session with at least one senior manager and a pool of selected middle managers. Senior management — usually the CEO — guides a discussion of strategy at a high level, typically beginning with some history to put the current challenges in perspective. A major part of this discussion is the value proposition — the ways in which the organization will competitively differentiate itself — and what it will need to do to make that competitive differentiation happen.

With the strategic perspective established, breakout groups can identify the work processes critical to strategic success. The breakout groups then identify what is currently working well in those processes and also where there are issues that could affect the execution of strategy. Each breakout group presents its findings and recommendations back to the larger group for discussion and decisions.

The workshop wraps up with each middle manager presenting to the full group — including the CEO — his or her plan for leading the execution of strategy in his or her area. During this presentation, the middle manager identifies the financial and customer outcomes that are owned in part by his or her area. Important pieces of the plan include potential systems barriers (especially the linkage with peer functions or departments) and the manager's plans for addressing those barriers.

Following up

Each middle manager in the process has a follow-up meeting with his or her supervisor to review the work products of the session and to delve deeper into any potential barriers to execution and the plans for addressing those barriers. An important part of this follow-up is the supervisor's assessment of the developmental needs of the middle manager as they relate to carrying out the strategy. Thus, the developmental plan for each middle manager is anchored in the strategy. We describe this developmental needs assessment in Chapter Seven.

Each middle manager then continues the handoff process with each of his or her team members, including linking their individual roles with strategic goals. Again, an important part of the continuing handoff is assessing the team member's developmental needs in light of the strategy.

For the process to work best, the discussions have to be open and two-way. Indeed, the discussions in the workshop and breakout

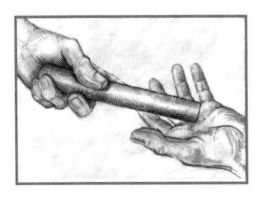

...it is critical to focus on the work in the handoff zone between management levels.

groups we lead usually get pretty lively. And if they are really working well, then not only is there two-way dialogue, but there is also two-way learning. That is to say that, ideally, the senior manager is learning as much from the dialogue as each member of the team is.

As such, the most common feedback that we receive after the process is that it was mutually beneficial for the senior and middle managers involved. Middle managers often report a better grasp not only of the strategy but also of the reasoning behind it and the implications for their roles and priorities. Senior managers often report a deeper appreciation of the specific challenges and points of confusion that exist out in the organization. Whether you use a structured process like the one described here or some other approach, it is critical to focus on the work in the handoff zone between management levels.

The First Handoff Zone at Biggs & Bucks: Senior to Middle Strategy and Themes

Because the financial and customer results are driven by internal processes, the handoff should be built around the internal process objectives. The reasoning is that if we have figured out the drivers correctly and we achieve those internal objectives, the customer experience and financial results should follow.

On the Biggs & Bucks strategy map in Figure 6.1, we can trace upward and see a clear link to customer and financial results for each of the eight internal process goals, as well as trace downward to see how the culture and competencies in the organization support the strategy. Here we begin to make the translation from strategic goals to activities and accountabilities. For example, we can see that the goal of channeling clients to the right product and service mix would likely involve Marketing, Finance, IT, Consulting and Sales, and HR. Marketing should provide data about client purchasing patterns and help in creating the product and service mix for each tier. Finance would have to work with Marketing to provide the profitability data for those tiers. Once the plan for selling to each tier has been developed, IT would create systems support in the form of user-friendly screens showing current and recommended services and products for each client. HR would provide training support in using the new systems.

Another theme would begin with the internal process goal of excelling at product and sales training. Looking at Figure 6.1, we see that theme highlighted as it appears in the Biggs & Bucks strategy map. We will use this one theme to follow the handoff process from the senior ranks down to middle management, and from there down to the front lines, from the perspective of the HR department, especially the Training and Development staff.

Looking upward from this internal process objective, we see that it is one of the drivers of a key customer goal: that of being valued for a high level of product knowledge. We also assume that Training and Development will play an important role in preparing consultants to carry out two other customer goals: becoming the trusted advisor for tiers two and three, and increasing the number of tier one clients who have the minimal core services portfolio. Looking upward from the customer perspective, we see that all of these objectives roll up into the financial goal of increasing revenue from current accounts. Finally, looking to the bottom of the map, we see that

Strategy Map
Lasting Value for Clients and Shareholders

Financial Goals

Cost Management Goals
Overhead expenses at or below x%

Revenue Goals
$xxx in total sales by 20xx

- Productivity: $xxx revenue per FTE by 20xx
- Improve Profit per Location: x% profit per office by 20xx
- Current Accounts: Increase revenue from current accounts to $xxx by 20xx
- New Accounts: $xxx from new accounts by 20xx

Customer Goals

Convert the unprofitable | *Expand the profitable*

Relationship Strategy

- Trusted advisor for tiers two and three
- Core portfolio for tier one accounts

- Provide a full array of self-help on-line options
- Charge fair fees for value-added services
- "One Company" products and services
- Valued for our product knowledge

Service Strategy | *Sales Strategy*

Internal Process Goals

- Channel clients to right product/service mix
- Establish accurate costing and pricing processes
- Segment client acquisition activities
- Develop one-client management system

- Standardize administrative processes
- Establish uniform compensation and HR systems
- Excel in product and sales training
- Create strong product research and selection

Culture and Competency Goals

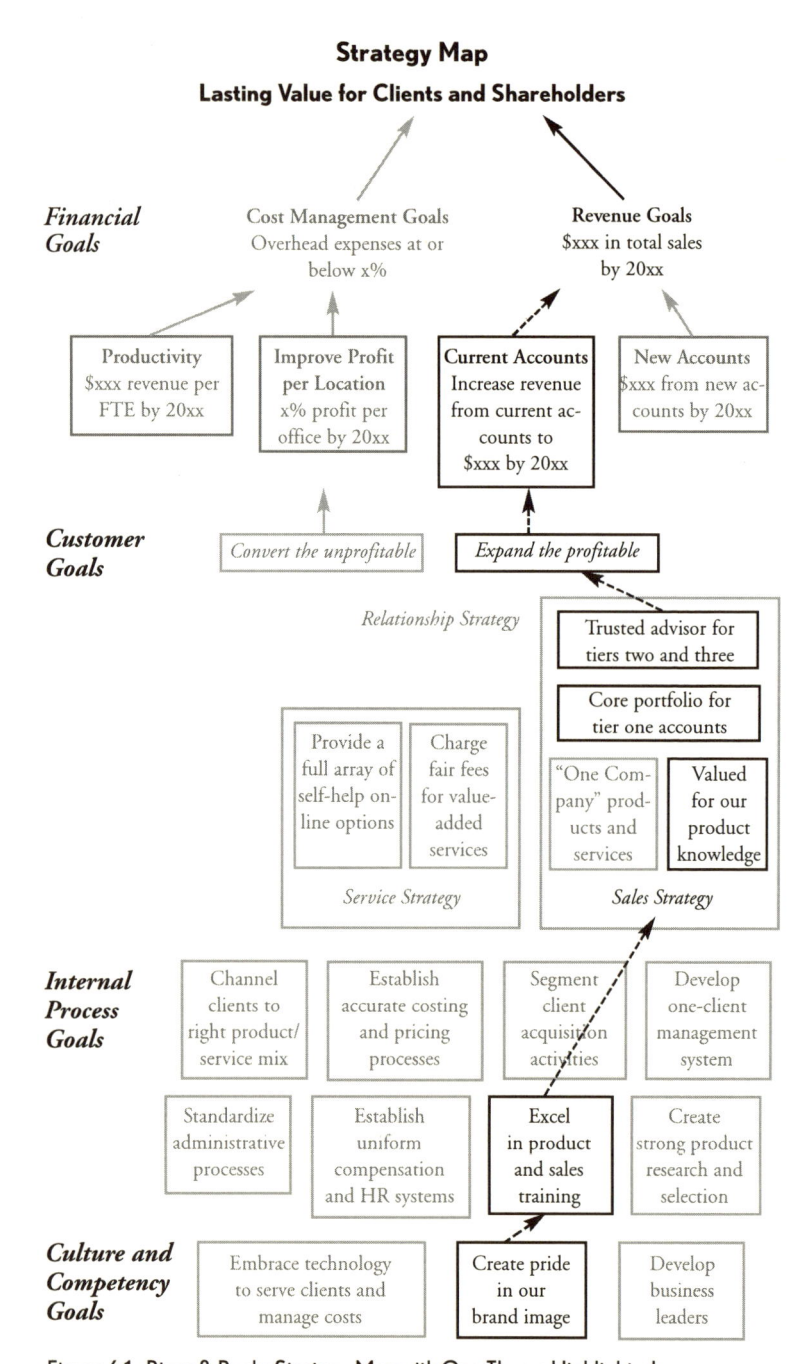

- Embrace technology to serve clients and manage costs
- Create pride in our brand image
- Develop business leaders

Figure 6.1 - Biggs & Bucks Strategy Map with One Theme Highlighted

all of these objectives depend in part on creating pride in the Biggs & Bucks brand as part of the culture. Without that pride, the "one company" look will be a difficult sell to the many branches that have enjoyed a fair amount of autonomy since the early days of the company.

2. Look at Your Team, but Remember That Not All Runners Are Equal

Before we move on, let's recap. We have created a strategy map and identified the critical paths within that map. The next step will be to translate the strategy map into expectations for departments and, ultimately, for individuals. Before we go more deeply into that translation process, however, let's look back at our initial assessment of the team from Chapter Four. Looking at that assessment, presented again in Figure 6.2, we see that all of the runners in each functional area are not equally able to participate in the handoff zone or, ultimately, to take the handoff.

Two alert warnings should sound in our minds as we look at the strategy map and then at the talent bench. The first is that the vice president of operations and the vice president of client services can-

Role Alignment and Handoff Model

	Finance	Consulting/Sales	T & D	IT	Marketing
Ideal Senior Role	CFO	VP - Client Services	CEO / President		VP Operations
Ideal Middle Role	Middle	Middle / Middle	Middle	Middle	Middle
Ideal Line Role	Line	Line	Line	Line	Line

Figure 6.2 - The Talent Bench at Biggs & Bucks

not just toss the baton to IT and to the local office directors who are the middle managers in Consulting and Sales. Those two functions will need much closer support in the handoff zone in order to make the high-level translation that we are about to cover. They will need more coaching in the strategic aspects of their roles than will the director of training and development. The second alert is that once the baton is passed, follow up will still be critical. Do you really want the success of your strategy depending on the unsupported performance of managers who are just getting their arms around their role?

There are more subtle challanges that emerge with a little more study. One is that, even though our director of T&D seems well-aligned in his role from a vertical perspective, we should not assume that the vice president of operations can pass the baton and go on to something else. After all, the Training and Development role will need support from Consulting and Sales, Marketing, and IT. Even though the director of T&D is clear on expectations and there are no apparent personal barriers (commitment, skill, confidence) to fulfilling his role, we might anticipate external barriers on any work that requires support from other departments.

With this context in mind, let us move on to a more detailed look at the handoff process as it rolls through the Training and Development Department.

3. Drill Down to the Individual

The first major outcome of working in the handoff zone is the translation of strategic goals into functional initiatives and individual accountabilities. Figure 6.3 uses our Biggs & Bucks example to show one way of managing the translation from the strategic goal to the more specific functional initiatives and individual accountabilities for the goal of excelling in product and sales training. Note that there should be a similar document for each of the seven remaining internal process goals.

Internal Process Goal: To Excel in Product and Sales Training

Theme From Strategy Map	Measure	Target	Solution Path (Initiatives)	Accountabilities
Financial Goal: Increase revenue from current accounts	Fees per account per year	to $xxx by 20xx		
Customer Goals: Become a trusted advisor for tiers two and three	Average products per customer	From x to y		
Provide core portfolio for tier one accounts	Percentage of accounts with core portfolio	From x to y		
Become valued for our product knowledge	Percentage of consultants passing assessment at 90% or greater	From x to y		
Internal Process Goals: Excel in products and sales training	Rated usefulness of training Lift in sales after training	90% or better excellent ratings Product line sales up 25% after training	Initiative #1: Product Mastery Series Initiative #2: Online help Initiative #3: Mentoring Process	T&D (Consulting and Sales, Marketing) T&D (IT) T&D (Consulting and Sales)
Culture and Competencies Goal: Create pride in our brand image				

Figure 6.3 - Translation from Strategy to Initiatives

To illustrate the drilldown, we will follow one department in particular. Remember Jim Newman, director of training and development, whom we introduced at the end of Chapter Four? Later in this chapter, we will follow the handoff to Jim's direct report, Myra Bennis, and ultimately to Myra's direct report, Tracey Collins. Though others on the executive team might have had input, Figure 6.3 would result primarily from discussions between Jim and his manager, the vice president of operations. Jim is the middle manager who will carry the lion's share of meeting this goal. Let us say that, after debate and discussion, the two agreed on three broad initiatives for meeting the goal: 1) the development of The Product Mastery Series, a training program to promote mastery of the entire range of Biggs & Bucks products; 2) an online help process to provide information and cues to consultants when they access client records; and 3) the development of a mentoring process to support the development of consultants. In Figure 6.3, these initiatives are listed in the Solution Path (Initiatives) column.

It should be easy to envision a senior team using a document like that in Figure 6.3 to monitor execution of strategy. There is enough detail for a senior team to know what initiatives are planned and who is on point for those initiatives. For example, we see that T&D is primarily on point for the three initiatives above, but with support from Consulting and Sales, IT, and Marketing. The detail is not excessive, however, so that executives are not drawn into the pit of micromanagement.

Figure 6.4 provides an example of the translation of strategic goals into an accountability and development plan for Jim Newman, the director of training and development. This plan contains the three initiatives from Figure 6.3, which have all been delegated to him, along with weights to indicate the importance of these three deliverables. In the Current Ability Assessment column in Figure 6.4, however, note that the vice president of operations (senior level) and Jim Newman as the middle manager have assessed potential barriers to execution. As we mentioned above, this assessment begins

Jim Newman's Accountability and Development Plan

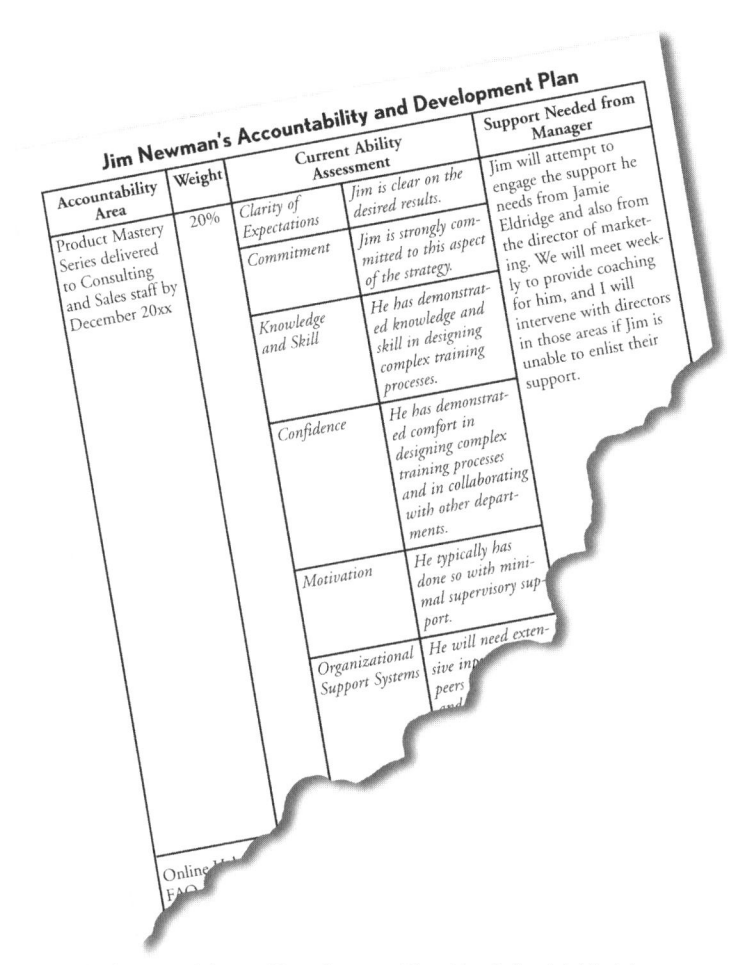

Accountability Area	Weight	Current Ability Assessment		Support Needed from Manager
Product Mastery Series delivered to Consulting and Sales staff by December 20xx	20%	Clarity of Expectations	Jim is clear on the desired results.	Jim will attempt to engage the support he needs from Jamie Eldridge and also from the director of marketing. We will meet weekly to provide coaching for him, and I will intervene with directors in those areas if Jim is unable to enlist their support.
		Commitment	Jim is strongly committed to this aspect of the strategy.	
		Knowledge and Skill	He has demonstrated knowledge and skill in designing complex training processes.	
		Confidence	He has demonstrated comfort in designing complex training processes and in collaborating with other departments.	
		Motivation	He typically has done so with minimal supervisory support.	
		Organizational Support Systems	He will need extensive in... peers	
		Online...		

Figure 6.4 - Accountability and Development Plan: Handoff to Middle Management for Jim Newman, Director of Training and Development

with clarity of expectations and commitment, then considers skill and knowledge to do the work, and finally ends with assessment of the potential systems barriers to execution. The expectations — commitment, skills, and knowledge — appear to be there, so we see that Jim is basically able to work at the ideal middle manager role (Figure 6.2).

But zooming out from Jim's role as an individual runner and looking at the whole team, a strong caution emerges. There are potential systems barriers beyond Jim's control. Two of the three priority initiatives require substantial support from Jim's peers. The Product Mastery Series initiative will need input and support from Marketing and from Consulting and Sales, and there are no champions in those areas to make this a priority. The online help initiative will require substantial work with IT, and that department has strongly resisted having any new initiatives assigned. Thus, the role of the vice president of operations will have to shift accordingly from routine supervision to closer monitoring and coaching as needed with all three of his middle managers.

Notice for a moment the middle column of Figure 6.4, labeled Current Ability Assessment. We devote the entire next chapter to this critical step in the process. For now, be aware that an essential part of the handoff is this assessment of an employee's ability to deliver on delegated tasks.

Translation of Strategy: Middle Management to Line Management

Meet Myra Bennis, Supervisor of Training and Development

Let's continue the translation process down to the next level to Myra Bennis, a line supervisor of training and development who oversees the work of several trainers. In Figure 6.5, we once again see the importance not only of translating the strategic initiatives into accountabilities, but also of identifying potential barriers in the ability of the recipient to deliver. Myra has successfully developed sales process training in the past, but it would be a mistake to assume that she would easily transfer that experience to the requirements of developing the Product Mastery Series. The latter requires much more fa-

The Fifth Challenge: Translating Strategy into Expectations

miliarity with actual product and service details, which means that she will have to work closely with Consulting and Sales to develop those aspects of the training. Consequently, her current ability to deliver the work is judged as moderate; her Accountability and Development Plan is tailored to provide her with closer supervision from Jim Newman, director of training and development, as well as support from someone in Consulting and Sales as reflected in Figure 6.5 in the column labeled "Support Needed from Manager."

To fully appreciate what can happen even to the best of strategic plans, look back for a moment at the Accountability and Development Plan for Myra's manager, Jim Newman. Jim also was seen as having moderate ability to execute the aspect of his accountabilities having to do with the Product Mastery Series because of the lack of priority placed on this work by Jim's peers in Marketing and Consulting and Sales. With likely barriers to execution (defined in the Current Ability Assessment column) in the first two handoff zones, it is unlikely that the Product Mastery Series would deliver the needed results without closer support from higher in the organization. By assessing the potential barriers to execution, the vice president of operations can develop Jim's ability to enlist support from peers in other departments. That way, the work gets done, and Jim grows in his role. Failing that, however, the vice president can at least intervene personally to ensure that the needed support comes from Marketing and Consulting and Sales, thus removing a potential barrier to execution of this one aspect of strategy. With that barrier removed one way or the other, Jim is now in a position to ensure that Myra gets the input she needs from the Marketing and Consulting and Sales staff to develop the Product Mastery Series. By translating not only accountabilities but also potential barriers, management at each level can take appropriate action to avoid potential fumbles in the handoff of strategy from level to level.

We can imagine the response of many managers that such a process is too time-consuming or is redundant with existing organizational processes such as job descriptions and appraisal systems. As

Myra Bennis' Accountability and Development Plan

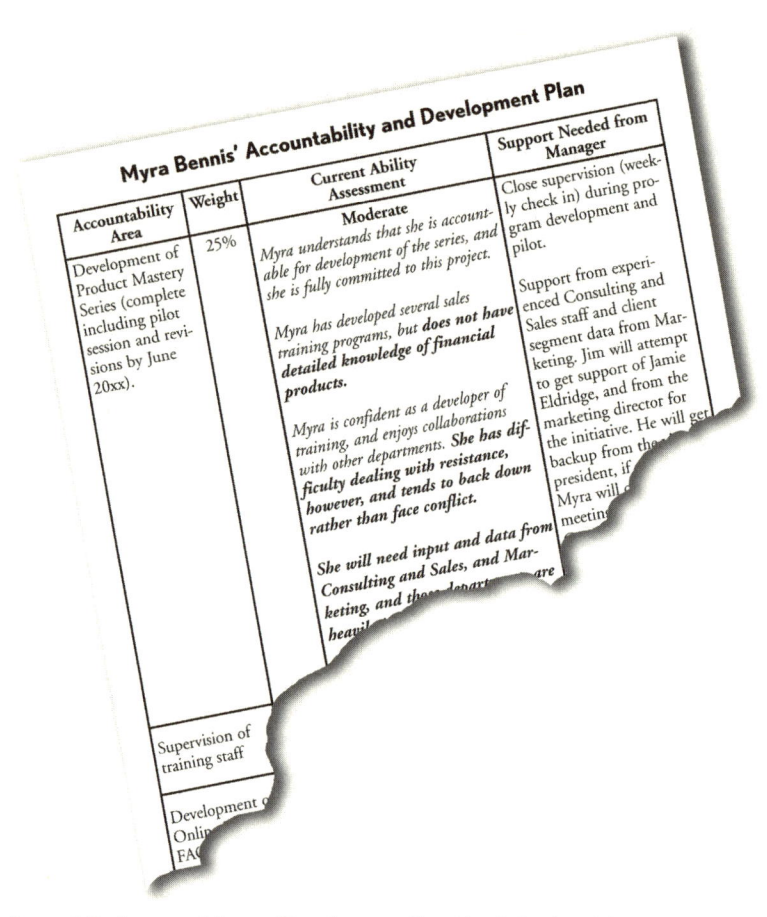

Accountability Area	Weight	Current Ability Assessment	Support Needed from Manager
Development of Product Mastery Series (complete including pilot session and revisions by June 20xx).	25%	**Moderate** Myra understands that she is accountable for development of the series, and she is fully committed to this project. Myra has developed several sales training programs, but *does not have detailed knowledge of financial products*. Myra is confident as a developer of training, and enjoys collaborations with other departments. *She has difficulty dealing with resistance, however, and tends to back down rather than face conflict.* She will need input and data from Consulting and Sales, and Marketing, and th...	Close supervision (weekly check in) during program development and pilot. Support from experienced Consulting and Sales staff and client segment data from Marketing. Jim will attempt to get support of Jamie Eldridge, and from the marketing director for the initiative. He will get backup from th... president, if Myra will... meetin...
Supervision of training staff			
Development... Onli... FA...			

Figure 6.5 - Accountability and Development Plan: Handoff to Line Management for Myra Bennis, Supervisor of Training and Development.

to the time objection, we can only respond by saying, "That's your job! That's what managers do." If managers do what's required of them in their roles as discussed throughout this book, most managers can find the time to think in detail about the role and development of each direct report. As to the second objection, if your organization's systems already support this kind of thinking and discussion, then you're ahead of the game.

But many job descriptions do not clearly link to strategic goals, and that is the purpose of the Accountability and Development Plan and the assessment of potential barriers to execution. And many performance appraisal processes are retrospective; they provide the slow-motion replay of the dropped batons over the previous appraisal period. The Accountability and Development Plan above is proactive, serving to avoid the dropped baton in the first place. At each handoff, the supervisor can use each potential barrier to execution as a developmental opportunity for the manager taking the handoff if the barrier is within the control of that manager. If the barrier proves to be beyond the control of the receiving manager, however, the supervisor is then in a position to intervene rapidly at the appropriate level in the organization to ensure execution.

Now let's look at the final handoff from the supervisor of training and development to the staff trainer charged with developing the materials for the Product Mastery Series.

Translation of Strategy: Line Management to Organization

Meet Tracey Collins, Anchor Runner

We are now ready for the final handoff from the line supervisor to someone in the organization who carries out the bulk of the work. In this case, that someone is Tracey Collins, a training and development specialist who recently joined Biggs & Bucks. She will take the handoff for the materials design portion of the Product Mastery Series. The weights on her Accountability and Development Plan reflect the relative size of these assignments for her current work plan. Note that, once again, the supervisor has estimated the current ability and created a supervision and development plan to ensure execution. Because Tracey is new, her supervisor Myra will work closely with her even though Tracey has a good background in materials design.

The logic of this approach is compelling. How often have you seen someone do a job correctly in a technical sense, but step right into some organizational tripwire because they failed to involve the right people or because they did not know how to get things done in the culture? Imagine for a moment the impact on execution of the strategy if the baton is fumbled in this last leg of the race. If the materials are not up to par or if they are not delivered in a timely manner, the Product Mastery Series suffers. And the ability of the consultants in the field offices to become trusted advisors for clients in tiers two and three depends heavily on the Product Mastery Series. With so much riding on a new person, albeit an experienced and talented one, Tracey's supervisor errs on the side of caution by holding onto the baton longer here to ensure a smooth handoff.

We have described the handoff process as it moved from the strategic goal to excel in product and sales training right down to the role of the anchor runner who will design the materials. Before we move on, let us just note that the vice president of operations would go through a similar process of defining accountabilities and assessing the coaching and development needs of the directors over IT and Marketing.

Meanwhile, Just Down the Hall...

If you are Jim Newman, director of training and development, there should be no doubt in your mind by this point how important the Product Mastery Series is to strategic execution and to your success as a manager. That same sense of urgency should apply as well to Myra Bennis and Tracey Collins in Training and Development.

But what if you are Jamie Eldridge, the local office director we introduced in Chapter Four? Remember that Jamie rose through the ranks from senior financial consultant to local office director because of her expertise in financial products, her knowledge of the local market, and her skill with clients. She has thrived in the atmosphere of local autonomy that characterized the early growth of Biggs &

The Fifth Challenge: Translating Strategy into Expectations

Tracey Collins' Accountability and Development Plan

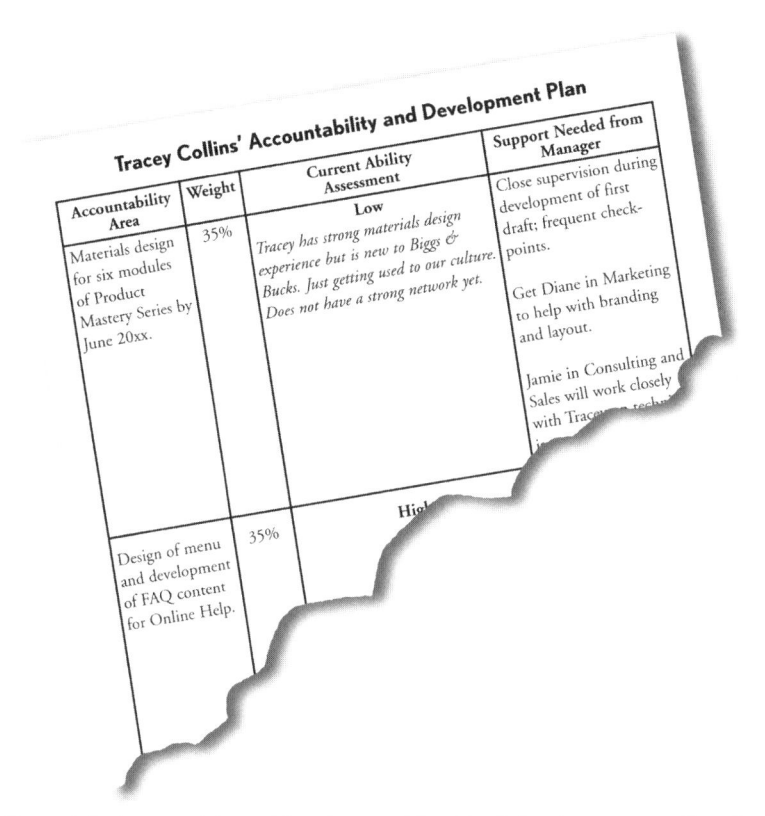

Accountability Area	Weight	Current Ability Assessment	Support Needed from Manager
Materials design for six modules of Product Mastery Series by June 20xx.	35%	**Low** — Tracey has strong materials design experience but is new to Biggs & Bucks. Just getting used to our culture. Does not have a strong network yet.	Close supervision during development of first draft; frequent check-points. Get Diane in Marketing to help with branding and layout. Jamie in Consulting and Sales will work closely with Tracey...
Design of menu and development of FAQ content for Online Help.	35%	**High**	

Figure 6.6 - Accountability and Development Plan: Handoff to Organizational Level for Tracey Collins, Staff Trainer.

Bucks. In a sense, we might say that her pride is in her local office's brand image more than in the Biggs & Bucks brand. Consequently, she is worried that the new strategic direction sounds the death knell of her ability to run the local office her way. When she hears about a new Product Mastery Series and other efforts to standardize the Biggs & Bucks approach across local offices, what is her likely reaction?

Now let's spice things up by supposing that Jamie is also the point person from Consulting and Sales who is selected to provide advice and support to the Training and Development Department on two of the initiatives to meet the internal process goal of excelling in product and sales training. Jamie was chosen because of her internal reputation as a product expert. Two of the initiatives in Figure 6.3 — development of a Product and Mastery Series and development of a mentoring program — require that Consulting and Sales provide technical input and advice to Training and Development. Let's assume that Jamie is a seasoned professional and would not deliberately undermine the effort. But then again, she doesn't have to. She only has to put a higher priority on activities other than providing technical support on a project outside of her own area, and she can do so with a clean conscience. After all, she has other responsibilities within her vertical chain of command, such as managing the local office and doing business development.

We just want to emphasize here a hard reality of life in middle management. Jim Newman can have the support of his boss for this project, and he may do a great job of managing the handoff down through his own Training and Development domain. But much of his ability to execute depends on the actions of Jamie Eldridge, a peer whose priorities and pressures are quite different from those of Jim and his department. We have heard countless times the frustrations of middle managers in wrestling with the differing priorities in their peer relationships. Once again, if the baton is tossed to Jamie from her manager — "just get to that project when you can" — it will be low on her to-do list. As long as Jamie delivers on her major responsibilities in the vertical scheme of things, she is unlikely to feel much pressure about the Product Mastery Series.

The good news is that Jamie's boss, the vice president of client services, understands the importance of the handoff process and has worked with her to create an Accountability and Development Plan similar to those that we have covered previously. Jamie's plan, shown in Figure 6.7, includes the Product Mastery Series and mentoring program along with Jamie's other accountabilities. As you would expect, providing technical support to another department gets a relatively small weight in comparison with running her local office and

The Fifth Challenge: Translating Strategy into Expectations

Jamie Eldridge's Accountability and Development Plan

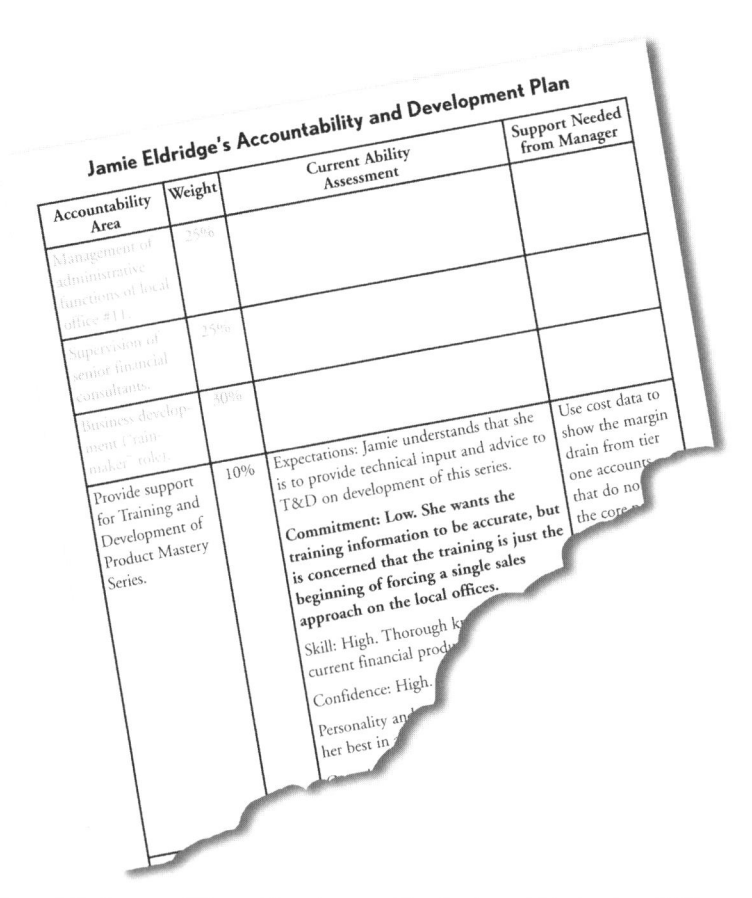

Accountability Area	Weight	Current Ability Assessment	Support Needed from Manager
Management of administrative functions of local office #11.	25%		
Supervision of senior financial consultants.	25%		
Business development (rain-maker role).	40%		
Provide support for Training and Development of Product Mastery Series.	10%	Expectations: Jamie understands that she is to provide technical input and advice to T&D on development of this series. Commitment: Low. She wants the training information to be accurate, but is concerned that the training is just the beginning of forcing a single sales approach on the local offices. Skill: High. Thorough k[nowledge of] current financial prod[ucts] Confidence: High. Personality a[nd...] her best in [...]	Use cost data to show the margin drain from tier one accounts that do not [use] the core [...]

Figure 6.7 - Accountability and Development Plan for Jamie Eldridge, Local Office Director

developing business. But note that the vice president of client services, who understands the strategy map and the importance of this project in execution, has identified commitment as a possible barrier as shown in bold lettering in Figure 6.7 and has a plan for getting Jamie on board. Note also how targeted the supervision approach is to the one potential barrier to execution: Jamie will get only routine check-ins on her other inter-departmental accountability, providing support for the development of a mentoring process. Because Jamie is more committed to this latter project, she will likely give it a higher priority.

Now let's look at the process of assessing developmental needs for individual managers and adapting your management style accordingly.

Chapter 7

The Sixth Challenge: Coaching for Performance

We have looked at what an ideal alignment looks like and reviewed some of the more common problems in managing the handoff from the senior to the middle ranks, and from there to the front lines — and we've discussed the crucial skills and actions at each level. Now let's take a closer look at coaching for performance. After all, even top talent requires effective coaching and development.

Anyone who has ever supervised or mentored someone else knows that performance can depend on a number of personal and organizational factors. But you don't have to make performance assessment and coaching more complicated than it needs to be. If the person has the potential to succeed in a given role, reasonable efforts to coach that person will pay off well. If the potential is not there, even heroic efforts on your part will yield little payoff.

Factors to Consider before You Start Coaching

Two Kinds of Performance

Let's define more clearly what we mean by "performance." In practice, there are two kinds of performance that are needed to get optimal results. We can think of these as *what* is to be done and *how* it

> If citizenship ends up in performance, it ends up in the P&L.

is to be done. As we will show, you have to be able to coach in both areas if you want to get full performance.

The first consideration in managing performance is what is required in the task or the role. This consideration includes the task or technical aspects of performance, the familiar "knowledge, skills, and ability" factors that are needed to perform a given task or to succeed in a role. Does a salesperson have sufficient product knowledge, and does he understand the selling process? Does a branch manager in a bank understand the fundamental procedures and guidelines for retail banking? Does an engineer have sound engineering skills? Clearly, sound technical skills are a must for good performance.

But sound technical skills alone are not enough. All of us know people who get good results on the task or technical side, but the way they get those results has negative repercussions. A common problem we see in executive coaching is someone whose technical skills are superior, but who creates a lot of pain in the organization because of personal and interpersonal skill issues, such as being seen as argumentative, overbearing, arrogant, or too demanding. One senior executive described a technically brilliant but interpersonally difficult subordinate this way: "For several years, I've been trying to avoid the pain of losing this guy. But he leaves such a wake of ticked-off people that the pain of losing him and the pain of keeping him are now about equal." The senior executive then went on to describe, in essence, how the subordinate's personality was having a negative impact on the P&L:

- "He gets great results, but then I have to spend quality time doing damage control with the people he worked with."
- "Several times I've had to talk others out of leaving because of him. Maybe they weren't brilliant, but they were solid performers, and it would hurt to lose them."
- "Though his teams are highly successful, people who have been on a team with him once don't want to be on another team with him."

Most of us probably could come up with a list of names that fit that description (and some of us hope that our name doesn't show up on somebody else's list).

Studies of the relationship between personality and performance have identified a number of personal and interpersonal skills that are important to success in one's role. In one line of research, these personal style factors are described as *citizenship*.[24] Being a good citizen in the organization has value of its own, independent of task skill. These citizenship qualities include persistence, willingness to volunteer and help others, following procedures, taking initiative, and supporting the organization's goals. One study of Air Force personnel used three separate ratings of each individual by different supervisors.[25] One supervisor rated the individual's overall effectiveness. A second supervisor rated the individual's task performance, and a third supervisor rated the individual's citizenship. The findings indicated that supervisors gave about equal weight to task performance

---

24 Borman, W. C. & Penner, L. A. in Roberts, B.W. & Hogan, R. (Eds.) (2001). *Personality in the Workplace.* Washington, DC. American Psychological Association.

25 Motowidlo, S. J. & Van Scotter, J. R. (1994). Reported in Borman and Penner chapter of Roberts, B.W. & Hogan, R. (Eds.) (2001). *Personality in the Workplace.* Washington, DC. American Psychological Association.

and citizenship when judging someone's overall performance in the organization. But in terms of the chances of someone getting promoted, citizenship actually weighed more heavily than task performance.

It makes sense that a major factor in promotion should be the personal and interpersonal characteristics we described as good citizenship. But obviously, we would be unlikely to promote someone who just does not have the task skills. This study and others strongly support the need to pay attention to *citizenship factors as well as task factors* in managing performance. If citizenship ends up in performance, it ends up in the P&L.

Other studies have supported the idea that personal characteristics such as customer service or integrity in the workplace have been correlated with personality factors such as the ability to handle stress, ability to manage conflict and disagreement, and reliability in following through on commitments.[26] These formal studies make the case that personal traits — how someone works with others in accomplishing tasks — can be as important as what the person accomplishes. In our own practice, we have seen this confirmed time after time in working with executives and their teams. To be successful in a leadership role, it is important to understand and learn to manage one's own personality. As we said earlier, this personal growth curve in part shapes role performance, and role performance drives organizational results.

People and Systems

Another key aspect of the executive role is identifying and managing potential barriers to execution. Those barriers may be the communication between levels, inside the people taking the handoff (commitment, knowledge, skills, motivation), or external barriers in the organization's systems. Misreading the readiness of any of those areas

---

[26] Ones, D. S. & Viswesvaran, C. Studies cited in chapter of Roberts, B.W. & Hogan, R. (Eds.) (2001). *Personality in the Workplace*. Washington, DC. American Psychological Association.

almost guarantees a fumble of the baton. Our assessment process looks at the three kinds of potential barriers or hurdles to execution and the developmental needs they indicate:

Hurdles in Communication

The first level of assessment is the clarity of communication between supervisor and direct report about strategy and expectations. Barriers here are low-hanging fruit in that they can be addressed fairly quickly by taking the time to discuss and clarify expectations. Though this sounds easy enough, executives often underestimate the need for such an investment of time.

Hurdles within the Direct Report

If the direct report and supervisor are on the same page about expectations and priorities, the next level of assessment has to do with factors internal to the direct report. Where's the level of commitment? Does he or she have the needed knowledge and skill? If the knowledge and skills are there, is there a confidence barrier that indicates the need for closer support from the supervisor? Are the critical skills a comfortable fit with the personality and motivation of the direct report? Barriers within the direct report indicate the need for coaching, mentoring, or other forms of skill development. Again, busy executives often underestimate the need for developing the capacity of their team.

Hurdles in the System

You will also need to determine if there are systems barriers outside of the control of the direct report. For example, are there competing priorities that cannot be met by improved efficiency? Are there resources outside of the control of the direct report that require the support of the supervisor? Barriers here usually require the decision-making authority and intervention of the supervisor.

We see the linking of developmental planning and strategy as essential for several reasons. First, the organization can target its developmental resources to efforts that are most likely to support improved execution. Second, the developmental work has a high level of relevance as it is tied to success in the current role, so people are likely to retain what they have learned in the process. Finally, because of the cascading of the work from one level to the next, the developmental work is aligned from the senior to the line level in the organization. This cascading helps in the translation process from strategic language to day-to-day actions.

A Guide to Performance Development

For a person to perform well, and to ensure that the baton is handed off cleanly and not fumbled, there are Six Performance Hurdles© that the runner must clear. It does little good to clear five of them, only to slam into the sixth one, drop the baton, break a leg, and be hauled off the track on a gurney. In business, it is the coach's responsibility to ensure that the runner clears each of these hurdles so that the runner is there for the handoff of the baton to the next runner. Figure 7.1 lists the Six Performance Hurdles that we will cover in detail.

For each of the Performance Hurdles, we will provide you with a simple tool in the form of a Decision Tree (see Figures 7.3 – 7.8). In Chapter Nine, we will pull all of this together into a method and set of coaching tools for you to use with your people for all the Performance Hurdles discussed in this chapter.

Performance Hurdle #1: Expectations

People have to know what is expected of them on a particular task or in their role, both in terms of the results that they are to achieve and the methods they may use to get those results. If they aren't on the same page with you to begin with, their motivation and skill

The Sixth Challenge: Coaching for Performance

> **Six Performance Hurdles**©
> 1. Expectations
> 2. Commitment
> 3. Skill
> 4. Confidence
> 5. Personality and Motivation
> 6. Organizational Supports

Figure 7.1 – Six Performance Hurdles

won't matter. As obvious a point as this might seem to you, we are frequently amazed at how often this is a primary hurdle to execution of strategy. Both authors could retire in luxury if we had a nickel for every time we have heard something like, "I don't know what's expected of me! I do what I think is right, but then I get criticized for doing the wrong thing. Well, no one told me!"

In working with organizations, we usually find that people are clear about their goals. There are always exceptions, of course, but setting clear, measurable goals is a pretty fundamental management practice. When we talk about the need for clarity of expectations, however, there is much more involved than clarity of goals. In order to pass the strategic baton from senior level to the middle and line levels, the strategy itself needs to be understood. The goals have to connect with strategy and with other goals in the organization; otherwise you are at risk for the goals appearing to be isolated and arbitrary. When we do interviews in organizations to help identify drivers and restrainers of strategic execution, two of the most common restrainers we hear are:

- "I understand the organization's goals, but I'm not at all clear on our plan for getting there."
- "I know my goals, but my goals don't seem to mesh with the goals of my peers."

So when you work toward having clear expectations as part of the handoff of strategy, your territory will range from understanding strategy right down to defining the expected personal performance level.

Defining the Scope: Specific Skills versus Role

Our coaching approach will work for assessing someone's needs with respect to specific skills, such as closing the books at the end of the month. The first question is whether the person understands what is expected in closing the books. But you can also use our coaching approach to address larger issues, such as when someone is not working at the right level for their role. For example, if someone is personally closing the books when they should have trained someone else and delegated that task, then you are addressing the issue of role fit. But you still begin with ensuring that they understand what is expected. Do they know that, at their level in the organization, they should be supervising the closing of the books instead of doing it personally?

To help with thinking about broader role issues, we have included a very brief summary of the Four Dimensional Leadership© model (Figure 7.2). It should be very useful in assisting you in getting your arms around the different role expectations required of the individual you are coaching, depending on where they fall within one of the three major levels of management.

Four Dimensional Leadership©

The Four Dimensional Leadership model is a conceptual representation of the shift in leadership competencies and personal characteristics required at the three levels of management. This model can be used to visualize effective alignment of management with respect to the leadership that is required for any organization. That is, each level of management in the organization should have people with the right mix of leadership characteristics and competencies. Additionally, this model can be used to better understand the necessary shift in leadership competencies as one moves up within the management levels of an organization.

Before going into the model, let's first define our terms — *management* and *leadership*.

Management and Leadership [27]

The term *manager* usually refers to a position having the authority to get work done through other people, including such functions as planning, organizing, directing (or commanding), controlling, and coordinating. These skills are distinct from technical, financial, and other specialty functions in the organization.

As such, competence in specialty technical areas, such as engineering or accounting, would not necessarily prepare one for the work of manager. Highly skilled engineers or other specialists may

---

[27] Kotter, J. P. (1990). *A Force for Change: How Leadership Differs from Management.* New York, NY. Simon & Schuster.

struggle when promoted into a managerial role unless they develop a new set of managerial skills.

The term *leader* is broader. Though it can certainly overlap with the role of manager, leadership may not always involve the positional authority of the manager. Thus, leadership can involve influence deriving from sources outside of one's formal position. For example, these sources of influence can include one's personal characteristics and interpersonal skills. Both involve planning and forward thinking. But planning in the manager role is usually shorter term and more focused on the details of execution, while planning in the leader role is more visionary and tends to be longer term.

Management:
- Planning in terms of detailed steps, resources, timetables
- Providing structure, staffing, clear roles and procedures
- Tracking planned vs. actual performance and addressing gaps
- Delivering predictable, orderly results and goal attainment

Leadership:
- Creating conditions to induce people to follow or be influenced by you
- Planning in terms of direction, vision, scenario planning, developing strategy
- Communicating the vision and values; making the case for the vision

- Inspiring and energizing others, fostering commitment
- Creating change, often innovation

Given these descriptions of management and leadership, we can now predict some outcomes for a team or organization with strong management but weaker leadership.

The strong management should result in safe, predictable execution of a plan. But without strong leadership, the plan may simply reflect goal setting without vision or strategic positioning. Good managers may get compliance, but without strong leadership skills they won't get commitment and enthusiasm.

Teams or organizations with strong management *and* strong leadership, on the other hand, enjoy the benefits of the vision and have the ability to engage and energize others in pursuit of that vision along with the planned, steady execution that comes with strong management.

In our Four Dimensional Leadership model, we break leadership into four broad dimensions of skills and attributes:

Implementational Leadership comprises skills needed to lead or influence others in the implementation of plans and tasks. Consequently, technical expertise and detailed knowledge of work procedures are essential. No one wants to trust or follow someone who isn't viewed as competent in their job.

Personal Leadership describes the ability to understand and manage one's own personality so that personal ego does not get in the way of sound business practice. In particular, it involves management of stress and emotional reactions in problem situations. There is a strong emphasis on ethics and integrity.

Interpersonal Leadership is defined as influencing others through skills such as communicating, negotiating, giving (and receiving) feedback, facilitating discussions, coaching, and mentoring.

Directional Leadership comprises the skills needed to think and act strategically, understand and manage complex systems, and other skills related to managing the boundaries with the external environment, setting direction for the organization, and guiding the execution of that direction.

Our model is designed to depict, at a glance, the shift in leadership skills and attributes at different levels of management. In essence, the model shows the shift from leading others by virtue of technical competence (Implementational Leadership) to leading others by shaping the vision and strategy for the enterprise (Directional Leadership).

Working from the bottom of the model, a non-manager who is highly skilled will have influence in a team even without supervisory authority. The non-manager with strong technical expertise will emerge as the go-to person and will be known as someone who contributes greatly to getting the job done (Implementational Leadership). The line manager must demonstrate high levels of detailed knowledge and technical skill. In middle management, understanding and translating strategy are more central to success in the role. Middle managers, of course, still need technical knowledge and skill, but these will no longer pay off the way they did in line management. After all, the middle manager is likely to have responsibility for several functions outside of their area of technical expertise. Finally, a senior manager's role is heavily dependent on Directional Leadership skills.

Personal and Interpersonal Leadership are important at all levels of management. Inability to manage the stress of work or to reign in the ego (Personal Leadership) will limit the effectiveness of even the most talented expert. Difficulty in communication, negotiation, and other forms of influence (Interpersonal Leadership) likewise will impair performance at any level. But we should note that the impact of Personal and Interpersonal Leadership increases at higher levels because the span of control has increased along with one's power, status and authority. For example, the personal trait of impatience in a line manager may mean that a shipment goes out before it is ready. The same trait in a CEO may mean that an acquisition is made without full due diligence.

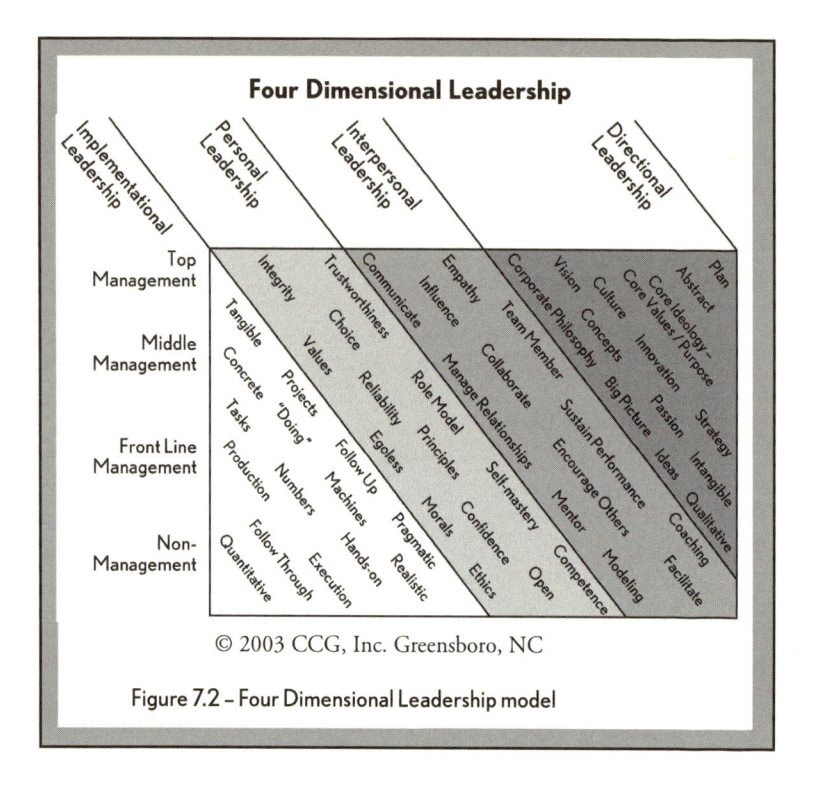

Four Dimensional Leadership

Implementational Leadership / Personal Leadership / Interpersonal Leadership / Directional Leadership

Top Management — Integrity, Trustworthiness, Communicate, Empathy, Corporate Philosophy, Vision, Culture, Concepts, Core Ideology – Core Values/Purpose, Plan, Abstract

Middle Management — Tangible, Values, Choice, Influence, Team Member, Collaborate, Innovation, Big Picture, Passion, Strategy, Intangible

Front Line Management — Concrete, Projects, Reliability, Role Model, Manage Relationships, Sustain Performance, Encourage Others, Ideas, Qualitative

Non-Management — Tasks, "Doing", Follow Up, Egoless, Principles, Self-mastery, Mentor, Coaching

Production, Numbers, Machines, Confidence, Morals, Competence, Modeling, Facilitate

Follow Through, Quantitative, Hands-on, Execution, Pragmatic, Realistic, Ethics, Open

© 2003 CCG, Inc. Greensboro, NC

Figure 7.2 – Four Dimensional Leadership model

If you are looking at the entire role of the individual instead of coaching about a more specific skill, you may find it helpful to break the role into its largest chunks and walk through each of the four dimensions in the Four Dimensional Leadership model: Directional, Interpersonal, Personal, and Implementational. Because the leadership dimensions in the model are clusters of similar skills and characteristics, it is fairly easy to drill down to a potential barrier in one of the dimensions.

The following is a breakdown of the leadership role from the Four Dimensional Leadership Model as applied to a middle manager.

- Directional Leadership
  - Understanding the corporation's strategy and the key trade-offs
  - Systems thinking, seeing the "big picture"

- Translating the strategy into long-term functional goals and plans
- Interpersonal Leadership
  - Communicating vision, strategy, values
  - Coaching, mentoring and counseling
  - Managing conflict and negotiation
  - Managing vertical relationships
  - Managing horizontal relationships
  - Team membership skills
  - Team leadership skills
- Personal Leadership
  - Managing emotional tensions effectively
  - Living by the corporation's core values
  - Integrity, honesty
- Implementational Leadership
  - Technical knowledge
  - Understanding of key metrics
  - Understanding and use of organizational processes and procedures

Suppose that on the first pass you discover that a middle manager seems to struggle most with understanding and translating the key trade-offs of the strategy into functional plans and priorities. That is, maybe he focuses so much on perfecting the technical features of a new product that he seems to lose sight of how much value the customer places on those features and the financial consequences of delaying the product launch. Then as you think about it, it occurs to you that you have no idea whether this particular manager understands the key metrics of the organization, which are important in defining the trade-off issues. Do you know for sure that this manager can translate "weeks of delay" into "lost sales"? So now you would have two targets to explore in more detail: one is understanding the trade-off between product perfection and launch date, and the other is understanding key organizational metrics.

A few minutes worth of deliberate, focused thinking about someone's role and performance could yield surprising clarity about their developmental needs. If you are like most managers, however, you get pulled so heavily into the day-to-day that you underestimate the need for a planned approach to developing your people.

In assessing clarity of expectations, some good questions to consider are:

Goals and Role Definition
- Are they clear on their goals — the measurable outcomes they are to achieve?
- Do they understand how their goals and activities roll up into the organization's strategy (in particular how their goals tie to customer experience, cost management, and/or revenue growth)?
- Are they clear on priorities so that less important work consistently gives way to more important work?
- Are they clear on where their time and effort should be spent, in particular what they should do versus what should be delegated?
- Are they clear on the people development and performance management aspects of their role?
- Do they understand how their role affects others vertically (supervisor and direct reports) and horizontally (others in the work flow)?
- Do they have a clear picture of how those vertical and horizontal relationships need to be managed?

Skill Clarity
- Do they understand the skills needed for success in their role?
- Do they have a realistic understanding of their current performance and how they can grow in their role?

Personal and Interpersonal Clarity
- Do they understand and appreciate the organization's core values as they apply in day-to-day work?
- Do they understand how they should manage themselves and their relationships in order to be most effective?
- Do they have a realistic understanding of how they can grow and develop in terms of personal management and interpersonal skills to enhance their effectiveness?

What If Expectations Aren't Clear?

The basic coaching tool here is simply teaching or explaining. Clarity about goals and role definition is not hard to achieve. Too often, problems in this area are simply the result of assumptions and lack of attention. You may assume that a subordinate is on the same page you are about expectations, so conversations you have in this area are brief and lacking in detail. But don't assume that because you and a direct report are using the same words that those words carry the same meaning. "Run this territory like it's your own business" means one thing to someone with a bold explorer personality and something quite different to someone who is cautious, practical, and risk-averse. The bottom line: err on the side of over-communication if you want to avoid a fumble early in the race.

In each of the following decision tree tables (Figures 7.3 – 7.5), we will offer some common tools and approaches for you to consider when a manager reporting to you has a Performance Hurdle to clear. The list of questions and suggested approaches and tools are meant only to give you the concept of what you need to do, and it is not meant to be exhaustive. For our purposes here, they are meant to be general enough that you can use them as a guide for working with managers from the line to the senior level. Some will be simple and obvious; you just have to remember to do them. Others will take more time and effort. Of course, you would have to adapt your presentation to accommodate the person with whom you are working. You will find that our list of tools and approaches will serve to

Decision Tree for Performance Hurdle #1: Expectations

Question	Decision Point	Coaching Tools
• Does this person understand his role and what is expected of him? Note: This includes *what* he is expected to accomplish and *how* he is expected to accomplish it (cultural fit).	No → Yes ↓	• Role Definition: *Use The Leadership Pipeline.*[28] • Use Four Dimensional Leadership for guidance.
• Is this person clear on his goals and how he will be measured?	No → Yes ↓	• Define goals that are specific and measurable, with target dates for completion.
• Does this person understand how his goals and activities roll up into the organization's strategy?	No → Yes ↓	• Use a strategy map to draw "line of sight" between his goals and strategic goals. • Be sure he understands key metrics used to measure overall organizational performance (e.g., efficiency ratios, etc.)
• Is this person clear on where his various responsibilities fit in the Importance – Urgency Grid? URGENCY HI X LO X HI LO IMPORTANCE	No → Yes ↓	• Identify any areas where his work affects multiple goals on the strategy map (e.g., a project that would both drive down cost and enhance customer experience at the same time). • Use a pie chart to show the relative proportion of time to be allocated to each of his key responsibilities. • Ask him to walk through his current to-do list and ask him to rate the priorities. It is most useful to let him describe his reasoning so you can listen for areas of misunderstanding. So don't jump in and correct his list too soon.
• Is this person delegating appropriately?	No → Yes ↓	• The rule of thumb here is that if it is something that can be done at a lower level of responsibility and authority, it should be delegated. • Our Four Dimensional Leadership model should be helpful in determining what responsibilities are appropriate to the level of management under consideration. • Charan's Leadership Pipeline model is useful as well.[28]

28 Charan, R., Drotter, S. & Noel, J. (2001). *The Leadership Pipeline: How to Build the Leadership Powered Company.* San Francisco, CA. Jossey-Bass.

The Sixth Challenge: Coaching for Performance

Decision Tree Hurdle #1 (continued)

• What is this person's understanding of how his role affects others vertically and horizontally?	Yes ↓ No →	• Walk him through the linkage of his role with yours and the supervisor, making sure to explain what you need from him to support you in doing your job. • Have him go through the same process with his direct reports. • Walk through each step in critical work processes and note who is involved in or affected by that step. Do not assume that he knows how his work fits into the whole, or who the go-to people are in each department to get issues resolved. In complex organizations with work broken out into many specialties, people often concentrate just on getting work out the door and miss easy opportunities to improve the process itself.
• Does this person understand his role in managing both vertical and, often more importantly, horizontal relationships?	Yes ↓ No →	• Have him prioritize the other relationships that are most crucial in the work flow and develop a brief vision of how each should work. • Work with him to develop one or two positive strategies for improving relationships that are especially difficult. In particular, coach him on the importance of asking more questions to better understand the other person's or department's role and challenges. • Especially for those in middle management roles, identify the crucial trade-offs between departments (e.g., design features vs. service capacity, etc.). • Go through several examples to guide him in understanding where the balance should be in order to line up with the organization's strategy.
• Does this person understand the skills needed for success in his role?	Yes ↓ No →	• Check to see if your organization has competency profiles for each role. (We have seen situations in which these had been done but not widely shared). • Use the Four Dimensional Leadership model, and/or *The Leadership Pipeline* to clarify skills appropriate to the role. • Draw his attention to someone who does the role well and discuss the skills and attributes that contribute to success.

Decision Tree Hurdle #1 (continued)

• What is this person's understanding of how he needs to manage himself and relationships in order to be the most effective?	No → Yes ↓	• Reading *First Break All the Rules* [29] will help him understand the business outcomes obtained by the most effective managers.
• Does this person have a realistic understanding of how he can grow and develop in terms of personal management and interpersonal skills to enhance his effectiveness?	No → Yes ↓	• Give honest and clear feedback about how his behavior affects others in the workplace. Focus on the behavior-effect aspect to avoid judging the behavior itself. The emphasis is on whether the behavior has a desirable effect. (There's less room to get defensive about the behavior if the result is clearly undesirable.)
USING THIS TABLE AS A MODEL FOR HOW YOU MIGHT APPROACH THIS COACHING OPPORTUNITY, CONTINUE WITH THE QUESTIONING PROCESS UNTIL YOU HAVE EXHAUSTED ALL POSSIBILITIES FOR ADDRESSING PERFORMANCE HURDLES RELEVANT TO EXPECTATIONS.		

Figure 7.3 - Decision Tree for Performance Hurdle #1: Expectations

spark ideas of your own that will best fit your particular situation.

With that in mind, Figure 7.3 is our first example of a potential decision tree process for addressing the Performance Hurdles for setting and confirming expectations. Again, it is not intended to be exhaustive, but merely to provide a model for you to use and adapt as needed.

Performance Hurdle #2: Commitment

The first step was concerned with making sure we have clarity about expectations. We were less concerned with whether we had buy-in. Separating these two elements is most important when there is resistance to the desired performance, because it breaks the discussion down into smaller steps. First you get clarity (which can be hard enough in itself), then you can work on getting commitment.

---

[29] Buckingham, M. & Coffman, C. (1999). *First Break All the Rules: What the World's Greatest Managers Do Differently.* New York, NY. Simon & Schuster.

Think of commitment in terms of coming from two sources: external rewards and internal rewards. External rewards include bonuses, promotion, staying employed, and other incentives that can be controlled by the manager. It is sometimes argued that these kinds of incentives can lead to compliance but not commitment. The idea is that if the external reward is removed, the performance drops off. That's probably true. But as long as you control the external incentives, you can get compliance that is pretty passionate. Internal rewards include things the manager can influence and leverage but not control, such as belief in the importance of what is expected, personal satisfaction, desire for success, and other motivators inside the person. If you are able to stimulate the inner motivators as well as manage the external incentives, that's ideal.

In essence, commitment depends in part on believing that the outcome is the right outcome to get. Someone may know that she is expected to have a particular product ready for launch by the end of the year, but if she believes that the product is not right for the market, her commitment will be reduced. We have seen this break between clarity of expectations and commitment when organizations are straining to move into a new stage. Often there is an "old school" faction within the organization that thinks the new direction is wrong, even though they clearly understand the direction. There may not be open rebellion, and some of their concerns may be valid. Even so, unless people believe their direction is the right direction, you won't see much focus and initiative in carrying it out.

Commitment also depends on believing that you are on the right track to get to the outcome. Sometimes we describe this track as the solution path — the methods and actions we have planned to get to the desired outcome. If someone agrees with the outcome but thinks the solution path doesn't get you there, you are unlikely to see the focus and initiative that you need. For example, if someone believes that the business has to drive down the cost of servicing existing accounts, he is showing both understanding of the outcome and belief that the outcome is important. But if the organization's solution path is to develop a call center to handle service calls, and the person strongly prefers the earlier method in which each salesperson was the customer's go-to person, you won't see full commitment.

Finally, to be committed to the outcome and the path, an individual must see what's in it for him. As we noted earlier, this can include external and internal incentives — some type of personal payoff if you want to see full commitment. It's ideal if he perceives that he will experience some personal reward by delivering on the outcome, but if that's not possible, then he has to see that he will experience something negative if he doesn't achieve the outcome.

Some questions to consider in assessing the degree of commitment include:

- Do employees believe that the expected outcome is important to the success of the organization?
- Do they believe the solution path (i.e., that the methods you want them to use) will lead to the outcome they are expected to produce?
- Do they see any personal benefit from achieving the expected outcome?
- Do they see any personal threat from failing to achieve the outcome?

Breaking through Barriers to Commitment

Remember that we are talking about commitment to a particular goal, task, or role. We are not talking about developing commitment in a general sense, as that probably belongs more to the notion of citizenship that we discussed earlier. Some people just are more inclined from the start to give the organization the benefit of the doubt, and that's a basic part of their personality. So we are not coaching to have a more committed person, but instead to have a person who is more committed to a particular plan of action. There are two basic approaches to breaking through barriers to commitment.

Building the Commitment to Outcome and Solution Path

The first approach to breaking through barriers to commitment is to develop commitment to the outcome and the solution path — in other words, making the business case for the outcome. You make the business case by relying on hard data, not on charismatic speeches and exhortation. When you develop this skill as a coach, you will reap numerous rewards. Making the business case is an important step in building commitment to the goal and the solution path. It also forces you, as the coach, to educate the people you are coaching about the business. If you are perceptive as a coach, you will notice that some people really seem to appreciate the information more than others. They ask good, thoughtful questions. They may even point out potential pitfalls or barriers to overcome that you hadn't considered.

Take note of these people, because they can become your ambassadors with the rest of the team. Their enthusiasm and problem-solving approach, especially during times of major change, can be just as contagious as the carping and resistance that you may get from others. Another reason to take note of these people is that they may be candidates for succession. Interest in the logic of the business as well as the reasoning behind your plans may be evidence of someone who can make the transition from individual player to coach. Finally, the time and energy you invest in teaching pays off indirectly because they are more likely to see you as making a personal investment in their development.

We witnessed a skilled use of this approach while facilitating a strategic planning retreat. The division president needed to convince the sales force to target more strategic customers, which would mean giving up a large group of customers who bought in small amounts. These smaller customers ran up good total sales for the salespeople and thus paid nice total commissions, but the overhead on small sales was hurting the company by squeezing margins. The president walked through example after example on the white board to show that the company lost money on each sale below a certain dollar

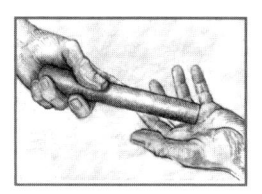

> Successful leaders don't trust the success of the handoff to assumptions about what the team knows.

amount because of the overhead. From there he added the total number of yearly sales below that amount, finally arriving at the business case for change. (Of course, we had to address the impact on sales commissions, but that was the next step.)

In another case, we had just finished a presentation to new partners in a large accounting firm on the need to shift from thinking like star players (which got them to the partner ranks) to thinking like coaches. The response was skeptical: "Yes, but I don't have time to coach because I've got to keep producing in order to remain a partner." A senior managing partner then used the flip chart to make the case by reviewing the business volume in market after market in which the growth was impressive. He then asked each of them to compare their individual targets to the numbers on the flip chart. You could feel the impact as the point sank in that the most successful markets were led by partners who did only a small percentage of the actual billing themselves. The rest was done by the team, which meant that the partner was a successful recruiter, developer, and manager of people.

While these examples may seem simple and obvious to a manager, you should not assume that they are obvious to others in the organization, especially those in lower ranks. Someone just promoted to partner is still thinking like a producer, not a partner. A salesperson is thinking in terms of commission, not in terms of cost of sales. Successful leaders don't trust the success of the handoff to assumptions about what the team knows.

Some issues to address in making the business case may include:
- What is the marketplace telling us about how we're doing currently? What do we learn from sales patterns, customer feedback, lost business, or other market indicators?
- Who are our target customers, and why do we target them? What are those customers looking for? If the customer's expectation is changing, how is it changing, and what does that mean for us?
- What are our competitors doing? What effect could competitor actions have on us? Where do we see competitive threats?
- What do we need to understand about our internal processes and costs? (Use specific examples of current work flows, proposed work flows, and the cost differences of each.)
- Where are our opportunities? How can we adapt and position ourselves to leverage our opportunities?

Building Commitment by Way of Internal and External Rewards

The second approach to breaking through barriers to commitment has to do with the notion that regardless of personality factors and internal motivation, most people will pay attention to things that affect their performance appraisal as well as bonuses and other aspects of career success. Tying performance to bonuses and appraisals is a pretty fundamental management practice, so we won't get into that here. We will note, however, that many people are more motivated when they see how their performance on a given project may be noticed by the "powers that be" in the organization. For others, a difficult task or assignment may be more motivating if you draw attention to the importance of having that kind of assignment under your belt or in your portfolio.

Sometimes, as a last resort, you have to rely on the negative results of failing to perform rather than the positive effects of performing well. One of the best examples we've seen of a manager convincing a small team of the need to aggressively pursue new revenue sources was a simple presentation of the true costs of keeping that team on the payroll: "When we add salaries, benefits, and indirect costs, here's what it will cost to keep this team in the organization for another year. Here's what we've got in projected revenue." The negative difference in those two figures can be a realistic and powerful motivator. But if you have to rely on this kind of stick instead of the carrot very often, you may have the wrong people on your team.

With regard to establishing commitment, Figure 7.4 provides the decision tree process with suggestions for interventions for these kinds of questions. Experiment with these tools and methods to see what feels most natural and comfortable for you. The idea is to make them your own so that they don't look or feel artificial, forced, or contrived to you or the person you are coaching.

Performance Hurdle #3: Skill

If the individual you are coaching isn't clear on what you expect, or if he's not convinced he should do what you've asked, there are a number of things you can do to effectively address those hurdles. If there is a skill barrier, however, your options become more limited — you can teach the skills, or someone else can teach the skills. And if you use a few simple guidelines to make sure the teaching is effective, then the individual will either learn the skill adequately or not.

If a reasonable effort has been made to teach a skill and the person has not learned it, you are probably up against an intellectual ability or talent barrier. There's not much you can do there other than try to work around the talent barrier if you have that option. Because so many talents relevant to work performance are tied to personality, we address this later in this chapter under Performance Hurdle #5: Personality and Motivation.

Decision Tree for Performance Hurdle #2: Commitment

Question	Decision Point	Coaching Tools
• Does this person believe that the expected outcome is important to the success of the organization?	No → Yes ↓	• Make the business case using market, competitor, customer, cost, or other hard data. To make this alive and most relevant, remember to draw clear links back to the day-to-day work of the individual or team. • Make the personal case (importance to his career goals).
• Does this person believe the solution path, (i.e., that the methods you want him to use) will lead to the outcome he is expected to produce?	No → Yes ↓	• Facilitate a process to draw out the step-by-step connection to how the proposed actions lead to the desired outcome. • Use your organization's strategy map.
• Does this person see any personal benefit from achieving the expected outcome?	No → Yes ↓	• Use traditional incentives, bonuses, and performance appraisals. • Draw attention to visibility or career benefits of succeeding (e.g., What's in it for him?).
• Does this person see any personal threat from failing to achieve the outcome?	No → Yes ↓	• (Last resort) Draw attention to negative consequences of failure (e.g., impact on job or career).
USING THIS TABLE AS A MODEL FOR HOW YOU MIGHT APPROACH THIS COACHING OPPORTUNITY, CONTINUE WITH THE QUESTIONING PROCESS UNTIL YOU HAVE EXHAUSTED ALL POSSIBILITIES FOR ADDRESSING PERFORMANCE HURDLES RELEVANT TO COMMITMENT.		

Figure 7.4 – Decision Tree for Performance Hurdle #2: Commitment

The basic considerations here are very simple:
- Does the individual have the basic skills to perform the task or carry out the role?
- Does he or she have the knowledge needed?

Addressing Skill Barriers

There are a handful of pointers that will help if you identify a skill barrier. As we noted earlier, reasonable efforts will usually pay off if both the raw talent and intellectual capability are there. If the talent and capability are not there, then you will get limited return on your time and effort.

Sometimes we tend to assume that everybody has the capability to do everything, when this simply is not the case. We have worked with a number of clients where we had to deal with individual executives who just did not have the capability to develop the skill needed to meet the role expectations of their position. Try as we might to support them in getting there, when the CEO of this client and the authors realized that we were trying to "teach pigs to sing," we pursued other options for correcting the situation. If we had not

---

Parable of the Singing Pig

A favorite parable of one of the authors has to do with the insane task of trying to teach a pig the skill of singing. (Trying to teach this same author the skill of singing is about the same as trying to teach a pig to sing!)

Anyway, it goes like this:

Never try to teach a pig to sing. All it does is annoy the pig, and frustrate the heck out of you.

changed our course, the consequences would have been disastrous to the stakeholders of the company.

To teach a specific skill, there are several things that the coach can do. One is to arrange for the person learning the skill to observe a role model or someone who is proficient at the skill. From watching someone do a monthly closing to observing a skilled team leader running a meeting, an interested observer can pick up both the technique and the feel for the skill. Once the individual is ready for the hands-on part where they have to actually go out and do it themselves, you may need to break the overall task down into smaller steps. An individual subjected to the information overload of learning an entirely new and complex skill by observing a model may eventually stop absorbing information, thereby wasting their time and that of the coach. By breaking the overall task down into smaller steps, you avoid this problem. The individual can later combine the smaller steps into the overall skill.

Another useful point to remember is that people learning a new skill may tend to overestimate how much they have absorbed. They see themselves improving and the coach is still there to offer help, so confidence increases pretty quickly. The problem arises when coaches see the improving performance and the signs of confidence, and assume that they can now delegate the task. But when the individual returns to the task the next time, especially after some delay, there has often been some pretty significant loss of what they learned earlier. This is normal, but it can cause frustration for the coach who has delegated prematurely and now thinks ". . . but I thought we had this covered." The point is not to rush the delegation, but to provide ample practice sessions to build skill over time.

Often, as you get closer to the actual handoff of responsibility for the task, it is tempting for the coach to step in and help if the individual encounters a problem. Unless the stakes are high, it is a good idea for the coach to let the individual struggle or face a setback. Allowing some struggle is hard for many managers; they have to manage their own impatience and desire to keep things moving,

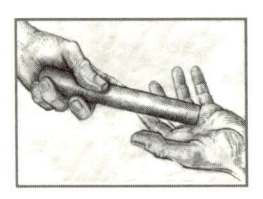

> Your role is to ensure that your direct reports get the skill development they need. Nothing says you have to be the one who does the development.

as well as avoid thinking about the prospect of a mistake that can have significant downstream effects in the organization. You can learn a lot by seeing how a person handles a setback. Do they even catch their mistake? If they do, do they panic and turn to you? Do they spot problems early and approach them logically? The better the recovery, the stronger the chances that you can delegate without having unpleasant surprises in the future. If the individual flounders and shows little sign of working their way through the setback, that's a reliable sign that he's not ready to accept the handoff from you.

Typically, as managers move up into the middle ranks, they make the mistake of assuming that they have to be the primary coach for their direct reports. Their dilemma is that by the time you're in middle management you usually have people reporting to you who are in specialized functions. We have often seen managers either avoid coaching with these specialized direct reports or, sometimes worse, try to coach but "wing" the parts that are out of their own specialty. The solution to the dilemma is simple. Your role is to ensure that your direct reports get the skill development they need. Nothing says you have to be the one who does the development. You can use your network of associates to pair the person you want to develop with someone who has the skills.

The Sixth Challenge: Coaching for Performance

Decision Tree for Performance Hurdle #3: Skill

Question	Decision Point	Coaching Tools
• Does this person have the basic intelligence to be able to grasp the knowledge and understanding of what is required of him?	No → / Yes ↓	• Though difficult to acknowledge in our current politically correct society, this is a fact of life. We have seen many situations where an individual was just not capable, intellectually, of handling the required skill. See the Parable of the Singing Pig. • Determine ways to work around the person's skill area deficits by allocating those responsibilities to another person. • If you determine that the intellect just isn't there and you are not able to allocate as discussed in the preceding bulleted point, reassign the person to a position in the organization that will fit his capability. • If you cannot reposition him in the organization, arrange to outplace the person.
• Does this person have the basic knowledge and understanding of what is required to have developed the skill?	No → / Yes ↓	• Provide the education required for him to get up to speed. This can be provided through formal education or through your own teaching and modeling efforts.
• Does this person have the necessary skills for the role or task? Can he do it?	No → / Yes ↓	• Demonstrate and coach in the required skill area. Arrange for the individual to observe someone who has the desired skills. For more complex skills, arrange shadowing of someone who is highly skilled.
USING THIS TABLE AS A MODEL FOR HOW YOU MIGHT APPROACH THIS COACHING OPPORTUNITY, CONTINUE WITH THE QUESTIONING PROCESS UNTIL YOU HAVE EXHAUSTED ALL POSSIBILITIES FOR ADDRESSING PERFORMANCE HURDLES RELEVANT TO SKILL.		

Figure 7.5 – Decision Tree for Performance Hurdle #3: Skill

You can still use our generic decision tree for developing complex skills or helping someone to better define and fulfill their role. Your best approach there is to break the role or complex skill into component parts, and then use the decision tree on each of the components. For example, a sales role could be broken into prospecting, cold calling, product knowledge, and then the actual sales process. If you discover that the barrier to ideal performance is in, say, the actual sales process, you can then break that down into further steps and skills.

The key here is to be purposeful and disciplined in developing the skills of the people you're counting on to execute their part of the strategy. Just by devoting some time to thinking about and planning the development of your direct reports, you'll be stepping up to the coach role.

Figure 7.5 shows what the decision tree process might look like for Performance Hurdle #3, having to do with a skill deficit.

Performance Hurdle # 4: Confidence

Though it is evident that confidence is fundamental to high performance, confidence is an intangible concept. It is not unusual to see someone who knows what is expected, is committed to it, and has the skill, but who still doesn't do what he needs to do. Nagging self-doubt or uncertainty gets in the way. A frequent sign that there is a confidence barrier is constant checking for reassurance on ideas or actions that are usually right. Fortunately, unless the confidence barrier is pervasive, an effective coach or mentor can usually help someone through this barrier.

If you are convinced that the individual is clear about what is expected and why, that he is committed, and has the skill — but you're still not seeing the performance you need — then the next logical barrier has to do with his level of confidence.

The sources of confidence barriers are varied. Most are rooted in two basic fears:
- Fear of failure on the task or in the role, and experiencing negative consequences. These can include failure to gratify a need for achievement while experiencing yourself as inadequate, stupid, not measuring up, etc. We see this most frequently in people with strong achievement drives.

- Fear of disappointing others and losing face or social standing with others. We sometimes see this in people who have a strong need to be liked and to please others.

Of course, virtually all of us have each of these two fears. And when these fears well up, they overtake our rational minds and drive us into behavior patterns that are ineffective. Recognizing those fears in the person you are coaching will be important in your decisions about how to coach him.

All of us have some degree of self-doubt. This is normal. And some have more than others. Sometimes people bring with them the legacy of a previous boss who was controlling and critical, and they assume that they still have to run everything by their current boss. Whatever the reason, you'll see a familiar pattern. You may see indecision and delay when confronted with decisions, or frequent checking for reassurance. Yet, when you check out their thinking or ask them for a recommendation, you find that their inclination is right most of the time. They know what to do and how to do it, they just aren't confident of either. When you provide reassurance, they perform reliably.

Minor confidence issues are a normal part of learning a new skill or role and can be addressed easily by a skilled coach. More serious confidence issues, however, require more investment of time and energy by the coach. You will probably see more success if the issues come from specific work experiences or setbacks, such as a critical and volatile boss in a previous role or a one-time stumble on a major project. If the confidence issue looks more like a consistent personality trait that shows up in a variety of situations, you will have a much harder time making significant progress.

Note that in discussing confidence issues so far, we have assumed that there were no barriers in clarity of expectations, commitment, or skill. You will sometimes see an interesting pattern in which the expectations and skills are questionable, but the confidence level is high. We see this often in people whose personalities are brimming

> Mistaking confidence for skill has burned many an inexperienced manager who delegates prematurely and then has to do damage control.

with confidence and energy in the first place. Their confidence may hinder them from making an accurate appraisal of their skill.

We also see it when an experienced employee joins the company from another company. We may assume that because the person has made a successful career, say, in commercial lending, that he is ready to do commercial lending with us. The more he chomps at the bit to get started and the busier we are, the easier it is to forget the basics. This employee's previous company may have had a very different value proposition and corporate culture. Suppose he was rewarded for making the loan at all costs with his previous company, but your company puts a higher premium on credit worthiness. Mistaking confidence for skill has burned many an inexperienced manager who delegates prematurely and then has to do damage control.

Addressing Confidence Barriers

Let's start with confidence barriers that are minor or related to specific circumstances. Usually clarification of expectations and simple affirmation of skill will have good results. Remember that breaking a new task into a series of simpler steps often increases confidence, as the task appears less daunting and complex. We have also found it helpful for the manager to have more frequent touch points as a way of handling mild anxiety about failure or disappointing others. Instead of asking someone to handle a customer complaint, for example, you might ask him to contact the customer and gather more information and then meet with you to develop a plan for addressing the complaint.

You may also find that a person's confidence is improved by walking through several scenarios with you prior to a difficult assignment or event. You can follow a simple, "What would you do if…" process. By presenting possible situations he might encounter and developing a plan, you help him feel more prepared and confident. This method is especially helpful if you present the scenario and he can generate a response. If the confidence issue is minor, you should quickly see that you can back off on the support.

If the confidence problem resulted from specific experiences, such as a difficult boss in the past or a project or task that has gone poorly, your task as a coach is to broaden perspective and use the negative experience as a learning opportunity. Sometimes spending some time with the person on lessons learned from the negative experience may seem like opening an old wound, but this process is especially important when the person contributed in some way to the negative experience. In reality, though, translating that negative experience into productive learning can boost confidence by providing a plan to avoid the experience in the future.

In many ways, negative experiences that were beyond the person's control can be more difficult to overcome, particularly for people with very strong achievement drives. For example, suppose the person headed a project that failed because of unforeseeable changes in resources. Though he knows rationally that he was not at fault, he is still keenly aware that he has a failure on his record, and so he may have trouble letting go and moving on. This situation is harder, because there are no specific lessons to be learned in order to avoid a repeat of the negative experience. In these situations, the lessons to be learned are not about the specific event but about career and life. Like a good coach, you can share experiences of your own or tell stories about others who went through a difficult experience and recovered. Either way, your goal is to teach the art of shaking it off and refocusing on the future.

The hardest confidence barriers to coach are those deeply rooted in personality. If the person seems to be hesitant in a number of different kinds of situations, you may be observing a personality trait rather than a reaction to a specific event. Though you may make some degree of progress over time with continued coaching, you may need to fall back on other approaches as suggested by the per-

Decision Tree for Performance Hurdle #4: Confidence

Question	Decision Point	Coaching Tools
• Does this person demonstrate his own personal sense of self-assuredness in being able to carry out what is needed from him?	No / Yes ↓	• Discuss with him where he feels insecure or unsure. • Discuss with him and agree on what he needs to do or experience in order to gain confidence. This might mean frequent check points with you as he executes a project, or it might mean more hands-on coaching with him regarding the specific tasks under consideration (similar to teaching your child to ride a bicycle, where you run along side, holding on, and gradually withdraw your supporting hands.)
• Is this person confident in his decisions?	No / Yes ↓	• Generate possible scenarios and have him respond. Clarify and teach where needed, and affirm when his decisions are good. • Use stories and personal experience to broaden perspective after a negative experience. Focus on getting over the experience and refocusing on future opportunities.
• Is this person confident in his skills?	No / Yes ↓	• Affirm for good performance. Provide external benchmarks for him to evaluate his own skill.
USING THIS TABLE AS A MODEL FOR HOW YOU MIGHT APPROACH THIS COACHING OPPORTUNITY, CONTINUE WITH THE QUESTIONING PROCESS UNTIL YOU HAVE EXHAUSTED ALL POSSIBILITIES FOR ADDRESSING PERFORMANCE HURDLES RELEVANT TO CONFIDENCE.		

Figure 7.6 – Decision Tree for Performance Hurdle #4: Confidence

formance decision tree process. Figure 7.6 provides the decision tree process for dealing with performance hurdles as they relate to issues of confidence. Again, remember to modify the decision tree to reflect the hurdles facing you or your company so this tool is comfortable to work with.

Performance Hurdle #5: Personality and Motivation

The task or role has to fit reasonably well with the person's personality and sources of motivation. By reasonably well, we mean that the degree of stretch between the person's natural comfort zone and what is required in the role is in the slight to moderate range. If the required stretch is slight to moderate, then there is a reasonable chance of learning new approaches and gaining some comfort over time. For example, a slightly reserved person can learn and practice techniques to manage the anxiety involved in leading a brainstorming session with a team.

If the stretch is extreme, however, the likelihood of success drops precipitously. Even if the skill is there, you are unlikely to see that skill put into practice if it runs counter to their personality and motivation. For example, a painfully shy person may have the intellect and commitment to learn a good sales process, but that degree of shyness would be a hard barrier to overcome. Later we will give you some simple tools for understanding those aspects of personality and motivation most likely to be relevant at work.

Figure 7.7 provides you with a very simple decision tree for determining if a person is managing his personality effectively. If your answer, as the coach, is that they are not, the following text on the Big Five Personality Model will undoubtedly be useful for you.

For clarity, what we are talking about here with regard to Performance Hurdle #5 has to do solely with current personality and sources of motivation, and not with basic, inherited talent and capability. (That was covered in a previous section in this chapter regard-

**Decision Tree for Performance Hurdle #5:
Personality and Motivation**

Question	Decision Point	Coaching Tools
• Does this person manage his personality effectively?	No → Yes ↓	• Refer to Coaching Pointers for Big Five Traits. • Read *The Owner's Manual for Personality at Work*,[30] by Pierce & Jane Howard.
USING THIS TABLE AS A MODEL FOR HOW YOU MIGHT APPROACH THIS COACHING OPPORTUNITY, CONTINUE WITH THE QUESTIONING PROCESS UNTIL YOU HAVE EXHAUSTED ALL POSSIBILITIES FOR ADDRESSING PERFORMANCE HURDLES RELEVANT TO PERSONALITY AND MOTIVATION.		

Figure 7.7 – Decision Tree for Performance Hurdle #5: Personality and Motivation

ing Performance Hurdle #3, where we discussed skill development.)

The Big Five Personality Model

Though understanding personality and motivation can get complicated, we have found that the Big Five model works well for most coaching purposes. This model is based on years of research that have identified five broad factors that are independent of one another and seem to comprise much of human personality.[31] These five factors show up across different cultures and are reflected in different languages all over the world. so they seem to be basic to human nature. In fact, though we do learn and adapt over the course of our lives, all five of these basic factors have been shown to have strong genetic predispositions.[32] We probably don't learn our personality so much as we learn to live with the personality we have.

---

30 Howard, P. J. & Howard, J. M. (2001). *The Owner's Manual for Personality at Work*. Atlanta, GA. Bard Press.

31 McCrae, R. R. & Costa, P. T. (1990). *Personality in Adulthood*. New York, NY. The Guilford Press.

32 McCrae, R. R. & Costa, P. T. (1997). "Personality Trait Structure as a Human Universal." *American Psychologist*, 52(5), 509-516.

Keep in mind that as a coach you don't want or need to play shrink, and we would certainly not encourage that. But there is no escaping the fact that personality shapes how people approach the world, including their work. If you are a good observer of people, as most effective coaches are, you can increase your skills in recognizing and managing common personality traits that show up in the workplace. Having a simple vocabulary for thinking about personality can help you in recognizing and making reasonable efforts to manage those common traits . . . in yourself and those you coach.

Let's look at the five factors as they have been described through years of personality study. Remember to think of each of these five factors as a continuum — or a scale from low to high — and that most of us are somewhere in between. All of us have some of each of these traits, so the important question is how we compare to the average person on each. After each of the factors, we include a description of someone who has a low level of that factor in his personality and someone who has a high level. We also describe how you might see those factors play out in their role.

Remember that each of these factors can have both advantages as well as potential disadvantages.

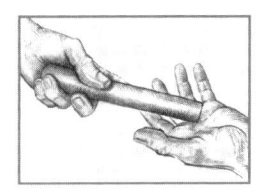

We probably don't learn our personality so much as we learn to live with the personality we have.

Big Five Personality Factors

Negative Emotionality: How a person reacts to stress and how easily a person experiences unpleasant emotions such as anxiety, worry, discouragement, hurt, anger, or impatience.

> *Low Negative Emotionality:* "Rolls with the punches" of life more easily than most people; not many situations cause stress; quick recovery from setbacks, frustrations, and disappointments; seen by others as cool-headed and calm; less worry and irritation than most people.

> *High Negative Emotionality:* More kinds of situations are stressful; shorter "fuses" for irritation, anger, worry, or other unpleasant emotions; longer time to recover from stressful events. Also seen as engaged, alert, on the lookout for potential problems.

Extraversion: How energetic, active, optimistic, and socially outgoing a person is.

> *Low Extraversion:* More reserved than most people; move and talk at a steady, more measured pace; quiet style may be viewed as thoughtful but also may come across as shy and withdrawn.

> *High Extraversion:* More energetic and talkative; enjoy a fast pace of activity; comfortable with groups; may come across as confident and assertive, but may dominate conversations and make it harder for others to express concerns or ideas.

Openness: Enjoyment of new ideas and new activities; curiosity and cultural interests.

> *Low Openness:* Seen as practical and no-nonsense; prefer the familiar and the tried-and-true; fewer interests than people at the higher end, but they are more likely to "drill deeper" in the areas that interest them; probably more comfortable during times of predictable growth along the organizational S-curve; may resist change or have difficulty accepting the need for change.
>
> *High Openness:* Preference for novelty and variety; open to new ideas or possibilities; may become bored with periods of steady and predictable functioning; in managing the details of execution, they often need someone at the lower end of the same trait to keep them grounded.

Agreeableness: How people handle power, conflict, and competition. Describes how easy a person is to get along with and work with. Style issues in managing the handoff often relate to this trait.

> *Low Agreeableness:* More competitive approach, interested in own needs; skeptical of those in authority; motivated by winning; may be seen as confident and sure of themselves and as willing to take a stand on tough issues but risk being seen as hardheaded and stubborn.
>
> *High Agreeableness:* Prefer a cooperative or even conciliatory approach to working with others; more comfortable making concessions to keep harmony; motivated to keep peace and harmony; often seen as good team players, but may concede in order to keep the peace when they needed to stand their ground.

Conscientiousness: How organized and goal-focused a person is.

Low Conscientiousness: More flexible approach to planning and organizing; more prone to acting on impulse and going with the moment, likely to welcome interruptions; comfortable in roles that require multi-tasking; may fail to plan far enough ahead and fail to push things through to completion.

High Conscientiousness: Prefer an orderly and planned approach to work; able to resist the distractions of the moment in order to pursue their goals; may find interruptions frustrating; motivated by order and by follow-through; may feel impatience when things grind down, pushing even harder to get through delays and setbacks; may set unrealistic goals and set the performance bar so high that their team rarely experiences success.

Addressing Personality and Motivation Barriers

Remember that we have provided a brief overview of something as complicated as human personality. For the purpose of development, however, we only need to recognize those traits that clearly stand out as influencing performance. If someone's Agreeableness is low enough to cause problems, you will probably see the signs if you stop to think about what you're witnessing.

Let's get back to our decision tree for each of the previously discussed performance hurdles. If all of the answers in our decision tree have been in the "yes" direction and you hit a "no" when you get to personality and motivation, your coaching role has just become more challenging. Of course, people can learn to adapt their behavior in order to be more successful in their role, but the more the desired behavior conflicts with their basic personality the bigger the challenge in learning to adapt. Remember our Pig Parable.

We have found that a handful of practical approaches can yield good results. If practical approaches from a supervisor don't work, then a professional coach may be needed. Begin by defining the personality and motivation issue in terms of what the person tends to do excessively or tends to avoid on a fairly consistent basis. It is also a good idea to note the consequences of the behavior.

Examples might include:
"Visibly shows irritation and frustration with others in team meetings. Tends to cause others to shut down and avoid discussing issues with him." (May be high on Negative Emotionality).

"Avoids conflict, failing to hold direct reports accountable. Accepts mediocre work, preferring to fix it himself." (Probably high in Agreeableness).

Sample Personality Assessment Chart

	Lower than most people	*About like most people*	*Higher than most people*
Negative Emotionality			X
Extraversion			X
Openness		X	
Agreeableness	X		
Conscientiousness			X

Figure 7.8 – Sample Personality Assessment Chart

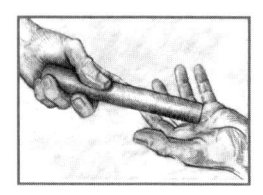

... personality eventually ends up in the P&L.

"Doesn't plan far enough ahead to anticipate resource needs or to allow for setbacks. Projects are delayed." (Possibly low Conscientiousness).

It may help you to organize your thinking by estimating where the person might fall on each of the Big Five personality factors. Again, these are broad traits and our point is just to organize your thinking so that you approach the coaching in a thoughtful and systematic way. You don't have to make exact hits in your estimates. Many executives we have worked with find it helpful to simply list the Big Five on a sheet of paper and estimate where the person might be with an "X" in Figure 7.8.

If you spend two or three minutes thinking about the above profile, you can easily imagine the things this person would have to learn in order to get the benefits of his personality and minimize the potential drawbacks. For example, if he is higher than most people on Negative Emotionality, Extraversion, and Conscientiousness, and lower than most people on Agreeableness, you would probably pay particular attention to whether he has learned to handle conflict without becoming disagreeable and argumentative. With another person, on the other hand, if the profile were identical on all factors except that he is high on the Agreeableness factor, you might note whether he has learned to hold his own in disagreements and not back down to please others.

Coaching Pointers for the Big Five Factors

Trait	In coaching, you might help "low" to...	In coaching, you might help "high" to...
Negative Emotionality	• Use expressive language to avoid seeming unconcerned and to engage others with more enthusiasm.	• Develop strategies for handling stressful situations (e.g., breathe and relax, and ask for more information instead of jumping to conclusions).
Extraversion	• Speak up more in meetings. • Show more enthusiasm when communicating so that people know what is important.	• Detect signs that they are dominating a conversation. • Ask more questions and enlist the views of others.
Openness	• Consider potential benefits of new idea or method before pointing out practical barriers.	• Challenge new ideas from practical perspectives. • Is it strategically critical or just new and interesting?
Agreeableness	• Be aware not just of what they say but how they say it (e.g., "Can I play devil's advocate for a moment?" instead of "But you've failed to consider this…"). • See the bigger picture ("Is this really a hill that you have to take?").	• Stand their ground when they're right. • Focus on what is right for everyone, not just what will make the conflict go away. • Remind them that "appeasement comes from the belief that throwing red meat to a tiger will eventually make him a vegetarian."
Conscientiousness	• Plan their work and work their plan. • Break large projects down into smaller chunks • Watch for tendency to over-commit.	• Watch for signs of burnout in self and others. • Challenge goals: "Is this really critical?" and "Is it worth this level of effort?"

Figure 7.9 – Coaching Pointers for the Big Five Factors

It is not our purpose to go into depth here on working with diverse personalities, but Figure 7.9 provides some simple coaching pointers for you to consider in coaching lows and highs on each of the factors in the Big Five.

Obviously we could go much deeper into specifics of how to work with diverse personalities, but to do so would be far beyond the intent and scope of this book. Hopefully, these simple tips can give you a practical framework for coaching if you see signs that someone's personality is limiting his success in his role. After all, personality eventually ends up in the P&L.

Now suppose you've done everything you can reasonably do as suggested in this section, and you don't find significant barriers to execution inside the person? Then there is a problem in the system, external to the person.

Performance Hurdle #6: The Organizational Support Systems

We understand that it is obvious that people have to have sufficient resources and other organizational supports. They can have all the knowledge, capability, skill, commitment, etc., in the world, but little good it will do them if they don't have the technical, financial, administrative, and people resources that they need in order to carry out their roles.

As such, we have purposely covered this one last, principally because people usually offer it first in explaining barriers to their own performance — for example, they'll complain that they didn't have the time or the resources to get the task done. Sometimes that is indeed the case — that the Performance Hurdle truly is outside the person in the form of conflicting priorities, lack of resources, or other organizational supports. But before you pursue those avenues with them in your coaching, you need to be sure all the other needed factors are in place, as we have covered them to this point in this chapter, before spending too much time looking at external system-wide Performance Hurdles.

If you are not seeing the desired performance and you have ensured that all the other hurdles have been cleared, then it is likely that you are dealing with a hurdle having to do with some component of the organizational system support. After all, if the person knows what is expected, is committed to the outcome, has the confidence, possesses the skills, and his personality and motivation fit with the job demands, the barrier is outside of the person you're coaching. At that point, your approach has to change from "developer of people" to "problem solver," because the barrier probably cannot be removed by the person you're coaching.

Examples of organizational barriers might include:
- Inadequate resources
- Technical limitations of equipment or processes
- Unrealistic expectations, plans, or timelines laid down by others
- Competing goals and priorities from others not in the direct line of supervision
- Too many priorities

Addressing Organizational Barriers

Again you see the logic of considering organizational barriers last. It is likely that the person you're coaching will raise organizational barriers before fully considering all the other options. The key consideration is whether the barrier is within the control of the person you're coaching. For example, if there is a problem with another department having competing goals and priorities, your first considerations are whether the person you're coaching understands the need to negotiate laterally regarding issues with peers, is committed to doing so, and possesses the confidence, skills, and motivation to do so. If all of these are in place, you can intervene at the appropriate level without fear of micromanaging or working at the level below you.

Decision Tree for Performance Hurdle #6: Organizational Support Systems

Question	Decision Point	Coaching Tools
• Does this person have adequate technical, financial, etc., supports provided to him from the organization to complete what is required? • Do the equipment and technical processes fully support the performance objectives?	No → / Yes ↓	• Discuss and determine where the insufficient resources are, and negotiate with the appropriate manager or executive to the degree and in the form appropriate to the particular situation. • Refer to the strategy map as needed and appropriate. • Identify the points of limitations, and determine if there is a work-around and/or what options are available to deal with this rate limiting factor.
• Are expectations, plans, or timelines defined by others realistic?	No → / Yes ↓	• Negotiate with the appropriate and responsible individuals who have the authority to re-define as needed. • Refer to the strategy map as needed in your negotiations.
• Are potentially competing goals and priorities removed from the path of implementation?	No → / Yes ↓	• Utilize the Urgency – Importance Grid in Figure 7.3 to assist in clarifying priorities. • If necessary and appropriate, negotiate with relevant managers or executives. • Refer to the strategy map.
• Are priorities clear and not competing with each other?	No → / Yes ↓	• Again, utilize the Urgency – Importance Grid to clarify priorities. • Assess and rank priorities by stepping back to a big picture, strategic perspective. • Refer to the strategy map.
USING THIS TABLE AS A MODEL FOR HOW YOU MIGHT APPROACH THIS COACHING OPPORTUNITY, CONTINUE WITH THE QUESTIONING PROCESS UNTIL YOU HAVE EXHAUSTED ALL POSSIBILITIES FOR ADDRESSING PERFORMANCE HURDLES RELEVANT TO ORGANIZATIONAL SUPPORT SYSTEMS.		

Figure 7.10 - Decision Tree for Performance Hurdle #6: Organizational Support Systems

Even as you intervene in the system to address the barriers, remember that you still have an important coaching opportunity. By letting the person you are coaching shadow you as you intervene — that is, by keeping them in the loop on your thinking and your methods — you are serving as a role model, helping them to understand how to get things done in the system. Figure 7.10 provides you with a way to approach this hurdle, with some key questions to pose along with possible tools and approaches to addressing the problem. Again, as with the other decision tree figures in this chapter, this is not meant to be exhaustive, but merely to communicate a concept. To flesh this out for application to all possible scenarios would be beyond the scope of this book, at best, and probably impossible to do anyway.

An Example of Coaching for Performance at Biggs & Bucks

Let's look at the application of this simple process with Jim Newman, the middle management director of training and development with Biggs & Bucks. In Chapter Six we saw the plan developed by Jim and the vice president of operations (reference Figure 6.4) to whom he reports. That plan linked Jim's role back to the internal process goal in the strategy map to excel in product and sales training. That goal rolls up into customer goals such as being valued for product knowledge and, ultimately, to financial goals of increasing revenue. Figure 7.11 shows Jim's plan as it relates to the Six Performance Hurdles.

Our intention here is simply to illustrate how it could be helpful to you to consider the Six Performance Hurdles for each of the accountability areas, if you wish to do so. We have chosen the first accountability area from the strategy map (Product Mastery Series delivered to Consulting and Sales staff by December, 20xx) to illustrate what the thought process of the supervisor might be. You may or may not decide to complete the entire table, depending on the person with whom you are working and the particular circumstances

Jim Newman's Accountability and Development Plan

Accountability Area	Weight	Current Ability Assessment		Support Needed from Manager
Product Mastery Series delivered to Consulting and Sales staff by December 20xx	20%	Clarity of Expectations	Jim is clear on the desired results.	Jim will attempt to engage the support he needs from Jamie Eldridge and also from the director of marketing. We will meet weekly to provide coaching for him, and I will intervene with directors in those areas if Jim is unable to enlist their support.
		Commitment	Jim is strongly committed to this aspect of the strategy.	
		Knowledge and Skill	He has demonstrated comfort in designing complex training projects.	
		Confidence	He has demonstrated comfort in designing complex training projects and in collaborating with other departments.	
		Motivation	He typically has done so with minimal supervisory support.	
		Organizational Support Systems	He will need extensive input from peers in Marketing, and Consulting and Sales, and there are no champions for this project in those areas.	
Online Help and FAQ to support Product Mastery Series up and running by December 20xx.	20%	**Low** Jim is clear on the need and has set up similar systems in other jobs. IT, however, is strongly resistant to taking on any new projects. Jim has little experience or relationship with IT here. He needs to develop better working relationships with his peers.		Jim will prepare a timeline that shows IT needs, and he and I will plan strategy for getting commitment from IT. Jim will use this work as an opportunity to develop his peer network.
Development of mentoring process for financial consultants.	20%	**High** Jim has championed mentoring processes in previous jobs.		Monthly check points so I can report to executive team.
Management of Training and Development Supervisors	40%	**High** Jim has demonstrated good results for several years in this area. He is planning to focus on succession in his area.		Will add succession planning to our agenda for monthly discussion.

Figure 7.11 - Current Ability Assessment Chart

in which you are working. But it is all there for you if and when you need it.

Note in Figure 7.11 that the vice president of operations not only worked with Jim to translate the strategy of Biggs & Bucks into accountabilities but also went through a careful analysis of Jim's ability to deliver on each of those. Notice how the supervisor's notes under the Current Ability Assessment column track with our coaching assessment described earlier in this chapter.

Imagine for a moment what would happen if the vice president of operations had not considered Jim's ability to deliver this critical aspect of the strategy. Given Jim's experience and interest in the project, it would be easy for the vice president of operations to assume that the path is clear and simply delegate the project to Jim. And certainly those elements of the project that Jim could do on his own would likely be carried out. But Jim's efforts to plan the project with Marketing and Consulting and Sales, however, would likely meet with delays and objections. Efforts to get information and resources from those two departments would likewise meet with protestations of heavy workload, short resources, and other signs that the project is not a high priority for those two other departments. Eventually, the project ends up back on the desk of the vice president of operations who supervises Jim and his peers. In the meantime, the execution of strategy has been delayed.

But the vice president of operations does not fall into this classic trap. Because of the careful assessment of potential barriers to execution, the vice president of operations settles on a plan that gives Jim a chance to drive the project with his peers, but also provides quick and focused backup for Jim if he encounters barriers.

Good thinking on the vice president of operations' part. But we now face one more key question. Whose project is this? How does the vice president of operations drive execution of this project without taking over the project? Because the challenge of driving execution without micromanaging is so crucial to smooth handoffs, we devote the entire next chapter to that challenge.

Chapter 8

The Seventh Challenge: Guiding Execution without Micromanaging

In Chapter Six, we followed the strategy as it was translated in handoffs from the senior ranks all the way to the employee who has to execute a critical piece of the strategy. At various points in this book, we have emphasized that the manager making the handoff has to guide execution without being pulled into micromanaging. But exactly when do we go from guiding execution to micromanaging? This distinction is probably one of the hardest that senior managers have to make, and the consequences of error are serious. Disagreements about the boundaries are also a common cause of complaints at the handoff boundaries between levels.

What's the Difference?

Guiding execution is an oversight process. It includes discussing and debating the potential paths to achieve a goal. It also includes regular monitoring to ensure that progress is occurring, as well as intervention when deviations are detected. Guiding execution can also include serving as a sounding board and resource for those actually doing the work. Guiding execution is in no way incompatible with good delegation; in fact, it is part of good delegation. Managers who are good at guiding execution know the status of work going on under them, and they know about barriers that have been encountered and what the plans are to overcome those barriers. To understand guiding execution, think of an orchestra conductor who coordinates the playing of a large number of individual experts, but does not, however, step out into the orchestra and pick up an instrument. (That would be micromanagement.)

Micromanagement is basically doing work that can and should be done by others. As such, micromanagement is a symptom of a deeper issue somewhere in the manager-subordinate relationship, such as:

- **Not trusting subordinates to deliver acceptable results in an acceptable way.** Several situations are common here. The lack of trust may occur because the subordinates have not been coached and developed to do their jobs without close supervision. Maybe the manager has been burned by prematurely trusting these or previous subordinates. Either way, a careful assessment of coaching needs such as those we presented in the last chapter can help.
- **Perfectionism on the part of the manager.** We encounter this pattern when several possible methods are acceptable and will achieve a goal, but the manager imposes his or her preference.
- **Excessive control needs on the part of the manager.**
  Some managers just need to have their hands in the action. Though the job of managers is to control things, the way in which control is exerted has to change at higher levels of management. Early on, the manager controls the content of work. At higher levels, because the manager is no longer an expert in many of the areas under his or her span of control, it is necessary to shift toward controlling the process of work. Either way, in delegating and holding people ac-

countable (as opposed to doing the work personally) the manager has to manage and redirect his/her control needs from controlling the content to controlling the process.

Guiding Execution at the Senior Management Level

Let's look first at the senior level. Because the leadership literature generally describes the senior leadership role as predominantly strategic or systems level[33], and because senior managers are so cautioned against excessive involvement in operational details, those at the top may underestimate the danger of overshooting in the opposite direction. Senior leaders who wait in frustration for results from the level below or who complain about under-communication may be confusing delegation and abdication. Delegation includes a general understanding of the solution path and monitoring to see that work is proceeding according to plan. But abdication is defining the direction without providing the guidance for execution. The simplest guidance we can give in making the distinction between guiding execution and micromanaging is that a senior leader who gets blindsided by an execution problem has been too removed from guiding execution, having essentially abdicated rather than delegated.

In clarifying the distinction between guiding execution and micromanaging at the senior level, it may help to look again at our role alignment description. A central feature of that description is the shift from being a "star player" to being a head coach at the senior level. At the risk of oversimplifying, we could easily see that a head coach of a football team who tackles an opposing player has stepped far outside of the head coach role. Tackling is the job of the players on the defensive team. In fact, even giving a lineman instruction about tackling methods would be micromanagement for the head

---

33 Zaccaro, S. J. (2001). *The Nature of Executive Leadership: A Conceptual and Empirical Analysis of Success.* Washington, DC. American Psychological Association.

coach, because that's the job of the defensive coach.

But how about the head coach questioning the quarterback on a specific play, or even sending in a play at a crucial point in the game? We would not see these actions as micromanaging (doing the quarterback's job) because the coach is guiding the execution of the game plan. If the quarterback actually calls the plays, it is still appropriate for the head coach to understand and agree with the plan and the reasoning behind those plays. In short, we see three general functions that most define the role of individuals and teams at the senior level:

- *Managing the boundaries* between the organization and the external environment (market trends, Wall Street, political bodies, etc.).
- *Scanning the environment* for threats and opportunities; interpreting the results in light of the organization's mission, vision, and capabilities; and developing a strategic adaptation to the environment.
- *Guiding execution* by aligning structure, systems, processes, resources, and culture to support the execution; monitoring and detecting problems in execution, understanding the sources of those problems, and ensuring that problems get resolved.

Now let's look once more at Biggs & Bucks for specific examples of guiding execution versus micromanaging in the handoff of strategy. We will continue to follow the development of the Product Mastery Series through the three handoffs, looking each time at examples of guiding execution versus micromanaging. Remember that developing and implementing a Product Mastery Series is one method for achieving Biggs & Bucks's strategic goal to excel in product and sales training. This goal, in turn, is essential to the sales strategy of being valued for product knowledge.

In Figure 6.4 we saw that the vice president of operations (senior level) had worked in the handoff zone with Jim Newman, the middle manager over training and development, to develop an Accountability and Development Plan. Figure 8.1 presents that the portion of that plan from Figure 6.4 that deals only with the Product Mastery Series.

In Figure 7.11 we saw how the vice president of operations and Jim had used our Accountability and Development Plan to identify the amount and kind of coaching support that Jim would need in order to successfully take this handoff. Though Jim understood the

Jim Newman's Accountability and Development Plan

Accountability Area	Weight	Current Ability Assessment		Support Needed from Manager
Product Mastery Series delivered to Consulting and Sales staff by December 20xx.	20%	Clarity of Expectations	Jim is clear on the desired results.	Jim will attempt to engage the support he needs from Jamie Eldridge and also from the director of marketing. We will meet weekly to provide coaching for him and I will intervene with directors in those areas if Jim is unable to enlist their support.
		Commitment	Jim is strongly committed to this aspect of the strategy.	
		Knowledge and Skill	He has demonstrated knowledge and skill in developing complex training processes.	
		Confidence	He has demonstrated comfort in designing complex training projects and in collaborating with other departments.	
		Motivation	He typically has done so with minimal supervisory support.	
		Organizational Support Systems	He will need extensive input from peers in Marketing, and Consulting and Sales, and there are no champions for this project in those areas.	

Figure 8.1 - Accountability and Development Plan for Delivery of the Product Mastery Series

expectations, was committed to the project, had the knowledge and skills, and had the confidence and motivation to achieve the goal, he still faced internal obstacles in other departments. He would need cooperation from Marketing and Consulting and Sales, and this project was unlikely to be a priority for those departments.

The vice president of operations could solve this simply by directly intervening with the heads of Marketing and Consulting and Sales, both of whom report to the vice president of operations. That would be quick, but it would not give Jim Newman much opportunity to demonstrate or develop his negotiating and networking skills as a middle manager. How then does the vice president of operations ensure execution on this critical strategic project without getting sucked into the black hole of operational details?

Figure 8.2 gives some indication of the difference between guiding execution and micromanaging in the senior-to-middle handoff.

In the senior-to-middle handoff level, then, the senior manager should focus on strategic outcomes and hold the middle manager accountable for functional plans and for handling functional details. The senior manager's perspective is strategic, budgetary, and systemic. Thus, in discussing issues related to a call center, the senior manager may appropriately be involved in discussions about acceptable customer wait times because wait times are an indicator of customer experience. But the same senior manager should not get pulled into debates about line speed and effect on wait times as that relates to technical details that should be handled at the next level down.

Guiding Execution at the Middle Management Level

Like successful senior managers, those who succeed in the middle are not really hands-off managers. They are quite hands-on, but they have their hands on the right things. Knowing the difference between guiding execution and micromanaging is just as important at

Guiding Execution versus Micromanaging

Senior Manager	
Guiding Execution	**Micromanaging**
• Asking Jim to develop a strategy for gaining the support of Consulting and Sales and Marketing. • Reviewing this plan and coaching Jim on approaches he might use. • Intervening with Consulting and Sales and Marketing if Jim's efforts fail.	• Bypassing Jim and going directly to Consulting and Sales and Marketing.
• Highlighting the strategic themes or paths that involve Training and Development. • Clarifying the thinking behind specific trade-offs, such as resources allocated to various projects. • Discussing and reviewing Training and Development's proposed annual plans and budgets until the senior manager understands the factors driving major decisions and the risks involved. • Raising potential problems with the plans. • Approving the plans.	• Directing, by *fiat*, the annual plan at a high level of detail. • Practically on a daily basis, active or frequent involvement in the development of the annual plan for Training and Development before those plans are proposed to senior management. • In-depth solving of problems relating to technical details instead of focusing on strategic outcomes.
• Reviewing materials for branding and image. • Do they support a "one company" image? • Reviewing and approving training proposals from a cost/benefit perspective. • Reviewing and approving learning objectives.	• Detailed reviews of training materials to ensure that they support the learning objectives.
• Monitoring execution and ensuring that Training and Development staff are held accountable for their performance. • Evaluating Jim's skill as a manager of people.	• Discussing details of the performance of specific staff members in Training and Development.
• Understanding and approving the logic and the processes guiding performance evaluation and compensation. • Ensuring consistency across functions.	• Making changes in performance reviews or compensation other than for legal concerns (e.g., documentation, liability) or organizational consistency across managers.
• Stepping in to fix an urgent technical problem and then figuring out why that problem was not solved at the appropriate level.	• Stepping in to fix a technical problem and then moving on to the next technical problem.

Figure 8.2 - Guiding Execution versus Micromanagement at the Senior Level

the middle level, but it may be harder. Middle managers are usually closer to their original areas of expertise, so the siren song of the daily firefight is always within earshot.

Of course, the boundary between guiding execution and micromanaging is not a clean one, and the specific circumstances of the organization require some flexibility. We often say that a single instance or decision that is below the ideal role does not necessarily qualify as micromanaging. But, as we showed in Chapter Four, if the role of management in a department or function overlaps too much with the level below, then over time that department or function can become the weak link in executing strategy. So it behooves the middle manager to be ever alert to the pull of the operational detail.

Let's follow the handoff of the Product Mastery Series from Jim Newman, Biggs & Bucks's director of training and development, to

Accountability and Development Plan

Accountability Area	Weight	Current Ability Assessment	Support Needed from Manager
Development of Product Master Series (complete including pilot session and revisions by June 20xx).	25%	**Moderate** *Myra understands that she is accountable for development of the series, and she is fully committed to this project.* *Myra has developed several sales training programs, but **does not have detailed knowledge of financial products.*** *Myra is confident as a developer of training, and enjoys collaborations with other departments. **She has difficulty dealing with resistance, however, and tends to back down rather than face conflict.*** *She will need input and data from Consulting and Sales, and Marketing, and those departments are heavily involved in other projects.*	Close supervision (weekly check in) during program development and pilot. Support from experienced Consulting and Sales staff and client segment data from Marketing. Jim will attempt to get support of Jamie Eldridge, and from the marketing director for the initiative. He will get backup from the vice president, if necessary. Myra will coordinate meetings and input from Consulting and Sales and Marketing staff assigned to the initiative and inform Jim if there are problems.

Figure 8.3 – Myra's Accountability and Development Plan for the Development of a Product Mastery Series

Myra Bennis, a supervisor of training and development. Figure 8.3 shows that portion of Myra's accountability and development plan from Figure 6.5 that addresses the Product Mastery Series.

Now let's look at guiding execution versus micromanaging in executing this plan. Figure 8.4 provides some examples that should be helpful in deciding what approach is appropriate for the middle management ranks.

Guiding Execution versus Micromanaging

Middle Manager	
Guiding Execution	**Micromanaging**
• Reviews the strategy map with Myra and emphasizes the importance of the Product Mastery Series. • Defines objectives for the series.	• Gives Myra an outline of training topics.
• Reviews Myra's plan for the project and coaches Myra on her project management skills.	• Provides a plan with timelines and resources and asks Myra to carry out the plan.
• Reviews materials for image, quality, and cost.	• Provides graphics for materials.
• Reviews Myra's plans for supervising Tracey Collins, the staff trainer who designs and produces training materials. • Ensures that Myra has assessed Tracey's abilities and needs in a methodical manner. • Meets with Myra to monitor Tracey's progress on the project and has the appropriate priorities.	• Checks with Tracey on status of project. • Changing Tracey's priorities to speed up the project.
• Attends a cross-functional team meeting involving Myra and marketing staff to assess Myra's progress in handling cross-functional teams. • Coaches Myra afterwards to develop her skills in this area.	• Convenes and runs a cross-functional team meeting with Myra and marketing staff.
• Intervenes with the director of marketing when staff in that department repeatedly reschedule the planning meeting with Myra.	• Calls staff in Marketing to schedule the planning meeting.

Figure 8.4 - Guiding Execution versus Micromanaging at the Middle Level

Guiding Execution at the Line Management Level

Finally, let's look at the distinction as it applies at the line manager level. This close to the player role, the pull that you experience back into that role can be almost overwhelming, especially when there are operational snags. Thus, it is especially important that line managers understand the shift in their role from one of actual implementation to one of guiding its execution by others.

Figure 8.5 below is the portion of the Accountability and Development Plan from Figure 6.6 that Myra Bennis developed with Tracey Collins, the staff member who will actually develop the materials for the Product Mastery Series.

As the accountability plan shows, Tracey's current ability to complete the design is estimated as low. She is strong in materials design, but has not yet developed a strong network among her peers in other departments. Myra will provide closer support and assistance for this project. Figure 8.6 continues our illustration of guiding execution versus micromanaging at the line level. Note that our examples of micromanagement are adjusted to take into account Tracey's

Accountability and Development Plan

Accountability Area	Weight	Current Ability Assessment	Support Needed from Manager
Materials design for six modules of Product Mastery Series by June 20xx.	35%	**Low** *Tracey has strong materials design experience but is new to Biggs & Bucks. Just getting used to our culture. Does not have a strong network yet.*	Close supervision during development of first draft; frequent checkpoints. Get Diane in Marketing to help with branding and layout. Jamie in Consulting and Sales will work closely with Tracey on technical issues.

Figure 8.5 – Tracey's Accountability and Development Plan for the Design of the Materials for the Product Mastery Series.

low current ability. Myra is pretty close to the action in our examples, but in this case she needs to be.

In particular, note the difference between guiding execution and micromanaging when the project falls several weeks behind schedule. The temptation is pretty strong for the supervisor to step in and begin designing materials in order to get the project back on track. That heroic act, however, misses the opportunity to better understand and coach Tracey. In both cases, the line supervisor gets the project back on track, which is perfectly appropriate. In one case, however, the line supervisor does so by better leadership of a key employee; in the other, the line supervisor does that employee's job.

For line managers who are new to the role or who struggle with micromanaging, it is essential to have a strong supervisor who understands and supports the transition from player to player/coach. Besides the longer term morale problems from a frustrated team, micromanagement at the line level usually means that the parts of the role that are neglected are those having to do with alignment of plans with strategic themes. In that case, we have the makings of a dropped baton in the last leg of the race.

Look back at the strategy map and the accountability plans and note that we can easily spot a potential fumble in the hand-

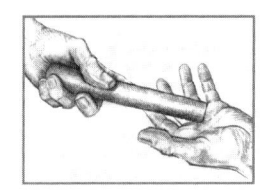

> The temptation is pretty strong for the supervisor to step in and begin designing materials in order to get the project back on track. That heroic act, however, misses the opportunity to better understand and coach Tracey.

Guiding Execution versus Micromanaging

Line Manager	
Guiding Execution	**Micromanaging**
• Uses the strategy map to educate Tracey about the importance of the Product Mastery Series. • Emphasizes the need for Consulting and Sales staff to have strong product knowledge in order to be viewed as trusted advisors. • Draws Tracey's attention to the importance of creating the materials in a way that supports the new emphasis on building pride in the brand.	• Starts the process by showing Tracey her own materials designed for a previous project. • Gives Tracey examples of how to brand the materials.
• Suggests that Tracey meet with Diane in Marketing and Mark in Consulting and Sales to enlist their help in the project. • Describes her own experience with Diane and Mark in the past and why she thinks they are good choices for help from those departments.	• Takes Tracey, Diane, and Mark out to lunch and describes how she would like for them to work on the project.
• Meets with Tracey shortly after the first meeting with Diane and Mark to check on the status of the planning. • Reviews Tracey's first draft of the project plan and asks about her plans for using Diane and Mark for input. • Inquires about what Tracey learned regarding Diane's and Mark's experience and skills. • Raises a concern that the timeline does not allow for unexpected delays and tells Tracey about how she learned the hard way to allow for the unexpected. • Has Tracey do a revision of the plan that addresses Myra's concerns.	• Meets with Tracey after the first meeting with Diane and Mark and reviews Tracey's plan. • Gives Tracey a new timeline that allows for unexpected delays. • Tells Tracey to get Diane's input first because Marketing has a vacant position and Diane could be pulled to fill that role.
• Checks with Tracey regularly about the status of the projects. • Reviews drafts of materials at each stage and gives feedback. • When the project falls several weeks behind schedule, gets Tracey to develop a plan for getting back on track and reviews the plan with Tracey. • Uses the experience to better understand Tracey's developmental needs in managing a large project. • Discovers that Tracey tends to avoid conflict, and so she has had difficulty holding Diane and Mark to their commitments. • Coaches Tracey on dealing with conflict.	• Checks regularly on the status of the project. • When it falls several weeks behind schedule, steps in and creates several of the more difficult modules to get the project back on track.

Figure 8.6 – Guiding Execution versus Micromanaging at the Line Level

off of this critical piece of strategy. Because of the moderate and low estimates of current ability to deliver at the line supervisor and employee levels, this strategic pathway will require close monitoring to ensure smooth handoffs and execution. In light of these concerns, the supervision and development approach has been tightened, key support people have been named, and the solution path has been clarified in more detail. All of these actions fall well within the range of guiding execution without micromanaging.

We have followed the handoff process from the strategic level down through the ranks. At each stage, we have used simple tools to assess the ability of the next level to take the handoff and to adapt the supervision strategy to avoid a handoff. In our final chapter, we offer a quick summary of the handoff process to support you in applying these tools to your own situation.

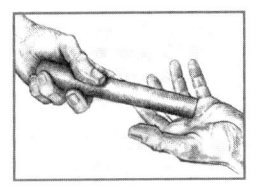

> Besides the longer term morale problems from a frustrated team, micromanagement at the line level usually means that the parts of the role that are neglected are those having to do with alignment of plans with strategic themes. In that case, we have the makings of a dropped baton in the last leg of the race.

Passing the Baton: Winning the Race for Strategic Execution

Chapter 9

Creating Your Handoff Plan

This chapter provides you with a planning format for addressing each of the challenges of the strategic handoff in your organization. Though no rigid format could possibly do justice to the diversity of organizations and the challenges they face, we hope that the following guide will help you organize your thinking about the particular challenges you face.

As you work your way through the planning process guided by this chapter, you might want to take notes as you create your own handoff plan. You will probably find it helpful to review the models and tools from earlier chapters – we reference them throughout this chapter where relevant. Where appropriate, we have included our own suggestions for addressing each of the seven challenges, based on experiences with our clients and our own business.

The First Challenge: Sizing up the Field

In Chapter Two, we argued for the importance of sizing up the field for the strategic race — analyzing the environmental and organizational context that shaped the formulation of the strategy. The following assessment will guide you not only in developing your strategy, but also in engaging your organization at the right times and at the right level. So, as you reflect on the following questions, give some thought to the best ways to ensure that people in your organization understand the environmental and organizational context in which their work will occur. This understanding not only will be important to developing commitment to needed change, but it also can help people participate in defining barriers and coming up with solutions.

It may appear at first glance that this first challenge is (or should be) handled only at the senior level, as they will likely have a deeper grasp of these issues. Certainly, the environmental and organizational scanning process should be driven by the senior level, but we believe that any manager in the organization should be able to discuss the following topics to some extent. Managers at every level must have a basic understanding of the strategic field, or they will not be able to make a convincing case to their team for pursuing priorities relevant to corporate strategy. So, if you are a senior manager, we recommend that you not only respond yourself, but also that you pause to reflect on how managers at the levels below you would respond.

Environmental Scan

- What major forces will affect our segment or entire industry over the foreseeable future? Watch for trends in these areas:
    - *Political, regulatory, legal* (the politics of health care, environmental regulations, defense spending, lawsuits, etc.)
    - *Macroeconomic* (interest rates, market trends, etc.)
    - *Demographic changes* (changes in customer and potential customer base, product and service needs driven by immigration, etc.)
    - *Consolidation/fragmentation* (impact of these trends on market share, niche opportunities, etc.)

- *Technological* (impact on production, service, infomation storage and retrieval, customer habits, etc.)
- *Other external forces affecting your particular organization*

Organizational Scan

- Looking back over the history of the organization, where do you see periods of continuous improvement? Where were there fundamental shifts in how the organization worked?
- What does this historical perspective tell you about how the organization got to its current state and what the future probably holds for the company?
- What are the major drivers of current success (our quick response to customers, our skill at innovation, our ability to drive down costs, etc.)?
- Where do you see restrainers building up (our larger size is slowing our speed of decisions, we're outgrowing our infrastructure, we don't have the depth of middle management needed to push decisions closer to the customer, etc.)?
- What kinds of organizational changes will minimize the restrainers (pushing decisions closer to the customer level, updating our infrastructure, developing stronger business leaders in the middle ranks, etc.)?
- Regarding our readiness for change, what is our urgency level?

If you are a *senior manager*, success at your level requires that you wrestle with questions like those above and guide the organization in coming to grips with the environmental challenges it faces.

If you are a *middle manager*, your role is to understand these challenges and to translate them into functional or departmental implications. It is also up to you to guide senior management in understanding the functional or departmental options in addressing the environmental challenges, along with the benefits and risks of each.

If you are a *line manager*, you are the final ambassador for management in gaining the understanding and commitment of the organization. People look to senior management for high-level descriptions of what is changing in the environment, but they often look to you at the line to see if senior management is credible.

The Second Challenge: Sizing up the Team

Your assessment of your team and your organization should continue throughout the handoff process. At this stage, you are primarily interested in identifying the level at which the individuals on your team should be working in order to receive the strategic baton effectively. At a minimum, you should lay out the ideal roles of those who report to you and over whom you have some responsibility. (And if you are in a position to do so, define the ideal roles for each level in the organization.)

A good way to begin is to identify the level for each individual you are assessing and list key elements of that person's role as it would ideally be in grappling with the issues identified in your environmental and organizational scan. In this book, we have listed general role requirements, so you will want to translate those so that they fit the language and roles of your organization. Do not be constrained by our general list, but be sure to adapt it to the realities of your organization.

In Figures 9.1 - 9.3, which will help you in this preliminary assessment, we have adapted information from the model we used in Figure 3.1 of Chapter Three. We recommend that you reproduce the following tables and complete them for each position reporting to you. We suggest comparing the individuals currently in those positions to your ideal description of the role in your organization.

Role Assessment for Individual Senior Management Positions

General Role Requirements	What does this requirement mean in our organization?	In general, how does this individual manager stack up?
• Managing external boundaries		
• Scanning the environment		
• Finding causal patterns		
• Being an effective team player		
• Visioning and strategic positioning		
• Aligning structure and systems		
• Guiding execution		
• Planning time horizon is measured in years		

Key Factors in General	What does this factor mean in our organization?	In general, how does this individual manager stack up?
• Mental complexity		
• Strategic thinking		
• Business skill		
• Interpersonal savvy		

Figure 9.1 – Role Assessment for Individual Senior Management Positions

Role Assessment for Individual Middle Management Positions

General Role Requirements	What does this requirement mean in our organization?	In general, how does this individual manager stack up?
• Translating strategy		
• Working with an intermedate time horizon		
• Functional visioning and planning		
• Managing internal boundaries		
• Developing line managers		

Key Factors in General	What does this factor mean in our organization?	In general, how does this individual manager stack up?
• Systems thinking		
• Basic finance		
• Tactical planning		
• Resource allocation		
• Negotiating		
• Role flexibility		
• Organizational savvy		

Figure 9.2 – Role Assessment for Individual Middle Management Positions

Role Assessment for Individual Line Management Positions

General Role Requirements	What does this requirement mean in our organization?	In general, how does this individual manager stack up?
• Planning work and tasks		
• Handling details		
• Managing resources		
• Supervising line employees		
• Working with a short time horizon		

Key Factors in General	What does this factor mean in our organization?	In general, how does this individual manager stack up?
• Technical skill		
• Organizational ability		
• Work planning		

Figure 9.3 – Role Assessment for Individual Line Management Positions

The Third Challenge: Anticipating Problems in the Handoff Zones

Now we turn from assessing individual team members against the ideal to looking more broadly at potential problems across the three primary handoff zones of the organization. It is not unusual for us to find noticeable patterns of strengths or weaknesses within a particular management level. Particularly as role demands change in a growing organization, you may find, for example, that a number of senior managers are pulled far more into daily operations than would be ideal. Or, as diversifying product lines requires a deeper bench of middle managers, you may find that the organization has not yet developed strong managers in the middle ranks. Whatever the case in your organization, a few moments of reflection time can help you zero in on likely fumbles as the strategic baton is passed from senior to middle to the line levels.

You may find it helpful to use the simple Role Alignment and Handoff Model we introduced in Chapter Four (ref. Figures 4.4 and 4.5) as a guide to reflecting about role alignment and handoffs in your organization. You can copy and use the assessment chart in Figure 9.4 for this exercise if you wish. If a department or function has managers working at the right level (and therefore are able to take and translate the strategic baton), just draw a circle within the bounds of that level. If, on the other hand, a department or function on the whole is working below its ideal level, then draw its role circle as overlapping with the level beneath it.

As you look at your results on this assessment, consider the following:

- **If a department or function appears to operate below the needed level, how did that situation evolve?** For example, did the organization outgrow the capabilities of the

Role Alignment and Handoff Chart

Senior Team	
Middle Teams	
Line Teams	
Organization	

Figure 9.4 – Role Alignment and Handoff Chart

management in a particular area? Does the organization's culture tolerate performance below the needed levels? Does micromanagement at one level force managers at the next level down into an inappropriate level of detail (e.g., excessive demand for detailed information)? Do management weaknesses at lower levels pull higher levels into firefighting?

- **What does your alignment graphic suggest about the weak points in your organization's ability to adapt effectively to the environmental threats and opportunities from your environmental scan?** Can you anticipate the likely effects of fumbles in one area on the functioning of other areas? For example, if your information technology department is a weak link, how will that affect the ability of other areas to execute against strategy? Who has responsibility for add-ressing the weak links?

- **How much time do you have before any weak links become critical?** Sometimes — especially when the role misalignment has resulted from the organization's failure to educate managers about their

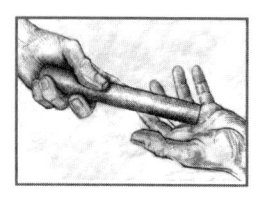

> If you see a critical role underperforming in your line of supervision – and if reasonable coaching efforts have not been effective – we suggest that you ask yourself honestly how likely it is that further efforts will work.

changing roles and when the levels above and below are fairly strong — you will see managers step up to the role requirements if they are provided with good coaching and mentoring. At other times — especially if the role misalignment has been known for awhile or if coaching efforts so far have proven ineffective — you have to face the possibility that key personnel have topped out in their personal performance S-curve.

In working with hundreds and hundreds of executives over many years, we have found that a difficult point of learning for many of them was how hard it is to try to force someone into a role that is not a good fit for them. If you see a critical role underperforming in your line of supervision — and if reasonable coaching efforts have not been effective — we suggest that you ask yourself honestly how likely it is that further efforts will work.

The Fourth Challenge: Defining the Strategic Baton

As we have noted throughout the book, a central management role at all levels is to translate organizational strategy into the language, metrics, and priorities appropriate to their level in the organization. Though senior managers should carry the bulk of the responsibility for communicating the organization's direction, people still go to their own managers for clarity and interpretation regardless of managerial level. So middle and line managers need to be able to discuss the overall organizational strategy intelligently without distorting the message. The second challenge for middle and line managers is then translating those portions of the strategy that are relevant for their areas of responsibility into the language, metrics, and priorities that make sense for their teams.

Whatever your level in the organization, remember to include the following seven elements of the strategic baton as you translate and communicate the strategic baton for your team:

1. The Business Context
2. Organizational Vision
3. The Strategy
4. Organizational Value Proposition and Major Trade-offs
5. Barriers to Execution and Solution Paths
6. Personal Implications and Performance Expectations
7. Organizational Values and Team Agreements

For each of these six communication and translation points, we are going to suggest some questions that will help you begin to create your action plan.

The Business Context

- Look back at your notes from the first challenge, sizing up the field. Regardless of your management level, which parts of the organization's environmental and organizational context are most critical for your team to understand? How will you bring your team up to speed?
- Which parts of the environmental and organizational context are most relevant for you and your team? For example, if you are in the customer service area, how will customer service need to adapt in order to be effective in the future? What will probably change for members of your team, and what will they need from you in order to commit to the changing direction?

People learn and remember in different ways. Don't rely on any one approach to communication, but use multiple methods. Team meetings, one-on-ones, formal presentations with slides, informal discussions with flip charts, and other approaches all add value for somebody. And remember that repetition helps the message to sink in.

Organizational Vision

- What is the vision for the organization? Are there key phrases or images used by senior managers that you need to be sure to support in your own communications?
- What is your vision for your area? That is, how do you hope to see your department or function contributing to the organization's success over the next three to five years? How can you enlist your team in understanding and sharing that vision?

People often ask us if the vision should be the result of a group process. Though the intention to involve people is laudable, you should ask yourself how much freedom your team really has to shape its own direction. Most of the time, the range of options is limited by the resource constraints and other realities of the organization. So, if the options for the functional or departmental vision are limited, we recommend that you make the case for the needed vision and not run the risk of inviting input that is unrealistic. There will be plenty of room for involving others in terms of how to achieve the vision.

The Strategy

We advocate developing a strategy map to meet several needs. First, the process encourages the senior team to wrestle with the hard decisions about trade-offs and priorities. Second, the map becomes an accountability tool for the senior team in terms of its ongoing focus. Third, the map can become a problem-solving tool for managers further down in the organization as they attempt to prioritize local actions that support the strategy. Finally, a strategy map is a powerful educational tool because it allows employees to see how the various organizational goals are related to one another. Key questions related to strategy include:

- If your organization has a strategic plan but has not mapped it, what would be the added benefit of taking the extra step to create the one-page map? Who would need to be convinced of the value?
- Whether or not your organization has a formal strategy map, how and where, organizationally, does your team's work affect:
    - Cost management?
    - Revenue growth?
    - Customer experience?
- What are the internal activities and processes that drive results in the above three areas?

- Which of those internal activities and processes are within your span of control, and how will you and your team need to run them in order to achieve the desired results?
- Which of those internal activities and processes are outside of your direct control but affect your team's ability to achieve its goals? What can you and your team do to improve the workflow between your area and these other areas?

Value Proposition and Major Trade-offs

The value proposition and trade-offs are, of course, embedded in the strategy map. They are the intentions that underlie the goals described on the map. We have found, however, that these aspects of the strategy are so critical that they need to be highlighted by management in any presentation of strategy. You should be able to clarify questions such as the following for your team:

- How will we differentiate ourselves from competitor in the minds of our customers. Will it be primarily in our price, our service, the innovative features of our products, or other drivers of customer preference?
- Where will we choose to be acceptable but not necessarily to differentiate? For example, if we are known for exceptional service, maybe our prices should be "competitive in our market" but not "lowest in our market."
- As we focus our priorities and resources on those things that are most critical to our customers, which activities become "nice-to-have" instead of "essential"? For example, if our primary value proposition centers on exceptional service, just how much ground can we yield on price?

Barriers to Execution and Solution Paths

- What barriers affect the ability of the entire organization to carry out the strategy? Does the culture need to change to fit changing circumstances? Are there limitations in the ability of your current infrastructure to support the strategy?
- What barriers affect the ability of your department or function to deliver your intended results? What are your plans for addressing those barriers? Whose help might you need to carry out those plans? How will you enlist their help?

It is here that you have the best hope of involving your team and enlisting their commitment. Once the goals are established, engage your team in identifying and prioritizing the barriers they anticipate and organizing their thoughts about ways of addressing those barriers.

A good process is to use a simple force field analysis with your team. Begin by stating a particular process goal, such as "improving production yield." Then have the group brainstorm those factors in the organization that are drivers (working toward the goal) and those that are restrainers (getting in the way of the goal). It is usually helpful to prioritize the resulting list and then to develop plans for overcoming the restrainers. For example, a driver of improved production yield might be "we purchased new equipment" and a restrainer might be "operators slow with changeovers."

Figure 9.5 provides an example of the force field analysis that you can use with your team.

Force Field Analysis

Drivers	Restrainers
→	←

Figure 9.5 – Force Field Analysis

Personal Implications and Performance Expectations

Make sure that each person on the team understands the personal implications of the baton that is being passed to him.

- How will the priorities, skills, and thinking of each person on your team need to change in order to carry out your functional group's part of the strategy? How will he be evaluated on carrying out his part?
- Especially for employees with high potential, what are the personal career implications of the changes? For example, a particularly difficult change in methods might be more tolerable for a high performer who sees the opportunity to prove her talents.

Organizational Values and Team Agreements

Because of the abstract nature of most values (e.g., integrity), it is essential that managers guide their teams not only in understanding what those values mean in day-to-day actions…but also what they *don't* mean. We also find it most useful to translate the organizational values into behavioral examples that fit the work environment of each team. For example, how does integrity play out in the daily work of Compensation and Benefits or of Manufacturing?

We suggest that you reflect on the following yourself, and then engage your team in a group discussion:
- What are the organization's explicit values?
- What are behavioral examples of each of these values in your team's day-to-day work environment?
- What do the values *not* mean? For example, saying that the company cares about employees might mean that it provides coaching and help for someone who is not performing up to speed, but it does not mean that the company will leave that person in their job if they fail to improve.

The Fifth Challenge: Translating Strategy into Expectations

In Chapter Six, we used an Accountability and Development Plan (ref. Figure 6.4) to illustrate the process of translating strategic language into individual accountabilities and development plans. It is not necessary for you to use this specific form, which we've duplicated for your use in Figure 9.6, but we strongly suggest that you make sure this information exists for each person on your team. Use of such planning processes does risk becoming bureaucratic if taken to extremes, but our experience has been that managers are more likely to err in the opposite direction — that of assuming that everyone is clear on how he connects with strategy — with negative consequences.

Therefore, for each person on your team, we suggest that you adapt the table in Figure 9.6 to fit the language and realities of your organization. Then, in the next section, we'll look at some ways to determine how to coach your team members through this plan.

Accountability and Development Plan

Accountability Area	Weight	Current Ability Assessment	Support Needed from Manager
		• Clarity of expectations? • Commitment? • Skill? • Confidence? • Personality and Motivation? • Organizational Supports?	

Figure 9.6 – Accountability and Development Plan

The Sixth Challenge: Coaching for Performance

The easier part of the handoff process is usually translating strategic priorities into specific accountabilities. The harder part is determining each individual's current abilities and her supervision and development needs. We often see managers make assumptions in haste about what their team needs from them in order to succeed. Managers tend to overestimate the importance of someone having the needed skills, and to underestimate other internal barriers to performance (clarity, confidence, and so on).

If you have been working the process described so far in this chapter, you now have:

- Clarified the environmental and organizational context in which the current strategy was developed.
- Clarified any changes in role requirements for yourself and managers above and below you in light of where the organization has come from and where it is heading.
- Paid particular attention to any obvious weak spots in the handoff process and, as far as you can within your span of control, developed plans for avoiding handoff problems.
- Identified the elements of the strategy that belong to you and your team.
- Identified potential barriers to carrying out your piece of the strategy and have engaged others as appropriate in developing plans to overcome those barriers.
- Translated all of the above into accountabilities for each person on your team in a format like that of Figure 9.6.

You are now ready to assess the current ability of each person on your team to deliver on their accountabilities and to create an accountability and development plan for each person. Before you begin, let us caution you that what follows may seem complicated and burdensome to you if you are a busy manager. The temptation will be to blow the coaching process off completely or to blow through it quickly. But our experience has taught us that it is here that the baton is most likely to be fumbled or dropped. So if you need an added boost to get you through this part of the process, just remember this wise old saying: "Go slow to go fast!"

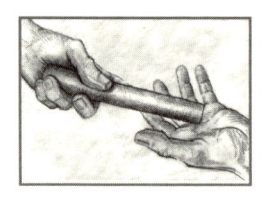

To support you in seeing the wisdom of going slow to go fast, consider the following:

- **If you have overestimated someone's ability to deliver on an important piece of the strategy and have tossed the baton at him, you'll end up with delays, errors, and wasted resources.** In the end, you'll get pulled into the problem anyway, only you'll have a conflagration on your hands instead of a small flicker of flame that you could have stomped out quickly.

- **If you have underestimated the person's ability, you'll spend time and effort providing unneeded guidance and supervision.** You'll create frustration on the part of team members who could take some of the weight off you, and you'll waste time that

you could have spent supporting those with less current ability.
- **If you take the time now to give serious consideration to the handoff, the worst case is that you will have spent a few minutes confirming that what you assume about your team does appear to be accurate**…and you'll score points with them for having taken their developmental needs seriously.
- **If you discover even one potential handoff problem and adapt your supervision style appropriately, you will have earned a tremendous return on a small investment of time.**

As you work through the accountability plans for each person, we have repeated for your convenience each of the decision tree figures from Chapter Seven in Figures 9.7 – 9.12 to help you in making a current ability assessment of each of your people and in adapting your supervision approach.

And remember, if you have made it this far in assessing someone's ability to deliver on an accountability without encountering a barrier inside the person, it is always possible that there are barriers outside the person that are up to you to address.

Clarity of Expectations Decision Tree

Question	Decision Point	Coaching Tools
• Does this person understand his role and what is expected of him? Note: This includes *what* he is expected to accomplish and *how* he is expected to accomplish it (cultural fit).	No → / Yes ↓	• Role Definition: *Use The Leadership Pipeline.*[34] • Use Four Dimensional Leadership for Guidance.
• Is this person clear on his goals and how he will be measured?	No → / Yes ↓	• Define goals that are specific and measurable, with target dates for completion.
• Does this person understand how his goals and activities roll up into the organization's strategy?	No → / Yes ↓	• Use a strategy map to draw "line of sight" between his goals and strategic goals. • Be sure he understands key metrics used to measure overall organizational performance (e.g., efficiency ratios, etc.)
• Is this person clear on where his various responsibilities fit in the Importance – Urgency Grid? URGENCY: HI [X] [ ] / LO [X] [ ] — HI LO IMPORTANCE	No → / Yes ↓	• Identify any areas where his work affects multiple goals on the strategy map (e.g., a project that would both drive down cost and enhance customer experience at the same time). • Use a pie chart to show the relative proportion of time to be allocated to each of his key responsibilities. • Ask him to walk through his current to-do list and ask him to rate the priorities. It is most useful to let him describe his reasoning so you can listen for areas of misunderstanding. So don't jump in and correct his list too soon.
• Is this person delegating appropriately?	No → / Yes ↓	• The rule of thumb here is that if it is something that can be done at a lower level of responsibility and authority, it should be delegated. • Our Four Dimensional Leadership model should be helpful in determining what responsibilities are appropriate to the level of management under consideration. • Charan's *Leadership Pipeline* model is useful as well.

34 Charan, R., Drotter, S. & Noel, J. (2001). *The Leadership Pipeline: How to Build the Leadership Powered Company.* San Francisco, CA. Jossey-Bass.

Clarity of Expectations Decision Tree (continued)

• Does this person understand how his role affects others vertically and horizontally?	Yes ↓ No →	• Walk him through the linkage of his role with yours, making sure to explain what you need from him to support you in doing your job. • Have him go through the same process with his direct reports. • Walk through each step in critical work processes and note who is involved in or affected by that step. Do not assume that he knows how his work fits into the whole, or who the go-to people are in each department to get issues resolved. In complex organizations with work broken out into many specialties, people often concentrate just on getting work out the door and miss easy opportunities to improve the process itself.
• Does this person understand his role in managing both vertical and, often more importantly, horizontal relationships?	Yes ↓ No →	• Have him prioritize the other relationships that are most crucial in the work flow and develop a brief vision of how each should work. • Work with him to develop one or two positive strategies for improving relationships that are especially difficult. In particular, coach him on the importance of asking more questions to better understand the other person's or department's role and challenges. • Especially for those in middle management roles, identify the crucial trade-offs between departments (e.g., design features vs. service capacity, etc.). • Go through several examples to guide him in understanding where the balance should be in order to line up with the organization's strategy.
• Does this person understand the skills needed for success in his role?	Yes ↓ No →	• Check to see if your organization has competency profiles for each role. We have seen situations in which these had been done but not widely shared. • Use the Four Dimensional Leadership model, and/or *The Leadership Pipeline* to clarify skills appropriate to the role. • Draw his attention to someone who does the role well and discuss the skills and attributes that contribute to success.

Clarity of Expectations Decision Tree (continued)

• Does this person understand how he needs to manage himself and his interpersonal relationships in order to be the most effective?	No → (Yes ↓)	• Reading *First Break All the Rules*[35] will help him understand the interpersonal effects obtained by the most effective managers.
• Does this person have a realistic understanding of how he can grow and develop in terms of personal management and interpersonal skills to enhance his effectiveness?	No → (Yes ↓)	• Give honest and clear feedback about how his behavior affects others in the workplace. Focus on the behavior-effect aspect to avoid judging the behavior itself. The emphasis is on whether the behavior has a desirable effect. There's less room to get defensive about the behavior if the result is clearly undesirable.
USING THIS TABLE AS A MODEL FOR HOW YOU MIGHT APPROACH THIS COACHING OPPORTUNITY, CONTINUE WITH THE QUESTIONING PROCESS UNTIL YOU HAVE EXHAUSTED ALL POSSIBILITIES FOR ADDRESSING PERFORMANCE HURDLES RELEVANT TO EXPECTATIONS.		

35 Buckingham, M. & Coffman, C. (1999). *First Break All the Rules: What the World's Greatest Managers Do Differently.* New York, NY. Simon & Schuster.

Figure 9.7 - Decision Tree for Performance Hurdle #1: Expectations

Commitment Decision Tree

Question	Decision Point	Coaching Tools
• Does this person believe that the expected outcome is important to the success of the organization?	No / Yes ↓	• Make the business case using market, competitor, customer, cost, or other hard data. To make this alive and most relevant, remember to draw clear links back to the day-to-day work of the individual or team. Make the personal case, making the link to his career goals.
• Does this person believe the solution path, i.e. that the methods you want them to use, will lead to the outcome they are expected to produce?	No / Yes ↓	• Facilitate a process whereby he draws out the step-by-step connection to how the proposed actions lead to the desired outcome. Use your organization's strategy map.
• Does this person see any personal benefit from achieving the expected outcome?	No / Yes ↓	• Use traditional incentives, bonuses, and performance appraisals. • Draw attention to visibility or career benefits of succeeding (e.g., What's in it for him?).
• Does this person see any personal threat from failing to achieve the outcome?	No / Yes ↓	• Last resort – Draw attention to negative consequences of failure (e.g., impact on job or career).
USING THIS TABLE AS A MODEL FOR HOW YOU MIGHT APPROACH THIS COACHING OPPORTUNITY, CONTINUE WITH THE QUESTIONING PROCESS UNTIL YOU HAVE EXHAUSTED ALL POSSIBILITIES FOR ADDRESSING PERFORMANCE HURDLES RELEVANT TO COMMITMENT.		

Figure 9.8 – Decision Tree for Performance Hurdle #2: Commitment

Skill Decision Tree

Question	Decision Point	Coaching Tools
• Does this person have the basic intelligence to be able to grasp the knowledge and understanding of what is required of him?	No → Yes ↓	• Though difficult to acknowledge in our current politically correct society, this is a fact of life. We have seen many situations where an individual was just not capable, intellectually, of handling the required skill. See the Parable of the Singing Pig. • Determine ways to work around the person's skill area deficits, by allocating those responsibilities to someone else. • If you determine that the intellect just isn't there and you are not able to allocate as discussed in the preceding bulleted point, re-assign the person to a position in the organization that will fit his capability. • If you cannot re-position him in the organization, arrange to outplace the person.
• Do they have the basic knowledge and understanding of what is required to have developed the skill?	No → Yes ↓	• Provide the education required for him to get up to speed. This can be provided through formal education or through your own teaching and modeling efforts.
• Do they have the necessary skills for the role or task? Can they do it?	No → Yes ↓	• Demonstrate and coach in the required skill area. • Arrange for this person to observe someone who has the desired skills. • For more complex skills, arrange shadowing of someone who is highly skilled.
USING THIS TABLE AS A MODEL FOR HOW YOU MIGHT APPROACH THIS COACHING OPPORTUNITY, CONTINUE WITH THE QUESTIONING PROCESS UNTIL YOU HAVE EXHAUSTED ALL POSSIBILITIES FOR ADDRESSING PERFORMANCE HURDLES RELEVANT TO SKILL.		

Figure 9.9 – Decision Tree for Performance Hurdle #3: Skill

Confidence Decision Tree

Question	Decision Point	Coaching Tools
• Does this person demonstrate his own personal sense of self-assuredness in being able to carry out what is needed from him?	No ↓ / Yes	• Discuss with him where he feels insecure or unsure. • Discuss with him and agree on what he would need to do or experience in order to gain confidence. This might mean frequent check points with you as he executes a project, or it might mean more hands-on coaching with him regarding the specific tasks under consideration, similar to teaching your child to ride a bicycle, where you run alongside, holding on, and gradually withdraw your supporting hands.
• Is this person confident in his decisions?	No ↓ / Yes	• Generate possible scenarios and have him respond. Clarify and teach where needed, and affirm when his decisions are good. • Use stories and personal experience to broaden perspective after a negative experience. Focus on getting over the experience and refocusing on future opportunities.
• Is this person confident in his skills?	No ↓ / Yes	• Affirm for good performance. Provide external benchmarks for him to evaluate his own skill.
USING THIS TABLE AS A MODEL FOR HOW YOU MIGHT APPROACH THIS COACHING OPPORTUNITY, CONTINUE WITH THE QUESTIONING PROCESS UNTIL YOU HAVE EXHAUSTED ALL POSSIBILITIES FOR ADDRESSING PERFORMANCE HURDLES RELEVANT TO CONFIDENCE.		

Figure 9.10 – Decision Tree for Performance Hurdle #4: Confidence

Personality and Motivation Decision Tree

Question	Decision Point	Coaching Tools
• Does this person manage his personality effectively?	No → Yes ↓	• Refer to Figure 7.9 - Coaching Pointers for Big Five Factors
USING THIS TABLE AS A MODEL FOR HOW YOU MIGHT APPROACH THIS COACHING OPPORTUNITY, CONTINUE WITH THE QUESTIONING PROCESS UNTIL YOU HAVE EXHAUSTED ALL POSSIBILITIES FOR ADDRESSING PERFORMANCE HURDLES RELEVANT TO PERSONALITY AND MOTIVATION.		

Figure 9.11 – Decision Tree for Performance Hurdle #5: Personality and Motivation

Organizational Support Systems Decision Tree

Question	Decision Point	Coaching Tools
• Does this person have adequate technical, financial, etc. supports provided to him from the organization to complete what is required?	No → / Yes ↓	• Discuss and determine where the insufficient resources are, and negotiate with the appropriate manager or executive to the degree and in the form appropriate to the particular situation. • Refer to the strategy map as needed and appropriate.
• Do the equipment and technical processes fully support the performance objectives?	No → / Yes ↓	• Identify the points of limitations, and determine if there is a work-around and/or what options are available to you to deal with this rate limiting factor.
• Are expectations, plans or timelines defined by others realistic?	No → / Yes ↓	• Negotiate with the appropriate and responsible individuals who have the authority to re-define as needed. • Refer to the strategy map as needed in your negotiations.
• Are potentially competing goals and priorities removed from the path of implementation?	No → / Yes ↓	• Utilize the Urgency – Importance Grid to assist in clarifying priorities. • If necessary and appropriate, negotiate with relevant managers or executives. • Refer to the strategy map.
• Are within function priorities clear and not competing with each other?	No → / Yes ↓	• Again, utilize the Urgency – Importance Grid on page __ to clarify priorities. • Step back and from a big picture, strategic perspective, assess & rank priorities. • Refer to the strategy map.
USING THIS TABLE AS A MODEL FOR HOW YOU MIGHT APPROACH THIS COACHING OPPORTUNITY, CONTINUE WITH THE QUESTIONING PROCESS UNTIL YOU HAVE EXHAUSTED ALL POSSIBILITIES FOR ADDRESSING PERFORMANCE HURDLES RELEVANT TO ORGANIZATIONAL SUPPORT SYSTEMS.		

Figure 9.12 – Decision Tree for Performance Hurdle #6: Organizational Support Systems

The Seventh Challenge: Guiding Execution without Micromanaging

If you have not identified barriers to execution by this point, you are about as safe as any manager can be in delegating. You still want to provide oversight, however, to ensure that the agreed-on plan does get carried out. But if you have identified barriers, you'll want to provide just enough supervision to ensure execution without micromanaging. As we have noted, this tightrope can be one of the trickier ones that a manager has to walk. Some reflections and suggestions in deciding your supervisory approach for any accountability or task include:

- How critical or urgent is this task to execution?

    The more critical or urgent the task, the closer your oversight should be. You want to allow your team members to learn, and learning involves errors. If those errors cause discomfort for the person you're developing, it's okay; discomfort is part of the learning process. But you should step in before failure on the task or accountability hampers execution of strategy.

- If you had to step in, why? Where is the learning opportunity?

    If no one else puts out the fire, then you have to put out the fire. Just don't forget to figure out why someone else didn't put out the fire. If you had to step in to solve a problem, use that event as a teaching opportunity. Why did someone else not address the problem? Did you overestimate their ability? If so, where? Or was the problem unforeseeable?

If you had to step in not because you overestimated their ability but because of some unforeseeable event, can you use your intervention to teach them about problem-solving? Don't let them sit back and wait for you to solve the problem. Walk them through what you're doing and make it clear that you want them to develop similar problem-solving skills.

- Are you *doing* their work or are you *supervising* their work?

    Watch for upward delegation when you elect to supervise closely. There can be a fine line between teaching someone how to do something and doing it for them. If you have been teaching, the result is that they should demonstrate improvement as a result of your efforts. If you have taken over the task, they are no further along in their learning.

    Probably the most common way we have observed upward delegation to occur is in a situation where the manager's personality is high on Agreeableness, and therefore, tends to be heavily influenced to be a pleaser/rescuer type of person. If the direct report is also a helpless victim type of person, you have almost the perfect storm for upward delegation.

    If there is less time urgency, err on the side of having them develop a plan for addressing a problem. That way, you can evaluate their plan without having to step in to solve the problem itself.

- Are you honest with yourself about your own motivation when you step in?

    Early in the book we described the path from player to player/coach and then to coach. We pointed out the difficulty in developing as a coach. If you find yourself repeatedly stepping in to solve similar problems, you should seriously question whether you are motivated by the quick feel-good of solving the problem instead of the longer term feel-good of developing others.

Some Final Thoughts

If you have followed our reflection and planning outline, you probably have a good handle on the handoff challenges that you face in your organization. Your objective now is to follow through on what you have planned. We have never met a manager who complained of not having enough to do — the to-do list is always daunting, and deciding where to spend your valuable time and energy can be difficult. If you are not deliberate in your follow through, any insights you may have had in reading this book may be lost six months from now.

Some ideas that may help you put these tools into practice:
- Enlist your supervisor and your direct reports in discussing the elements of the baton as we have presented them here. If you are working with the level above and the level below, you have a kind of mini-alignment that allows better communication and execution.
- Early on, err on the side of writing out your assessments and plans. The discipline of writing it out will take a little more time, but you will be forced to make sure that you have clearly thought through each potential barrier to execution and have a workable plan to overcome it.
- Remember that our work here is intentionally generic – it's drawn from many years of work with clients of a variety of sizes, purposes, and cultures. Be creative and adapt what we have presented to the language and realities of your own organization.

- Put time on your calendar to flip through this book again once a month for the next few months. Even a brief review will refresh your memory and make it easier for you to apply the tools.

And remember: persistence is the key.

References

Borman, W. C. & Penner, L. A. in Roberts, B.W. & Hogan, R. (Eds.) (2001). *Personality in the Workplace*. Washington, DC. American Psychological Association.

Buckingham, M. & Coffman, C. (1999). *First Break All the Rules: What the World's Greatest Managers Do Differently.* New York, NY. Simon & Schuster.

Charan, R. & Colvin, G. (June 21, 1999). "Why CEOs Fail." *Fortune Magazine*, 69-78.

Charan, R., Drotter, S. & Noel, J. (2001). *The Leadership Pipeline: How to Build the Leadership Powered Company.* San Francisco, CA. Jossey-Bass.

Collins, J. & Porras, J. (1997). *Built to Last: Successful Habits of Visionary Companies.* New York, NY. Harper Collins Publishers.

Greiner, L. E. (May-June, 1998). "Evolution and Revolution as Organizations Grow." *Harvard Business Review*. From Reprint 98308.

Howard, P. J. & Howard, J. M. (2001). *The Owner's Manual for Personality at Work.* Atlanta, GA. Bard Press.

Kaplan, R. & Norton, D. (2000). *The Strategy Focused Organization: How Balanced Scorecard Companies Thrive in the New Business Environment.* Boston, MA. Harvard Business School Publishing.

Kaplan, R. S. & Norton, D. P. (2004). *Strategy Maps: Converting Intangible Assets into Tangible Outcomes.* Boston, MA. Harvard Business School Publishing Corp.

Katzenbach, J. R. (1995). *Real Change Leaders: How You Can Create Growth and High Performance at Your Company.* New York, NY. Random House.

Kotter, J. P. (1990). *A Force for Change: How Leadership Differs from Management.* New York, NY. Simon & Schuster.

Kotter, J. P. & Heskett, J. L. (1992). *Corporate Culture and Performance.* New York, NY. Free Press.

Kouzes, J. M. & Posner, B. Z. (1987). *The Leadership Challenge: How to Get Extraordinary Things Done in Organizations.* San Francisco, CA. Jossey-Bass.

McCrae, R. R. & Costa, P. T. (1990). *Personality in Adulthood.* New York, NY. The Guilford Press.

McCrae, R. R. & Costa, P. T. (1997). "Personality Trait Structure as a Human Universal." *American Psychologist,* 52(5), 509-516.

Motowidlo, S. J. & Van Scotter, J. R. (1994). Reported in Borman and Penner chapter of Roberts, B.W. & Hogan, R. (Eds.) (2001). *Personality in the Workplace.* Washington, DC. American Psychological Association.

Ones, D. S. & Viswesvaran, C. Studies cited in chapter of Roberts, B.W. & Hogan, R. (Eds.) (2001). *Personality in the Workplace.* Washington, DC. American Psychological Association.

Porter, M. (November-December, 1996). "What is Strategy?" *Harvard Business Review, 61-64.*

Senge, P. M. (1990). *The Fifth Discipline.* New York, NY. Currency-Doubleday.

Walton, M. (1986). *The Deming Management Method.* New York, NY. Perigee Books.

Zaccaro, S. J. (2001). *The Nature of Executive Leadership: A Conceptual and Empirical Analysis of Success.* Washington, DC. American Psychological Association.

Passing the Baton: Winning the Race for Strategic Execution

List of Figures

Figure 2.1 - Example of an S-Curve .23

Figure 2.2 - Limits to Growth Applied to Rabbit Population
on an Island 24

Figure 2.3 - Limits to Growth Applied to Biggs & Bucks
Financial Services 25

Figure 2.4 - Systems Model of the Organizational
Challenges at Biggs & Bucks 37

Figure 2.5 - Systems Model of the Local Leadership
Challenges at Biggs & Bucks 38

Figure 2.6 - Systems Model of the Personal Challenges
at Biggs & Bucks 39

Figure 3.1 - Three Levels and Three Handoff Zones 58

Figure 4.1 - Ideal Alignment and Ideal Handoffs 68

Figure 4.2 - All Levels Working Beneath Ideal Role 74

Figure 4.3 - Senior and Middle Managers Underperforming
in Roles with Strong Line Management 77

Figure 4.4 - Fumbling in the Middle Ranks 79

Figure 4.5 - The Talent Bench at Biggs & Bucks 82

Figure 5.1 - Strategy Map for Biggs & Bucks 109

Figure 6.1 - Biggs & Bucks Strategy Map
with One Theme Highlighted 138

Figure 6.2 - The Talent Bench at Biggs & Bucks 139

Figure 6.3 - Translation from Strategy to Initiatives 141

Figure 6.4 - Accountability and Development Plan:
Handoff to Middle Management for Jim Newman,
Director of Training and Development 143

Figure 6.5 - Accountability and Development Plan:
Handoff to Line Management for Myra Bennis,
Supervisor of Training and Development. 146

Figure 6.6 - Accountability and Development Plan:
Handoff to Organizational Level for Tracey Collins,
Staff Trainer. 149

Figure 6.7 - Accountability and Development Plan
for Jamie Eldridge, Local Office Director 151

Figure 7.1 – Six Performance Hurdles 159

Figure 7.2 – Four Dimensional Leadership model 166

Figure 7.3 – Decision Tree for Performance Hurdle #1:
Expectations 170-172

Figure 7.4 – Decision Tree for Performance Hurdle #2:
Commitment 179

Figure 7.5 – Decision Tree for Performance Hurdle #3:
Skill 183

Figure 7.6 – Decision Tree for Performance Hurdle #4:
Confidence 188

Figure 7.7 – Decision Tree for Performance Hurdle #5:
Personality and Motivation 190

Figure 7.8 – Sample Personality Assessment Chart 195

Figure 7.9 – Coaching Pointers for the Big Five Factors 197

Figure 7.10 - Decision Tree for Performance Hurdle #6:
Organizational Support Systems 200

Figure 7.11 - Current Ability Assessment Chart 202

Figure 8.1 - Accountability and Development Plan
for Delivery of the Product Mastery Series 209

Figure 8.2 - Guiding Execution versus Micromanagement
at the Senior Level 211

Figure 8.3 – Myra's Accountability and Development Plan
for the Development of a Product Mastery Series 212

Figure 8.4 - Guiding Execution versus Micromanaging
at the Middle Level 213

Figure 8.5 – Tracey's Accountability and Development
Plan for the Design of the Materials for the Product
Mastery Series. 214

Figure 8.6 – Guiding Execution versus Micromanaging
at the Line Level 216

Figure 9.1 – Role Assessment for Individual
Senior Management Positions 223

Figure 9.2 – Role Assessment for Individual
Middle Management Positions 224

Figure 9.3 – Role Assessment for Individual
Line Management Positions 225

Figure 9.4 – Role Alignment and Handoff Chart 227

Figure 9.5 – Force Field Analysis 234

Figure 9.6 – Accountability and Development Plan 236

Figure 9.7 - Decision Tree for Performance Hurdle #1:
Expectations 240-242

Figure 9.8 – Decision Tree for Performance Hurdle #2:
Commitment 243

Figure 9.9 – Decision Tree for Performance Hurdle #3:
Skill 244

Figure 9.10 – Decision Tree for Performance Hurdle #4:
Confidence 245

Figure 9.11 – Decision Tree for Performance Hurdle #5:
Personality and Motivation 246

Figure 9.12 – Decision Tree for Performance Hurdle #6:
Organizational Support Systems 247

Index

A

Accountability and development plan: 142-151, 202-203, 209, 212-214, 235-237

Alignment and handoffs, ideal: 67-69

Anticipating problems in the handoff zone: 65-88, 226-228
    All levels working beneath ideal role: 73-75
    Fumbling in the middle ranks: 78-81
    Strong line, but senior and middle management underperforming: 75-78

B

Barriers to execution and solution paths: 70-71, 89, 118-120, 229, 233-234

Big Five Personality Factors (See Personality, Big Five Factors)

Borman, Walter: 155

Buckingham, Marcus: 172, 242

Business case: 92-97, 175-177, 179, 243
    Business case at Biggs & Bucks: 94-97

Business context: 66, 69, 89, 90-102, 128-129

C

Charan, Ram: 43, 170, 240

Coaching for performance: 153-204, 237-239
    Clarity of expectations: 159, 168, 173, 202, 209, 236, 240-242
    Coaching for performance at Biggs & Bucks: 201-203
    Coaching pointers for the Big Five Factors: 197
    Establishing expectations: 168-172, 240-242
        Goals and role definition: 168
        Personal and interpersonal clarity: 169
        Skill clarity: 168
    Factors to consider before you start coaching: 153-157
    Hurdles in communication: 157
    Hurdles for the direct report in communication: 157
    Hurdles in the system: 157
    Six performance hurdles: 158-203
    Two kinds of performance: 153-156

Coffman, Curt: 172, 242

Collins, James: 48, 59, 103

Colvin, Geoffrey: 43

Common problems in executing strategy: 7-10
    Avoiding accountability: 10
    Dumping and micromanaging: 9-10, 133
    Failure to develop managers: 9, 53-60
    Failure to prioritize: 8
    Lack of strategic focus: 7

Core ideology: 58, 59

Core purpose: 58, 59

Core values: 58, 59, 169

Costa, Paul: 190

D

Decision tree: 158, 170-172, 179, 183, 188, 190, 200, 239-247
    Clarity of expectations: 170-172, 240-242
    Commitment: 179, 243
    Confidence: 188, 245
    Organizational support systems: 200, 247
    Personality and motivation: 190, 246
    Skill: 183, 244

Defining the handoff zone at Biggs & Bucks: 81-85

Dropped baton (see strategic baton)

Drotter, Steve: 170, 240

Dumping: 6-7, 9-10, 68, 120, 133

E

Environmental and organizational context: 11, 66, 69, 219-220, 230, 237

Environmental scan: 45, 90-92, 108, 220-221, 227
    Environmental scanning at Biggs & Bucks: 91-92

Expectations, clarity of: 159, 168, 173, 202, 209, 236, 240-242

Expectations, establishing: 168-172, 240-242

F

Failure to develop managers: 9, 53-60

Five Factor Personality Model (see Personality, Big Five Factors)

Force field analysis: 233-234

Four Dimensional Leadership: 161-167, 170-171, 240-241

Directional leadership: 164, 165, 166
Implementational leadership: 163, 165, 167
Interpersonal leadership: 164, 165, 167
Management and leadership: 9, 161, 163
Personal leadership: 164, 165, 167

Fumbled baton (see strategic baton, dropped baton)

G

Greiner, Larry: 28-29

Guiding execution versus micromanaging: 60, 205-217, 248-250
    Guiding execution at the line management level: 214
    Guiding execution at the middle management level: 210
    Guiding execution at the senior management level: 207

H

Handoff plan: 219-251
    The fifth challenge: translating strategy into expectations: 235
    The first challenge: sizing up the field: 219
    The fourth challenge: the strategic baton: 229
    The second challenge: sizing up the team: 222
    The seventh challenge: guiding execution without micromanaging: 248
    The sixth challenge: coaching for performance: 237
    The third challenge: anticipating problems in the handoff zone: 226

Handoff process: 15-18, 65-67, 82-86, 133-144, 237
    Following through after the handoff: 17-18
        Seventh challenge: guiding execution without micromanaging: 18
        Sixth challenge: coaching for performance: 18
    Making the handoff: 6, 16-17, 205
        Fifth challenge: translate into personal expectations: 17
        Fourth challenge: translate the baton: 16
    Preparing for the pass: 15
        First challenge: size up the field: 15
        Second challenge: size up the team: 16
        Third challenge: anticipate problems in handoff zones: 16

Handoff zones: 5-7, 44-52, 57-58, 65-88, 145, 226-228
    Anticipating problems: 65-88, 226-228
    Invisible levels: 57-60, 65
    Three handoff zones: 5-7, 44-53, 57-58, 67-68

Heskett, James: 123

Hogan, Robert: 155, 156

Howard, Jane: 190

Howard, Pierce: 190

K

Kaplan, Robert: 12, 43, 46, 59, 113-114, 130

Katzenbach, Jon: 48, 93

Kotter, John: 123, 161

Kouzes, James: 103

L
Limits to growth: 24-25

M
McCrae, Robert: 190

Micromanaging: 6-7, 9-10, 17-18, 60, 120, 133, 205-217, 248-250

Motowidlo, Stephan: 155

N
Noel, James: 170, 240

Norton, David: 12, 43, 46, 59, 113-114, 130

O
Ones, Deniz: 156

Organizational scan: 221-222

Organizational values and team agreements: 89, 123-126, 229, 234-235

Organizational vision: 11, 89, 103-107, 229, 230-231

P
Parable of the singing pig: 180, 183, 244

Penner, Louise: 155

Performance development: 158-203, 237-247
    Defining the scope: Specific skills versus role: 160
    Performance Hurdle #1: Expectations: 158-172, 240-242
    Performance Hurdle #2: Commitment: 172-179, 243
        Breaking through barriers to commitment: 174, 175, 177
        Building commitment by way of internal and external rewards: 177
        Building the commitment to outcome: 175
    Performance Hurdle #3: Skill: 178-184, 244
        Addressing skill barriers: 180
    Performance Hurdle # 4: Confidence: 184-189, 245
        Addressing confidence barriers: 186
    Performance Hurdle #5: Personality and motivation: 189-198, 246
        Addressing personality and motivation barriers: 194
    Performance Hurdle #6: Organizational support systems: 198-201, 247
        Addressing organizational barriers: 199
    Six Performance Hurdles: 158-159, 201

Personal implications of strategy and performance expectations: 14, 67, 71-72, 89, 93, 121-123, 125-126, 229, 234

Personality, Big Five Factors: 190-198, 246
    Agreeableness: 193, 195, 197, 249
    Coaching pointers for: 197, 246
    Conscientiousness: 194-197
    Extraversion: 192, 195, 196, 197
    Negative emotionality: 192, 195-197
    Openness: 193, 195, 197

Personality Assessment Chart: 195

Personality to P&L: Three S-curves: 31-33
    How the personal ends up in the P&L: 33-36, 40
    Leadership S-curve: 32
    Organizational S-curve: 31, 193
    Personal S-curve: 32, 39
    Reasons why any individual is not performing: 35
    Three S-curves at Biggs & Bucks: 37-41

Porras, Jerry: 48, 59, 103

Porter, Michael: 12, 46, 130

Posner, Barry: 103

R

Roberts, Brent: 155

Role alignment and handoff model: 68, 74, 77, 79, 82, 139, 226-227

Role assessment forms: 223-225

S

Senge, Peter: 22, 24

Stages of growth and organizational history: 97-102
    Stages of growth at Biggs & Bucks: 98-102

Stages of organizational development: 28, 73, 98
    Delegation stage: 29, 76, 79, 91, 118
    Entrepreneurial stage: 28
    Systems stage: 28, 75, 79, 118

Strategic baton: 5-7, 9-17, 53-57, 66-67, 68-70, 82, 89-126, 128, 222, 226, 229-235

Index

Behavioral boundaries for execution: 14
Dropped: 6, 47, 53-57, 82, 130, 147, 215, 217
    Where line managers drop the baton: 56
    Where middle managers drop the baton: 55
    Where senior managers drop the baton: 54-55
Environmental and organizational context: 11, 66, 69, 219-220, 230, 237
Organizational values and team agreements: 89, 123-126, 229, 234-235
Organizational vision: 11, 89, 103-107, 229, 230-231
Performance expectations and accountabilities: 14, 71-72
Personal implications of strategy: 14, 71-72
Value proposition, major trade-offs, and strategic paths: 12-13, 89, 114-117

Strategy: 5-14, 108-123, 127-152, 231-232

Strategy map: 12, 59-60, 108-117, 122, 129, 137-139, 231-232
    Strategy map for Biggs & Bucks: 108-110

Systems and stages: the context for the race: 22
    Causal maps: 22
    Growing and limiting loops: 26-27
    Restraining forces: 24, 102
    S-curves: 22, 26-27, 31, 37-39
    Systems archetypes: 22
    Understanding systems: 22

T

Team, sizing up: 43-64, 222-225
    Line or operational level: 52-53
        Focus on work planning and task assignment: 52
        Handle details: 52
        Manage resources: 53

Supervise line employees: 53
 Work with a shorter time horizon: 53
Middle or organizational level: the first translators of strategy: 47-52
 Create a functional vision and plan: 48
 Develop line managers: 52
 Manage internal boundaries: 49-52
 Work with an intermediate time horizon: 48
Right runners, right roles: 43
Senior or systems level: 44
 Align structure and systems: 46
 Guide execution: 17, 46, 58, 60, 205
 Manage external boundaries: 44
 Measure the time horizon in years: 47
Three management levels and three handoff zones: 44
Team agreements and organizational values: 89, 123, 229, 234

Translating strategy into expectations: 127-152
Translation of strategy: line management to organization: 147-152
Translation of strategy: middle management to line management: 144-147
Translation of strategy: senior management to middle management: 130-133
Managing the handoff: 86, 133-144, 150, 193

V

Values and team agreements: 89, 123-126, 229, 234-235

Value proposition: 8, 12, 58-59, 67, 89, 110, 114-117, 128, 134, 229, 232

Van Scotter, J.R.: 155

Vision: 11, 46, 48-49, 55-56, 58, 66, 70, 89, 103-107, 128, 162-164, 167, 229, 230-231
    About vision statements: 105
        Relevance of vision at Biggs & Bucks: 106
    Elements of vision: 104

Viswesvaran, Chockalingam: 156

W
Walton, Mary: 22

Weakest links: 85

Z
Zaccaro, Stephen J.: 22, 44, 103, 207

Passing the Baton: Winning the Race for Strategic Execution